Are the Kids Alright?

The Impact of the Pandemic on Children and Their Families

Edited by Linda Rose Ennis

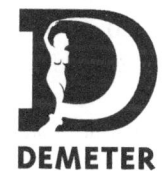

DEMETER

Are the Kids Alright?
The Impact of the Pandemic on Children and Their Families
Edited by Linda Rose Ennis

Copyright © 2023 Demeter Press

Individual copyright to their work is retained by the authors. All rights reserved. No part of this book may be reproduced or transmitted in any form by any means without permission in writing from the publisher.

Demeter Press
PO Box 197
Coe Hill, Ontario
Canada
K0L 1P0
Tel: 289-383-0134
Email: info@demeterpress.org
Website: www.demeterpress.org

Demeter Press logo based on the sculpture "Demeter" by Maria-Luise Bodirsky www.keramik-atelier.bodirsky.de

Printed and Bound in Canada

Cover artwork: *Colourful Chaos by* Linda Rose Ennis
Cover design and typesetting: Michelle Pirovich
Proof reading: Jena Woodhouse

Library and Archives Canada Cataloguing in Publication
Title: Are the kids alright?: the impact of the pandemic on children and their families / edited by Linda Rose Ennis.
Other titles: Are the kids alright (2023)
Names: Ennis, Linda Rose, editor.
Description: Includes bibliographical references.
Identifiers: Canadiana 20230157122 | ISBN 9781772584486 (softcover)
Subjects: LCSH: Child psychology. | LCSH: Child development. | LCSH: COVID-19 (Disease)–Psychological aspects. | LCSH: COVID-19 (Disease)–Social aspects. | LCSH: COVID-19 Pandemic, 2020–Psychological aspects. | LCSH: COVID-19 Pandemic, 2020–Social aspects.
Classification: LCC HQ767.9.A74 2023 | DDC 305.231—dc23

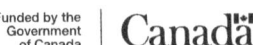

The publisher gratefully acknowledges the support of the Government of Canada

To Nathaniel James, Benny Wolf,
and Everett Dani with love, always

Acknowledgements

I thank all the contributors in this collection, who through their unique and thoughtful research, practice, and theory wrote informative chapters, from which we can all benefit immensely.

As always, I am grateful to Andrea O'Reilly for her unwavering support and friendship throughout the years. To Demeter Press, its editorial and design committees, much thanks and deep gratitude.

I will always be appreciative of my mentor, Dr. Otto Weininger, and how he, through his incredible insight, encouraged me to pursue the area of motherhood, as it relates to early childhood.

To my cherished parents, Dina and Wolf Tenenbaum, who lovingly modelled the importance of following dreams while enjoying life to the fullest.

Much love and appreciation to my daughters, Jessica and Jillian, who inspire me every day through their creativity and intelligence. Thank you for the privilege of being your mother. Thank you to Adam and Alex for their interest in my work.

Above all, I am deeply grateful to Alan for his love, support, and pride in all my endeavours.

Contents

Introduction
The Impact of the Pandemic on Children and Their Families
Linda Rose Ennis
11

Part I
Thinking about the Children during the Pandemic
23

1.
Failing Our Daughters: Teenage Girl Attempted Suicide, COVID-19, and the Broken Canadian Mental Healthcare System
Melinda Vandenbeld Giles and Rebecca Hughes
25

2.
Family Participation in the Development of Children with Intellectual Disabilities in the Pandemic
Vera Lúcia Mendes de Paula Pessoa, Francisca Charlenny Freitas de Oliveira, Virna Ribeiro Feitosa Cestari, Raquel Sampaio Florêncio, Thereza Maria Magalhães Moreira, Edna Maria Camelo Chaves, and Lêda Maria da Costa Pinheiro Frota
37

3.
Attachment and the COVID-19 Pandemic
Brianne Coulombe, Bridget Cho, and Tuppett Yates
49

4.

Taking Care of Children and Preadolescents in the Restrictive Home Stay: Caregivers' Actions during the Early Months of the Pandemic

Eny Dórea Paiva, Karina Rangel da Silva Garcia, Luciana Rodrigues da Silva, Maria Estela Diniz Machado, Paloma Gonçalves Martins Acioly, and Rosane Cordeiro Burla de Aguiar

71

5.

An Upside of Separation and Divorce: Mothering and Coparenting in the Pandemic

Rebecca Jaremko Bromwich

85

Part II
How Children and Their Families Felt
95

6.

Grandparents: Overlooked, Missing Links

Jacqueline Kolosov

97

7.

Paperwork: Mental Health Is Not New; It Has Just Been Filed Away

Hillary Di Menna

111

8.

Coping with COVID-19: Child-Parent Reflections on Perceived Stressors

Lisa H. Rosen, Linda J. Rubin, and Meredith G. Higgins

125

9.

Between the Screens: Pandemic Life and Therapy with
Children and Adolescents

Kiley Gottschalk, Tracey L. Hurd, Angela R. Jones, Laura Matlack

143

Part III
How We Helped Children Cope

159

10.

Gchi-Apptendaagoziwag akina Niizhigwag Idaanisag:
The Lives of My Two Daughters Are Precious

Renée E. Mazinegiizhigoo-kwe Bédard

161

11.

Noticing: A Story of a Mother's and Son's Arts-Based
Discussions about the Pandemic

Lauren E. Burrow and Ethan S. Burrow

183

12.

A Moment of Beauty: Verses of Hope for Children in a Pandemic

Mirelly da Silva Barros, Maria Wanderleya de Lavor Coriolano-Marinus, Bianca Rocha Gouveia, Adélia Karla Falcão Soares, Maria Ilk Nunes de Albuquerque, Weslla Karla Albuquerque, Talita Mendes Bomfim, Vitória Andrade Farias de Oliveira, and Brenda Elize Nunes da Hora

201

13.

Emotional Support and Academic Expectations:
How to Balance It During and After the Pandemic

Ronald Stolberg and Darlene Sweetland

217

Epilogue
Separateness and Connectedness in the Pandemic
Linda Rose Ennis
231

Notes on Contributors
237

Introduction

The Impact of the Pandemic on Children and Their Families

Linda Rose Ennis

It was the pandemic, and the children were not alright. The COVID-19 pandemic is presently in its seventh wave (July 2022), the third since the arrival of Omicron variant. During the early phase of the pandemic in 2020, the focus was on how education and social interaction with peers were integral to children's functioning. However, not enough attention was devoted to these lingering questions: How do children feel about the pandemic, and how do they process this experience? Why is it assumed that cognitive functioning and social interaction are the most significant areas of child development? Where do the emotional factors fit into this scenario?

When delivering advice to parents as to how they and their children should cope throughout the pandemic, educational and government officials referred to paediatric research, which concluded, through surveys and questionnaires, that children's mental health was affected by school closures and how this absence and online learning would result in lags in their future career. This research also communicated that children with special needs and those from low-income families would be the most affected by school closures, partly because they would not have access to school lunches. As such, there was an emphasis on the impact of school closure on children rather than on the deeper emotional repercussions of the pandemic on them.

This collection includes contributions from psychologists, academics, nurses, a lawyer, family mediators, and mothers, who explore how children emotionally experienced the pandemic. Their research and clinical work mostly draw from the early days of the pandemic in 2020, when schools and many businesses, other than essential services, were closed; children's schooling moved online, and extended families and friends were separated for fear of being infected with COVID-19. This was before vaccines were available and restrictions were gradually loosened. Through narratives, interviews, case studies, and qualitative research, this volume clarifies the impact that COVID-19 has had on children's emotional wellbeing and how the parents and caregivers in their lives helped them cope with this unusual and challenging time. Furthermore, this compilation examines the effect of pre-existing mental health issues in both children and their families. In addition, it explores how parents coped with the stresses of the pandemic, thereby affecting how their children did, in addition to other determining factors contributing to the mental health of children. It is important to highlight that not all children and their families were affected in the same way. Much depended upon whether there was COVID-19 exposure within the family, the stage of the pandemic and how it was dealt with by parents, the economic status of the family, and what kind of disadvantages they faced.

We are left with many questions when we examine the effect of the pandemic on children, which will be addressed in this collection. In terms of the pandemic, what supports do children have and need? What is their primary worry? How does the parents' stress affect children? How does intensive mothering fit into the pandemic experience? How have experiences of loss and fear of the unknown affected children during the pandemic? How do feelings of isolation affect child development? What is boredom and why was this feeling so prevalent during the pandemic? How can we explain the either-or thinking, that we utilized, to understand and cope with the pandemic? Why is the focus, so much, on what children do rather than who they are?

The Early Days of the Pandemic

As background to this collection, I cite here some research that examined the impact of the pandemic on children in the early days of COVID-19. One large cross-sectional study, during the initial phase of the pandemic, investigated the impact of the COVID-19 pandemic on the mental health of Canadian children and adolescents, using adapted measures from the CRISIS questionnaire and self-reporting. This study identified changes in children's mental health across six domains: depression, anxiety, irritability, attention, hyperactivity, and obsessions/compulsions due to social isolation (Cost et al). It concluded that "deterioration was associated with increased stress from social isolation" (Cost et al. 2). Much emphasis was made on the need to "balance the risk of infection with the deterioration in child and adolescent mental health, noted in this first wave, as decisions are made about re-entry to school and recreational activities and other normative activities" (Cost et al 13).

Another inquiry reviewed studies that measured, mainly through online surveys and questionnaires, the effects of the pandemic on children and adolescents. It noted that COVID-19 affected "the mental health of children and adolescents and that depression and anxiety are prevalent" (Wagner 3).

One report noted how families struggled to cope with the financial impacts of the pandemic. It recognized that "families see COVID as a threat to their financial well-being." It also identified how "recent immigrants, low-income families and families with children are disproportionately impacted by income loss" (Kaddatz 1).

Another article emphasized the impact of the pandemic on children five years old and younger through the RAPID-EC project, overseen by project director, Phil Fisher, which had conducted weekly surveys. The research recognized "how closely connected the emotional well-being of a caregiver is to the emotional well-being of a child" (Dastagir 1).

The first collection to "explore the impact of the pandemic on mothers' care and wage labour in the context of employment, schooling, communities, families and the relationship of parents and children" (O'Reilly and Green 24) paved the way for this volume to further expand and focus upon the emotional wellbeing of children and their families.

Considering the enormous impact the pandemic has had on children, as well as on their parents and other family members, I decided this collection should focus on the source of children's stress as well as what hindered or helped children and adolescents deal with their anxiety.

The Conflict Between the Mother's Needs and the Child's: The Impact of Parenting on Children

As a feminist and early childhood theorist, I have continually struggled with the compartmentalization of children's and mother's needs, as is apparent in the two disciplines, where the two camps rarely intersect (Ennis). However, the pandemic, inextricably, dissolved that illusion when the two worlds collided. It became apparent that motherhood and children's needs are interconnected and operate in a fine balance. Whether the mothering style was an intensive one, where children need and are entitled to constant maternal nurturing (Hays), or a more balanced form of mothering such as the "good-enough" approach (Winnicott), determined the degree of emotional stress that ensued during the pandemic. It must be acknowledged that this intensive form of parenting, with not enough supports in place, would escalate the stress levels in both mother and child, especially since intensive mothering was promoted at this critical time. Having said that, we must recognize that "there needs to be some realization that intensive mothering is neither good nor bad but, rather, an interplay of self-serving mothering practices due to individual and societal expectations" (Ennis 336)—which reflects the lived experience of mothers in collaboration with what is expected of them.

The Impact of Early Experiences on Later Ones

As early object relations (Klein; Winnicott) and attachment theorists (Bowlby; Ainsworth et al.) explain, the early mother-child relationship is integral to the development of a child, as is the impact of the early experiences and primary attachment relationships—a topic that will be further explored in this volume. Although the mother-child relationship has been broadened to include fathers, mothers are still often considered to be the primary caregivers, as they engage in more activities related to children, which was also the case during the pandemic, when mothers' careers often became jeopardized. Children were kept home from school for health and safety reasons, but they were still expected to continue with their studies through online learning while it was mothers who primarily supervised them. During this challenging time, children internalized parental messages and incorporated them into their thinking, feelings, and behaviours, which affected how children coped with adversity and whether they could become resilient.

Capitalism, Neoliberalism, and the Pandemic

In her recent work on mothering during the pandemic, O'Reilly noted; "The unequal distribution of paid work in the home and the increased burden of care throughout the pandemic has been particularly detrimental for mothers in the paid labour force" (21). A driving force behind this disparity is the neoliberal model, which emerged in the 1980s and 1990s, and has been defined as an individualized and economic one, when mothers are "positioning children as social capital to be invested in" (Vandenbeld Giles). This is the backdrop for the impact that COVID has had on mothers and, subsequently, their children, which will be further explored in this collection. Pressure placed on families through neoliberalism is most evident in anxieties related to children with learning difficulties.

Loss, Boredom, and Being/Doing during the Pandemic

Children, like adults, have experienced enormous anxiety during the pandemic. Some of their anxiety was expressed through boredom, the inability to fall or stay asleep at night; having nightmares; crying easily; feeling easily frustrated; experiencing loneliness; fearing getting the virus or transmitting the virus to vulnerable family members, and feeling hopeless and/or helplessness and lack of control, hypochondriasis (the fear of serious illness) or somatization (continuous complaints about physical symptoms). These issues are expanded upon in the following chapters.

Psychoanalytic thinking has a lot to teach us when it comes to the feeling of boredom and the capacity to be alone. As Adam Phillips says, "Boredom is merely the mourning of everyday life. Like all genuine transitional states, their destination is unclear" (72). He continues, "Boredom, I think, protects the individual, makes tolerable for him the impossible experience of waiting for something without knowing what it could be" (77). How apt these reflections are in understanding the uncertainty and emptiness of living in a pandemic. The (in)capacity to be alone is reflected in W. R. Bion's words: "Inability to tolerate empty space limits the amount of space available" (71). It is a form of claustrophobia, where one feels trapped in nothingness and lost and stuck in one place. These were the feelings about the pandemic for many, especially for children. Additionally, a child feels invisible or not fully understood when parents and teachers focus excessively on what children can do at the expense of who they are. The capacity "to be" is essential to prevent a child from taking on a false self and a compulsive cycle of "doing" to conceal the absence of "being" (Winnicott).

During the pandemic, children experienced enormous changes to their routine; they lost contact with their friends, their grandparents, and extended family. As a result, they experienced a general sense of mourning over what could and should have been, as reflected by many of the chapters in this volume. For the adolescents, dreams related to travel, university experiences, and social interactions were all put on hold and lost to them at that time—and perhaps forever. Additionally, new losses brought back old unresolved losses, which put children more at risk.

Resilience during the Pandemic

Children's previous experience with adversity, their pre-existing mental health, and parental, teacher, or therapeutic support will determine the child's ability to be adaptable and flexible in riding out the pandemic storm.

One academic study discussed how the pandemic "poses an acute threat to the well-being of children and families due to challenges related to social disruption such as financial insecurity, caregiving burden, and confinement-related stress" (Prime, Wade, and Browne 1). It also talked about processes of risk and resilience within families, with a focus on pre-existing characteristics that put them at risk, such as "economic hardship, racism and/or a history of other trauma or adversity." This study noted that family well-being and children's adjustment "is largely contingent on the general climate and relationships in a family" (3).

Resilience is defined as the ability to adapt to stress and the capacity to recover quickly from difficulties Building resilience in children will be fully explored in the last section of this collection, where supports and strategies will be offered.

The Lived Experience of Adolescents and Their Parents during the Pandemic

Adolescence is a unique time, as children go through a developmental milestone called the "second individuation," which leads them to seek out their peers as a way to separate themselves from their parents (Blos). As a result, adolescents' inability to connect with their peers during the pandemic left them emotionally at risk. While isolation and anxiety are contributing factors, specifically for teenage girls, a large part of this issue is the lack of mental health resources.

Overview of Chapters

To explore the impact of the pandemic on children, this collection examined it through three lenses: Thinking about Children during the Pandemic; How Children and their Families Felt; and How We Helped Children Cope. The first section draws upon research and theory in the area; the second section gives us a snapshot of the ways children and their families felt about the pandemic, and the last section reflects upon what has been learned from this experience and future implications. This collection has been authored by academics from various disciplines, from the US, Canada, and Brazil. They bring their passion, interest, scholastic expertise, and lived experience to this volume.

Thinking about Children during the Pandemic

The chapters in this section explore the impact of the pandemic on children, through various theoretical lenses, beginning with concepts of neoliberalism and ending with thoughts about mothers, who are separated or divorced, managing better than married mothers during the COVID-19 pandemic.

In the first chapter, "Failing Our Daughters: Teenage Girl Attempted Suicide, COVID-19, and the Broken Canadian Mental Healthcare System," Melinda Vandenbeld Giles and Rebecca Hughes focus on the concepts of neoliberalism, individuality, and the lack of publicly funded services for mental health in Canada. They also examine the influences of technology and larger neoliberal narratives of individuality and self-expression that sound positive but also have the adverse effect of leading to self-harm.

In "Family Participation in the Development of Children with Intellectual Disabilities in the Pandemic," Vera Lúcia Mendes de Paula Pessoa and colleagues, through qualitative research with sixteen parents of children with intellectual disabilities in Brazil, establish dialogue and partnership between the parents and the school, which enhance opportunities for educational improvements. The objective was to understand the family's role in the cognitive development of children with learning disabilities during the pandemic.

In "Attachment and the COVID-19 Pandemic," Brianne Coulombe, Bridget Cho, and Tuppett Yates consider the development and implications of attachment security in the context of COVID-19. They discuss how stay-at-home orders, and the attendant disruptions in caregiving, might have altered caregiving quality and resultant parent-child attachment among infants and toddlers born before and during the pandemic, as well as how children's and adults' attachment relationships may have shaped acute and ongoing responses to the COVID-19 pandemic. They draw on emerging empirical findings to support their theoretically informed recommendations for promoting positive attachment in the context of the ongoing global health crisis and to illuminate promising directions for future research.

In "Taking Care of Children and Preadolescents in the Restrictive Home Stay: Caregivers' Actions during the Early Months of the Pandemic," Eny Dórea Paiva and colleagues investigate through a nationwide online survey the immediate impact of the pandemic stay-at-home orders in Brazil. The authors analyze the type of care implemented by caregivers during the early months of the pandemic.

The last chapter in this introductory section, Rebecca Jaremko Bromwich's chapter "An Upside of Separation and Divorce: Mothering and Coparenting in the Pandemic," discusses the new legal and social contexts of co-parenting in Canada from a feminist perspective. She argues that mothers who are separated or divorced fare better than their married counterparts during the pandemic with respect to the unpaid labour burdens imposed by the lockdowns and childcare deprivations.

How Children and Their Families Felt

In the second section, the chapters explore the lived experience of children and their families in Canada, the US, and Brazil.

In "Grandparents: Overlooked, Missing Links," and using the genre of creative nonfiction, Jacqueline Kolosov looks at the impact of absent grandparents on children, particularly teenagers, during the pandemic.

In "Paperwork: Mental Health Is Not New; It Has Just Been Filed Away," Hillary Di Menna shares her family's story, using a feminist and class analysis. She writes how pre-existing mental health challenges have been exacerbated by the pandemic, the stigma around mental health, and the socially constructed barriers faced by children and their families based on their socioeconomic status.

The next chapter in this section, "Coping with COVID-19: Child-Parent Reflections on Perceived Stressors," by Lisa H. Rosen, Linda J. Rubin, and Meredith G. Higgins, is a multi-method study with children and parents. Their surveys include measures of stress, adjustment, and parent-child communication, which were completed by both children and parents. They focus on mother-child interviews, in which dyads discuss a problem specific to COVID-19, a peer problem during COVID-19, and the perceived effects of social distancing.

The last chapter in this section, "Between the Screens: Pandemic Life and Therapy with Children and Adolescents," Kiley Gottschalk, Tracey L. Hurd, Angela R. Jones, and Laura Matlack explore the way children and adolescents express their conflicted feelings about their lives during the pandemic, including their interior emotional experiences. Through presenting clinical excerpts, via pandemic telehealth and Zoom, of young, school age and teen patients, the clinicians demonstrate how children felt tensions between autonomy and belongingness and struggled to make sense of their place in pandemic life while remaining optimistic about the future.

How We Helped Children Cope During COVID-19

In this final section, the chapters discuss what coping strategies were and may be offered, looking out of the pandemic and towards the future.

The first chapter in this final section, entitled "Gchi-Apptendaago-ziwag akina Niizhigwag Idaanisag: The Lives of My Two Daughters Are

Precious," by Renée E. Mazinegiizhigoo-kwe Bédard, explores how the Seven Grandmother teachings are used by her family to ensure that her daughters continue to live through the pandemic as Anishinaabeg using traditional knowledge. Through these teachings, they learn how to articulate their mental health needs and allow culturally centred parenting to continue to create a holistic pathway for living in a good way.

In "Noticing: A Story of a Mother's and Son's Arts-Based Discussions about the Pandemic," Lauren E. Burrow and her son Ethan S. Burrow share their experience of the pandemic. To construct a mini-story that captures many big moments, Lauren uses multiple qualitative methods to both self-reflect and then, later, to interview Ethan in a discussion-based format. Primary data collection also includes photo elicitation, in which she uses family photo books to ask him about how he perceived their shared experiences of 2020. They then label those feelings through an arts-based association activity.

The next chapter by Mirelly Da Silva Barros and colleagues, "A Moment of Beauty: Verses of Hope for Children in a Pandemic" is a descriptive study that reflects on the construction of an e-book during the pandemic and its dialogue between sensitive care and aesthetics in the hope for a better world. It is also based on Brazilian folklore.

In "Emotional Support and Academic Expectations: How to Balance It during and after the Pandemic," Ronald Stolberg and Darlene Sweetland shed light on the challenge of maintaining high academic standards while prioritizing mental health. They discuss how depression, anxiety, self-harm, eating disorders, and substance abuse have all increased in children during the pandemic, which directly affects their learning and academic performance. They conclude by offering strategies for building resilience at home and in the classroom.

In the Epilogue, "Separateness and Connectedness in the Pandemic," I use the separation-connection model, which I introduced in previous work, to further understand the impact of the pandemic on children. I suggest that this model reflects the precarious balance that ensued during the pandemic, with phases of isolation and reconnection, where these dynamics were felt most deeply. Rather than an interplay of separateness and connectedness, this was an either-or experience of being together or apart. The chapter ends with a review of the central issues highlighted in this collection, what was learned from the pandemic, and how to move forward.

Conclusion

Are the Kids Alright? The Impact of the Pandemic on Children is a collection of chapters that examine, from different vantage points, the lived experience of children and their families throughout the pandemic. On this journey, what has been noted is the impact of the parenting experience on children's wellbeing as well as the need for supports to help ameliorate the stress that came with living through this challenging period of time. Further to that, as stated earlier, since early childhood and feminist strategies often seem at odds with each other, there is a need to look towards reconciling these disciplines by making them more compatible and building upon, expanding, challenging, and bridging the theories we have in place.

Works Cited

Ainsworth, M., et al. *Patterns of Attachment*. Erlbaum, 1978.

Blos, Peter. "The Second Individuation Process of Adolescence." *The Psychoanalytic Study of the Child*, vol. 22, no.1, 1967, pp. 162-86.

Bowlby, John. *A Secure Base*. Basic Books, 2005.

Cost, Katherine Tombeau, et al. "Mostly Worse, Occasionally Better: Impact of COVID-19 Pandemic on the Mental Health of Canadian Children and Adolescents." *European Child & Adolescent Psychiatry*, vol. 31, no. 1, 2022, pp. 1-14.

Dastagir, Alia. "During the Pandemic, Are the Little Kids All Right"? *USA Today*, 19 Aug. 2020, pp. 1-3.

Ennis, Linda Rose. *Intensive Mothering: The Cultural Contradictions of Modern Motherhood*. Demeter Press, 2014.

Hays, Sharon. *The Cultural Contradictions of Motherhood*. Yale Press, 1996.

Kaddatz, Jennifer. "Families Struggle to Cope with Financial Impacts of the COVID-19 Pandemic." *The Vanier Institute of the Family*, April 9, 2020, pp. 1-7.

Klein, Melanie. *Love, Guilt, and Reparation*. W.W.Norton & Co, 1964.

O'Reilly, Andrea, and Fiona Joy Green. *Mothers, Mothering, and COVID-19: Dispatches from a Pandemic*. Demeter Press, 2021.

Phillips, Adam. *On Kissing, Tickling and Being Bored*. First Harvard University Press, 1994.

Prime, H., M. Wade, and D. T. Browne. "Risk and Resilience in Family Well-being During the COVID-19 Pandemic." *American Psychologist*, vol. 75, no. 5, 2020, pp. 631-43.

Vandenbeld Giles, Melinda. *Mothering in the Age of Neoliberalism*. Demeter Press, 2014.

Wagner Dineen, Karen. "New Findings About Children's Mental Health During COVID-19." *Psychiatric Times*, 7 Oct. 2020, www.psychiatrictimes.com/view/new-findings-children-mental-health-covid-19. Accessed 1 Mar. 2023.

Winnicott, Donald. *Maturational Processes and the Facilitating Environment*. Hogarth Press, 1965.

Part I.
Thinking about the Children during the Pandemic

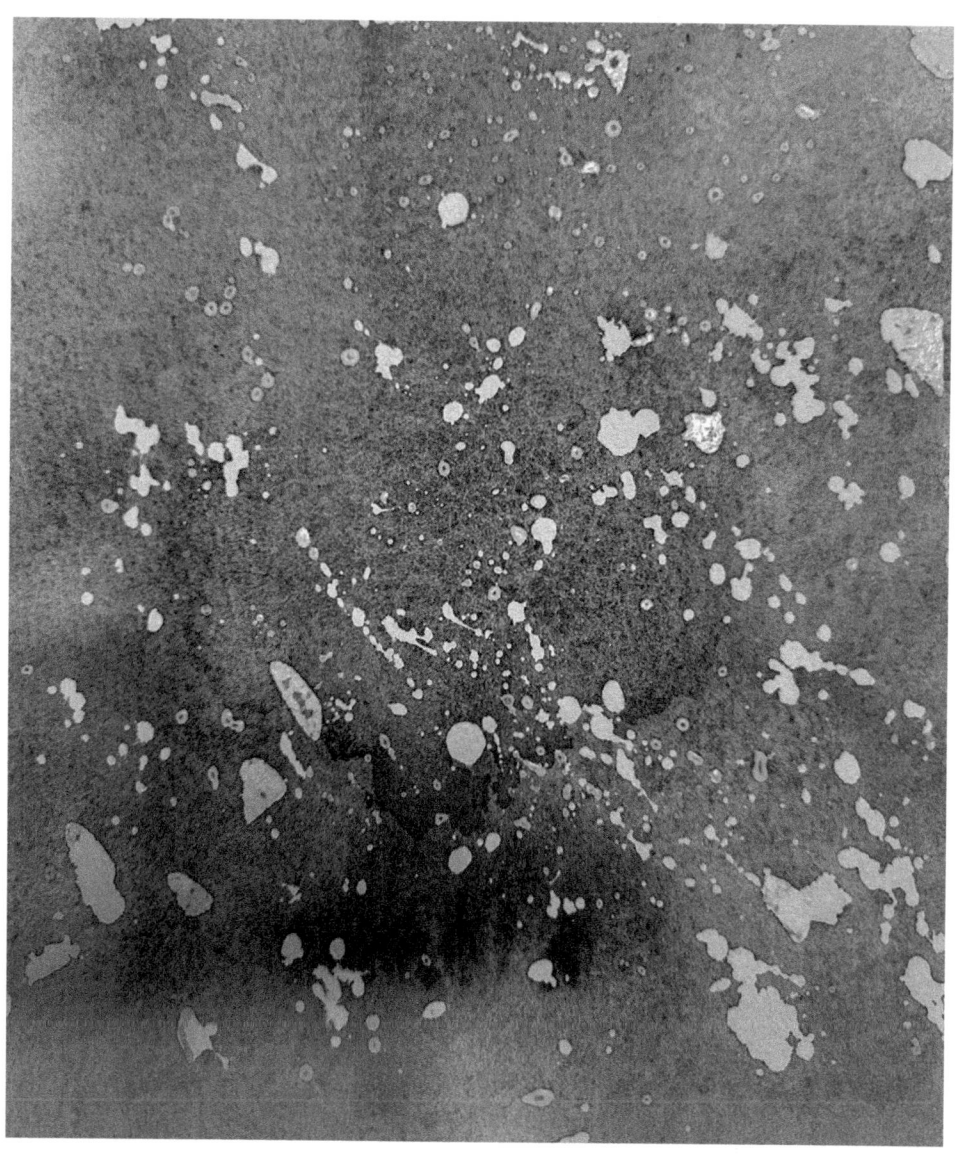

Chapter 1.

Failing Our Daughters: Teenage Girl Attempted Suicide, COVID-19, and the Broken Canadian Mental Healthcare System

Melinda Vandenbeld Giles and Rebecca Hughes

The pandemic struck a world that was already impacted by increasing economic inequities and political turmoil. This chapter seeks to make visible not only the devastating impact of broader neoliberal ideologies on the everyday lives of teenage girls in Canada but also the ways in which such ideologies have influenced current political thinking regarding social welfare spending, specifically in terms of investing in mental health.

Neoliberalism has produced a two-tiered system in terms of access to mental health supports. For the majority of people, access to publicly funded mental health services has become increasingly complex and difficult. Meanwhile, in response to demand, privatized mental health services have proliferated, giving the overall impression that help is available. Consistent with the neoliberal ethos in which representation becomes prioritized over reality, the apparent range of available mental health services obscures a dire reality. For many teenage girls experiencing mental health issues, little help or services are available. Additionally, the neoliberal offloading of societal responsibility for care onto the individual has placed the burden of self-care onto the shoulders of young girls without the necessary resources or follow up, leaving young girls and their parents abandoned in a dysfunctional mental healthcare system that can only provide emergency solutions.

A review of news media publications regarding teenage girl suicide attempts in Canada reveals a severe problem that has been building for years and has become a noticeable crisis during the COVID-19 pandemic. Examples of such articles include "Teen Suicide on the Rise among Canadian Girls" (Levinson-King), "More Teenage Girls Being Admitted to Hospital for Suicide Attempts" (CTV News), "Teen Suicide: Is There an Epidemic?" (Olson), "Number of Youth in Hospital after Suicide Attempt Tripled Over 4-month Period under COVID-19" (Brown), and "From Depression to Self-Harm, Teens Are Struggling During COVID-19" (Abma). While isolation, increased conflict at home, and inability to rely on friends for support were cited as major causes for increased emergency department (ED) admissions during COVID-19 lockdowns, alarming rates of attempted suicide, self harm, and eating disorders for teenage girls have been on the rise for over a decade now (Skinner and McFaull). Suffice to say, the kids are not alright: COVID-19 has only highlighted the increasing fractures in our already overburdened Canadian mental healthcare system, particularly when it comes to being able to provide support for teenage girls.

Teenage Girl Self-Harm and Attempted Suicide

Suicide is a leading cause of Canadian childhood mortality. For the age range, ten to nineteen years, suicide rates for females have increased since the 1980s yet decreased for males, making gender a crucial factor (Skinner and McFaull). LGBTQS2 youth in Canada are fourteen times more at risk of suicide than straight cisgender youth (Abramovich), and bisexual girls and lesbian girls have the highest levels of risk (Ferlatte et al. 8). Although suicide affects all populations, the 2016 *Suicide in Canada: Key Statistics Report* indicates that suicide attempts are three times higher among people born in Canada than immigrants to Canada. Suicide rates for First Nations people are three times higher than non-Indigenous people in Canada, and significantly, twenty-two times higher for Indigenous teen girls (Kumar and Tjepkema 5).

Despite evidence clearly illustrating the increasing rates of suicide incidences, attempted suicide, and self-harm for teenage girls and the significant amount of media attention, where are the resources to address this crisis? There is always a section at the end of any article about suicide listing where to get help: "If you're in an emergency, please call 911. If you or someone you know is suffering with mental-health issues, call Kids Help Phone at 1-800-668-6868" (Levinson-King). The increasing rates of ED admittance in Canada (Jaakkimainen et al.) reveal how emergency responses are becoming the primary points of accessing healthcare for many Canadians, specifically young girls. Although these responses deal with the immediate crisis, they do nothing to provide sustained integrative mental health support.

Canadians visit the emergency department when they are unable to receive appropriate care from their family physician. Canadian ED usage ranked the highest out of an international study comparing thirty-four developed nations (Jaakkimainen et al. 1). Given that ED admissions for teenage girls attempting suicide and self-harm have risen sharply, what exactly are the resources being provided? Calling 911 is what teenage girls and parents are told to do. However, when a parent of a teenage girl calls 911 in response to their child's suicide attempt, often the only help provided is the mandatory Form 1 requiring psychiatric consultation within 72 hours. What are the consequences of having to deal with police interrogation and forced isolated time spent in the ED waiting for psychiatric consultation after having attempted suicide or self-harm?

The way in which the healthcare system operates leads to many young girls falling through the cracks. Even when parents or teenage girls contact 911 clearly asking for help, the system is structured in such a way that such cries for help are often ignored. Even if the hospital psychiatrist determines admittance to the child and youth mental health ward, there must be a bed available. The teenage girl will have to wait in the ED until the bed becomes available, and once they are in the child and youth mental health ward, there will be other young girls waiting for their bed, making the system particularly fraught and perfunctory and only able to respond to those elegible in the most extreme circumstances.

This situation is not unique to teenage girls attempting suicide. They are caught up in the larger failures of a mental health system in Canada that has become inadequate and dysfunctional. There has been a 75 per cent increase in the number of mental health-related ED visits by children and youth aged between five and twenty-four since 2006/2007

(Moroz 283). In a study conducted regarding the experiences of individuals visiting emergency departments for mental health-related reasons, individuals increasingly visit the ED due to a lack of mental health services in the community, where wait times have become ridiculously long and few resources are available twenty-four hours a day, seven days a week (Vandyk et al. 587). "Having dedicated mental health practitioners in the ED to care for patients with psychiatric needs may be a more efficient and effective way to provide care. Evidence suggests that patients with access to designated psychiatric emergency services or advanced practice mental health nurses have better clinical outcomes" (595-96). Feeling that there is a health practitioner listening and available, rather than waiting up to seventy-two hours alone (after the initial doctor consultation in an ED after a suicide attempt), would certainly be preferable.

The other issue is the discharge plan. Due to lack of space available, many individuals are not admitted into the mental health ward and are discharged before they are ready to go. As one individual said, "It's usually only been like a night's stay. Just until they thought I was well enough to leave because they wanted the bed for someone else" (qtd. in Vandyk et al. 592). Another study regarding ED use and postvisit physician care for adolescents who self-harm revealed that once youth are discharged, 55 per cent received no follow-up care (Rosychuk et al. 3). Access to psychiatric care is only available to in-patients. Once discharged, follow up for medication and/or consultation is left to the family physician. But what happens if you have no family physician? And if you do have a family physician, as another report indicates, "In contrast to the receipt of a discharge note after a hospital admission, there are no established benchmarks for FPs [family physicians] receiving information about their patients' ED visits. In our study, not quite half of patients visiting the ED had information provided to their FP" (Jaakkimainen et al. 5). Additionally, despite 80 per cent of Canadians relying on their family physicians to meet their mental health needs, only 23 per cent of family doctors report feeling well prepared for severe mental health problems (Moroz 283).

There is the assumption that you only need to ask for help. However, as has been illustrated, asking for help is not enough. Due to the inherent malfunction of Canada's current healthcare system, teenage girls are being discharged home with all responsibility for care placed upon their own shoulders and their parents', creating a two-tiered healthcare system. Those who can afford it use privatized mental healthcare services, whereas those who cannot must suffer through repeated ED visits as their only available option for care, or worse. And even for those who can afford privatized mental health services, there is a severe shortage in access to psychiatric services (Moroz 283).

How can we position and understand this increasing crisis, which COVID-19 has only further exacerbated? The crisis is apparent, as is the need for increased funding towards mental health services (Moroz 283). However, the problem is deeper than that. To improve the current healthcare system, we need to illuminate where the fractures began, and begin to move beyond a neoliberal ethos.

The Effects of Neoliberal Practices on Public Health

The severe lack of mental health interventions, including access to psychotherapy (Moroz 283), has been increasingly impacted by neoliberal, cost-cutting policies. Neoliberal policies are characterized as including cost-effective restructuring of public healthcare and education systems, privatization of public entities, and the reduction of welfare spending (Wilkinson and Marmot 244). Proponents of neoliberalism support reduced taxation for wealthy individuals and corporations, privatization of public entities to further the interests of private entities, and the reduction of welfare expenditures to reduce governmental costs, deficits, and taxation. Neoliberal ideology purports that capital or surplus wealth accrued by wealthy individuals will eventually "trickle down" to poorer individuals (Wilkinson and Marmot 245).

Not only does neoliberalism reference the doctrine of capitalism or free market exchange, but it also infers a social and moral philosophy espoused by the mainstream dominant institutions. Thompson writes: "Neoliberalism is the intensification of the influence and dominance of capital; it is the elevation of capitalism, as a mode of production, into an ethic, a set of political imperatives, and a cultural logic" (23). Elizabeth Martinez and Arnaldo Garcia describe neoliberalism as a set of economic policies employed by conservative governments to restructure conservative policies as progressive, fiscally responsible, and socially advantageous rather than as inequitable for poor or marginalized demographic groups (1). More specifically, neoliberal policies include perceived cost-effective restructuring of public healthcare and education systems, privatization of public entities, and the reduction of welfare spending—all of which ultimately contribute in significant ways to lack of access to necessary healthcare interventions and economic hardship for the majority, and even more so for those that are marginalized.

Neoliberal policies and practices reflect a deeper penetration of capitalism into political and social institutions, and such trends have infiltrated our cultural consciousness (Harvey). Neoliberal conservative policies and practises are designed both to promote private enterprise and reduce social welfare expenditures. As such, they benefit only a select few. Noam Chomsky and Robert Waterman McChesney argue that such policies and practices are inherently grounded in issues of wealth and power: "One conclusion seems fairly clear: the approved doctrines are crafted for reasons of power and profit" (39). For low and middle-income families, decreased mental health expenditures result in individuals either paying out of pocket or forgoing mental health coverage, and/or relying on the ED as the only available source of care. If we consider the overall lack of access to publicly funded mental health coverage, particularly for therapy-related services, the two-tiered system becomes apparent. Although a select few can access private mental health services, for the majority, the cost is too high. The main tenets of neoliberalism include the support of free enterprise, the reduction of social services, the privatization of state enterprises, and the reduction of welfare benefits—all of which are promoted as "individual responsibility" or the moral responsibility of the ethically inspired citizen (Chomsky and McChesney 1). In other words, neoliberalism means offloading state responsibility for the increasing self-harm and attempted suicide crisis onto the already overly burdened shoulders of teenage girls and the shoulders of their parents.

The Advent of Neoliberal Personal Responsibility

In 1946, Saskatchewan was the first Canadian province to introduce universal healthcare coverage, which guaranteed free hospital care for residents of Saskatchewan. In 1966, the federal Liberal government of Lester B. Pearson extended this coverage to each province under the Medical Care Act (Granatstein et al. 181). The Canadian federal government played a pivotal role in promoting socialist nationalist movements during the decades after the Great Depression: "Because of the strength of [Tommy] Douglas's consensus, opposition to medicare was forced out of party politics" (181). The essential tenets underpinning Canada's universal healthcare system largely remained intact throughout the latter half of the twentieth century. In both 1984 and 1999, provincial leaders reaffirmed the earlier 1957 Canada Health Act: Leaders underscored the necessity of a universal, comprehensive, portable, and accessible health insurance program.

However, in more recent years, the Canadian social welfare state has undergone a series of philosophical shifts. Health institutions have increasingly framed healthcare in terms of personal responsibility (rather than state or governmental responsibility), and by doing so, they have been able to shift unwanted attention away from inequalities in the healthcare system and more into the realm of individual responsibility and personal choice (Lupton 44). In other words, parents have the personal choice to find the most effective therapy options for their suicidal teenage daughter even when the cost is prohibitive and increasing demand has made even privatized services difficult to obtain. As for publicly funded services, in Ontario, twelve thousand children and youth were reported to be waiting up to 2.5 years for services (Moroz 283). This means that if a thirteen-year-old girl attempts suicide, statistically, she will not receive any publically funded mental health services until she is almost sixteen years old. If we combine this discourse of individual responsibility with the increasing erosion of funding to mental health services, the combination becomes toxic and potentially life threatening.

Globalization of Neoliberal Health Policies

Neoliberal ideologies have created detriments to health for all. Neoliberal discourse has increasingly found its way into healthcare policy reform around the world: "This trend is especially evident in the United Kingdom, Canada, United States, Australia and New Zealand, where neoliberal philosophy resonates with policy makers and members of the private sector" (McGregor 82). Sue McGregor identifies neoliberal rhetoric including such phrases as:

> Spending cuts, dismantling, de-indexing, deficit cutting, haves and have-nots, competitiveness, downsizing, declining welfare

state, inefficiencies, inevitability, closures, chopping services, de-insured, user-pay fees, two-tier health care, for-profit health care, escalating costs, free markets, erosion of health care, being forced to make difficult policy choices, unfortunate necessities and justifiable sacrifices. (83)

Healthcare discourse has undergone dramatic change in recent decades throughout the United Kingdom, Canada, United States, Australia, and New Zealand. Neoliberal policies, practises, and directives have effectively shifted attention away from notions of public good, social justice, and universal care and have instead focussed public attention on the urgent need to promote accountability, cut governmental debt, and limit welfare spending. The Canadian socialized healthcare mandate asserts that all residents, regardless of their economic status, have equal rights to curative and preventive healthcare services. However, as has been revealed, this is sadly not the case. The lack of mental health services for teenage girls attempting suicide and self-harm is part of the larger breakdown of Canada's current healthcare system.

Conclusion

The current crisis in increasing teenage girl suicide attempts has been attributed by the media to COVID-19. Although the isolation and anxiety of COVID-19 certainly exacerbated the incidences of ED visits for teenage girls, it only highlighted a problem that had been occurring for the past several decades. It also starkly highlighted the extreme lack of mental health resources available to meet increasing COVID-19 demand. With EDs increasingly providing the only form of care, we will continue to see increasing ED visits. We need to pay more attention to how our mental healthcare system is structured. Not only do we need to provide the necessary funding, but we also must remove ourselves from the neoliberal ethos of individual responsibility that has governed our healthcare system. We need to restructure our mental health services, thereby allocating more funding at the community service level, as opposed to offloading responsibility onto family physicians. All mental health services including therapy should be publicly funded, with follow-up and monitoring under psychiatric (and not only family physicians) care for prescribed medications. As a society, we need to ensure that if a teenage girl resorts to calling 911, she will not become lost in a bureaucratically underfunded and dysfunctional administrative system, and will actually receive the help she requires.

Works Cited

Abma, Sandra. "From Depression to Self-Harm, Teens Are Struggling During COVID-19." *CBC News*, 15 Mar. 2021, www.cbc.ca/news/canada/ottawa/mental-health-teenagers-pandemic-1.5945851. Accessed 3 Mar. 2023.

Abramovich, Alex. *LGBTQ2S Youth Suicide*. City of Toronto. 2016.

Brown, Desmond. "Number of Youth in Hospital after Suicide Attempt Tripled Over 4-Month Period under COVID-19." *CBC Hamilton*, 18 March, 2021, www.cbc.ca/news/canada/hamilton/pandemic-safety-measures-children-teen-health-impact-1.5953326. Accessed 3 Mar. 2023.

Chomsky, Noam, and Robert Waterman McChesney. *Profit over People: Neoliberalism and Global Order*. Seven Stories Press, 2006.

CTV News. "More Teenage Girls Being Admitted to Hospital for Suicide Attempts: INSPQ." *The Canadian Press*, 31 Jan. 2022, montreal.ctvnews.ca/more-teenage-girls-being-admitted-to-hospital-for-suicide-attempts-inspq-1.5761098. Accessed 3 Mar. 2023.

Ferlatte, Olivier, Maxim Gaudette, and Celeste Pang. "2SLGBTQI Suicide Prevention Research in Canada: Evidence, Gaps, and Priorities. PHAC Suicide and its Prevention Final Report." *Egale*. L'École de Santé Publique de L'Université de Montréal. October, 2021.

Granatstein, Jack L., et al. *Twentieth Century Canada*. McGraw-Hill Ryerson Ltd, 1983.

Harvey, David. *A Brief History of Neoliberalism*. Oxford University Press, 2007.

Jaakkimainen, Liisa, et al. *The Receipt of Information by Family Physicians about Their Patient's Emergency Department Visits: A Record Linkage Study of Electronic Medical Records to Health Administrative Data*. BMC Family Practice, 2021.

Kumar, Mohan B., and Michael Tjepkema. "Suicide among First Nations People, Métis and Inuit (2011-2016): Findings from the 2011

Canadian Census Health and Environment Cohort (Can CHEC)." *Statistics Canada*, June 2019, www150.statcan.gc.ca/n1/en/catalogue/99-011-X2019001. Accessed 3 Mar. 2023.

Levinson-King, Robin. "Teen Suicide on the Rise among Canadian Girls." *BBC News*, 13 March, 2017, www.bbc.com/news/world-us-canada-39210463. Accessed 3 Mar. 2023.

Lupton, Deborah. *Medicine as Culture. Illness, Disease, and the Body in Western Societies.* Sage, 2003.

Martinez, Elizabeth, and Arnoldo Garcia. "What Is Neo-Liberalism?" *National Network for Immigrant and Refugee Rights*, 1 Jan.1997, www.corpwatch.org/article/what-neoliberalism. Accessed 3 Mar. 2023.

McGregor, Sue. "Neoliberalism and Health Care." *International Journal of Consumer Studies, Special Edition on Consumers and Health*, vol. 25, no. 2, 2001, pp. 82-89.

Moroz, Nicholas, Isabella Moroz, and Monika Slovinec D'Angelo. "Mental Health Services in Canada: Barriers and Cost-Effective Solutions to Increase Access." *Healthcare Management Forum*, vol. 33, no. 6., 2020, pp. 282-87.

Olson, Robert. "Teen Suicide: Is There An Epidemic?" *Centre for Suicide Prevention*, 2012, www.suicideinfo.ca/local_resource/teensuicide/.

Rosychuk, Rhonda, et al. "Does Emergency Department Use and Post-Visit Physician Care Cluster Geographically and Temporally for Adolescents Who Self-Harm? A Population-Based 9-year Retrospective Cohort Study from Alberta, Canada." *BMC Psychiatry*, 2016, www.ncbi.nlm.nih.gov/pmc/articles/PMC4940757/. Accessed 3 Mar. 2023.

Skinner, Robin, and Steven McFaull. "Suicide among Children and Adolescents in Canada: Trends and Sex Differences, 1980-2008." *Canadian Medical Association Journal*, vol. 184, no. 9, 2012, pp. 1029-34.

Suicide in Canada: Key Statistics. Public Health Agency of Canada, 2016.

Thompson, Michael J. "A Brief History of Neoliberalism – Democratiya." *Dissent Magazine*, 22 Jan. 2014, www.dissentmagazine.org/democratiya_article/a-brief-history-of-neoliberalism. Accessed 3 Mar. 2023.

Vandyk, Amanda Digel, et al. "Exploring the Experiences of Persons

Who Frequently Visit the Emergency Department for Mental Health-Related Reasons." *Qualitative Health Research,* vol. 28, no. 4, 2018, pp. 587-599.

Wilkinson, Richard, and Micheal Marmot, editors. *Social Determinants of Health: The Solid Facts.* World Health Organization. 2003.

Chapter 2.

Family Participation in the Development of Children with Intellectual Disabilities in the Pandemic

Vera Lúcia Mendes de Paula Pessoa, Francisca Charlenny Freitas de Oliveira, Virna Ribeiro Feitosa Cestari, Raquel Sampaio Florêncio, Thereza Maria Magalhães Moreira, Edna Maria Camelo Chaves, and Lêda Maria da Costa Pinheiro Frota

The family is an institution that greatly influences human development, as it helps to form and socialize individuals (Batista and Herzog 22). Currently, several different family arrangements and configurations exist, but not all of them offer a safe and supportive psychosocial environment (Ribeiro et al. 2). Family is where knowledge about different aspects of life and learning is developed and the appropriate choices are adopted for different daily situations, which also apply to families living with people with disabilities (Tomaz et al. 4).

Children with disabilities generate new demands for family members, such as more dedicated time to provide a family environment conducive to their development (Bossardi et al. 3). However, the lack of knowledge and stigma still hamper the proper development of children with intellectual disabilities.

According to the Diagnostic and Statistical Manual of Mental Disorders (DSM-V), intellectual disabilities, in general, begin in the developmental period and can include functional impairments, both intellectual—such as reasoning, problem-solving, planning, abstract thinking, judgment, as well as academic learning—and adaptive, which result in a failure to meet developmental and sociocultural standards regarding personal independence and social responsibility (American Psychiatric Association 10).

Without ongoing support, adaptation deficits limit functioning in one or more daily activities, such as communication, social participation, and independent living, as well as in multiple environments, such as home, school, workplace, and the community (Freitas and Ribeiro 59). Thus, parents have an essential responsibility for their children's learning (Benitez and Domeniconi 374). Encouraging children within the family is essential for the positive development of neurological, psychological, and motor aspects and enhances their skills (Gualda, Borges, and Cia 309). The family environment is a context that affects child development, especially for children with disabilities, who require greater involvement in their care and stimulation.

Daily tasks became intensified due to the COVID-19 pandemic and its social-distancing protocols, resulting in a greater number of activities for family caregivers. The confinement caused by the health situation directly affected the household and led to increased stress due to more caregiving demands (Heilborn et al. 6).

Faced with stress and uncertainties, some households required support to cope with relational difficulties and to strengthen protective processes, and to provide more didactic support for the learning of children with intellectual difficulties. The challenge of offering support and assistance so that these parents could provide better results to their school-aged children with intellectual difficulties raised the following question: How does the family encourage their child with ID in social distancing? Thus, we aimed to identify the family's participation in the cognitive development of children with intellectual disabilities during the pandemic.

Methods

This is an exploratory study—a type of research that aims to provide greater familiarity with the research problem and to build hypotheses. It is a qualitative study and was conducted with seventeen family members who accompanied their children to a specialty centre in the metropolitan region of Fortaleza, Ceará, Brazil.

We included family members aged seventeen or over who directly monitor the development of the child with intellectual disabilities, regardless of sex. Family members were invited to participate and, after agreeing, signed the informed consent term (TCLE) via Google forms.

Data was collected in May and June 2021 through online interviews via Google Meet, in which a semi-structured script was applied. All interviews lasted around twenty minutes and were recorded and transcribed to achieve the proposed objective.

Software IRaMuTeQ® was used for the accurate analysis of the information collected. It was chosen for textual data analysis as it calculates word frequency, classifies the descending hierarchical order, and analyses similarity (Camargo and Justo 2013). After organizing the discursive content, mediated by the software, a comprehensive analysis was conducted.

The research was approved by the ethics committee of a Brazilian university, under Registration N° 4.602.784, per Resolution N° 466/2012 of the National Health Council.

Results

The main characteristics found by the software indicated 71.9 per cent use of the textual corpus. Five classes were defined after scaling the complementary text units (CTUs). They were presented in the dendrogram and named according to their specific content (Figure 1, next page).

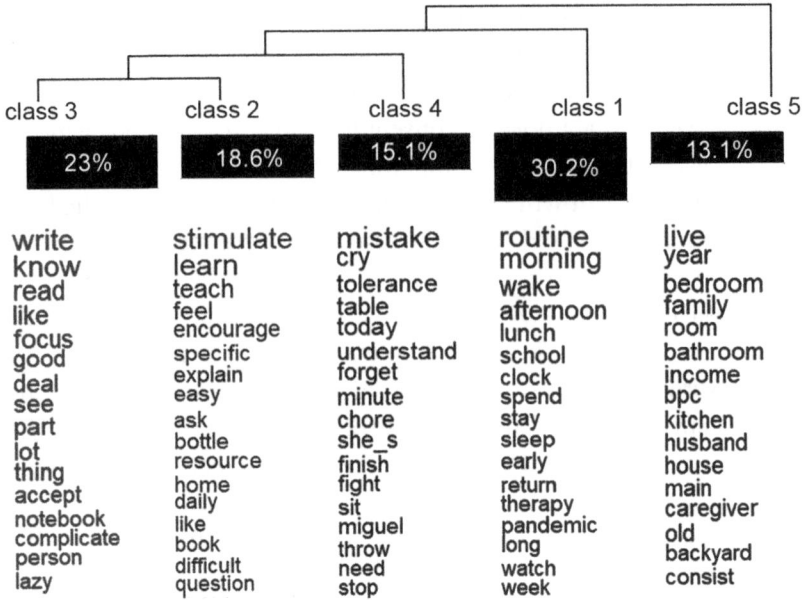

Figure 1. Descending hierarchical classification dendrogram

Thus, Class 1 categorized "routine" and "daily actions." We can infer that the difficulty in assuming a new routine, including social distancing in the analyzed statements, was one of the striking elements, as it pointed to the difficulty of this household in introducing a routine that considered all the attributions required for daily activities.

Subsequently, we observed that Class 4 (column 3), Class 3 (column 1), Class 5 (column 5), and Class 2 (column 2) together represented the greatest predominance, with a percentage of 74.9 per cent of CTUs. The classes demonstrated the family members' insecurity in fully participating in their children's home education. Family members expressed feeling overwhelmed by taking on the responsibility of becoming educators. Some parental narratives show us how family members, specifically mothers, see themselves stimulating the development of the home and the vulnerabilities experienced, as per the following statements:

> I see myself as my daughter's everything. I'm stimulating every day to see if she gets better. It's good, but complicated. The daily routine is very complicated.

It's my responsibility. I have the greatest pleasure in doing this teaching moment and carrying out the activities with her. I see it as a pleasant responsibility.

Today, there is a great difficulty because she is always at home, and everything is much more difficult. She got more agitated, so I have a hard time doing anything for her.

Such terms as "hard," "complicated," "knowing," "making mistakes," and "trying" found in the statements reveal that all the action developed with the child's home stimulation is improvised:

It's hard, because I don't know how to answer correctly.

The activities help to establish knowledge, but I don't really know how to do it. I'm doing what I think works.

The statements also highlight a discrepant reality in the conditions of the environment aimed at cognitive home stimulation.

I prepared a space, an environment: table and chair, books, and toys. She already knows what to do when she wakes up, and we do it together.

She doesn't have her own space. But I separate a table and chair in a corner so I can use it every day. It's not reserved, but that's what I can do.

Regarding the resources of the home learning environment, we observed the limited understanding of parents about the materials that can be used for the teaching and learning processes:

I consider school supplies and toys as a resource. We do activities with them. It's what we have. (M14)

I have books, the alphabet, and numbers. I put it on the table and ask him to tell me the letters and numbers. We do dynamics so that my child can develop.

We note from the terms "activity," "home," and "learning" that the other vertices manifest. Some appear more expressively, such as the terms "like," "process," and "understand." Symbolizing the starting point, the term "home" is crossed by "routine," which reveals that the participants' priority was wanting to know how to organize their children's daily activities (Figure. 2).

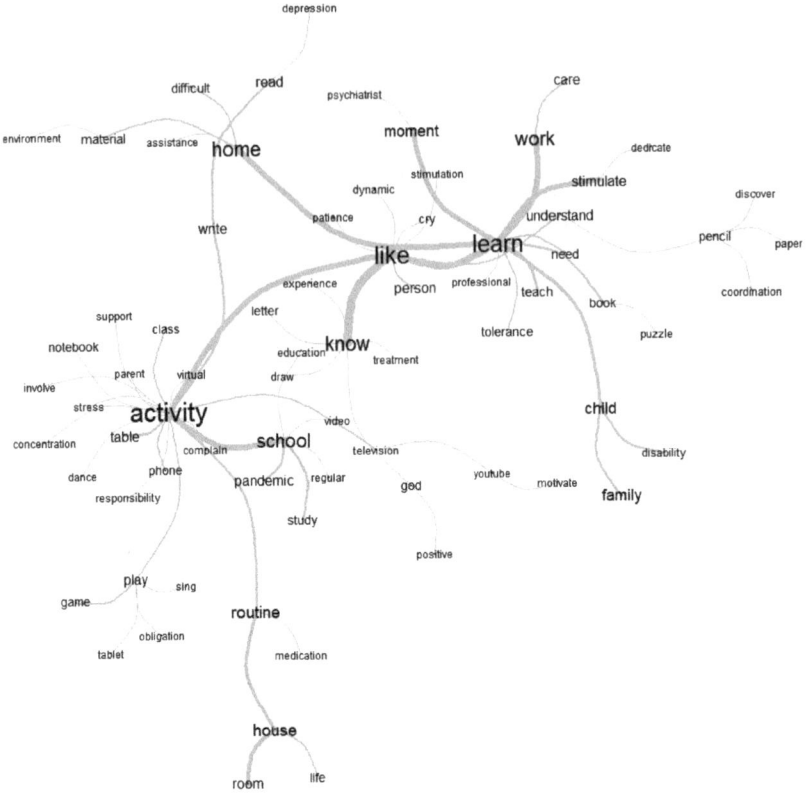

Figure 2. Similarity analysis

All other vertices stem from the term "home." Some appear more expressively and connect the terms "activity" and "learning." Symbolizing the starting point, the term "learning" is traversed by routine, revealing that family members prioritized the movement to adapt to their children's routine in the face of the pandemic. This "learning" aligned with "stimulating expressively" revealed the household's anxiety to be informed about what resources to employ to assist the several cognitive development aspects, such as reading. Anxiety is relevant and can be reduced by the guidance of trained professionals to family members so that they understand, help, teach, stimulate, and follow up on the learning process:

> Professionals say what is needed to carry out the activities. They explain how we should do it and what resources we can use, such as coloured pencils, crayons, markers, blunt scissors, paper, and bottle caps. It's very good; they teach us a lot, and then I can teach my son.

> She understands what we say, but I wanted her to read, write one day. However, professionals must help me in this regard.

Other words extend from the nucleating term "home," since there is a contextualized demonstration of the present for these mothers. Aggregate terms, such as "caring," "income," and "family," summarize the socioeconomic vulnerability in the daily lives of these families, regardless of the pandemic. However, this context aggravated these vulnerabilities, hindering their survival.

The vertex "time"—linked to "attention," "YouTube," "television," "paper," and "scissors"—appeared on the same axis. It summarizes the need to direct these households to encourage children with intellectual disabilities, offering only easily accessible resources but without defined and appropriate learning objectives.

The term "activity" is surrounded by the words "training," "class," "virtual," "monitor," "material," "drawing," "writing," "online," "write," "notebook," "develop," and "achieve." Even while recognizing the need to develop some activity, this segment may imply that collaborative work between the family, itself, and other equipment necessary to leverage learning is required. The link of a specialized institution (APAE) to the school allows support, ranging from specific guidance to the possibility of working at home with adequate resources.

Again, in the term "activity," we find the words "group," "tolerance," and "psychiatrist" in the ramification of the word "achieve," which evidences the need to control the tolerance of the child with a disability to the point of seeking medical support, since the current context has brought a lot of emotional instability of the whole family.

The software also made available the word cloud (Fig. 3), which highlights the words most evoked by the mothers, which are "being," "staying," "activity," and "home." We note, in the cloud, that words are randomly arranged in such a way that those that were calculated as the most frequent appear in larger sizes than others, thus showing their prominence in the research analysis corpus.

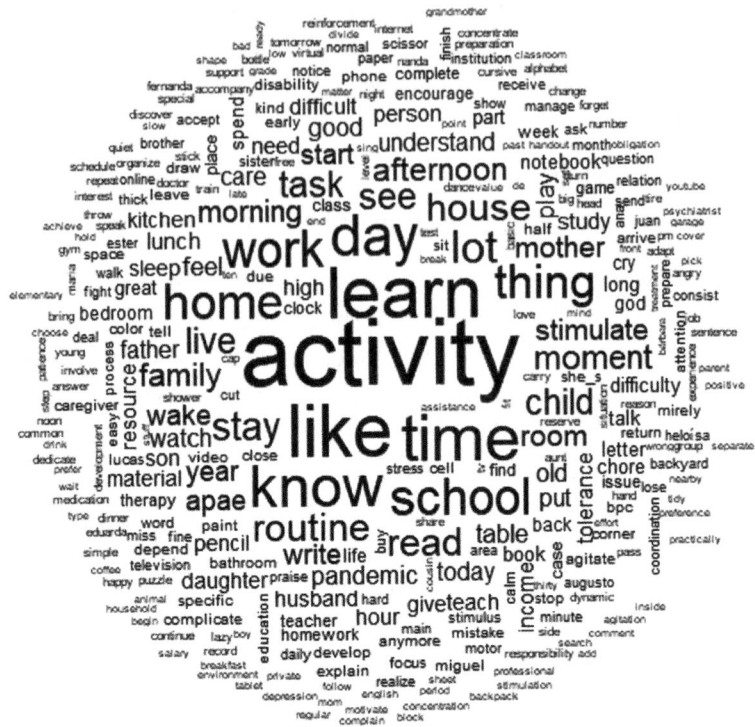

Figure 3. Word cloud

Discussion

The children's early learning occurs in the family. Thus, households assuming a significant role in its education is undisputed. Understood as the first and foremost educational agent, we can designate education as the core of the child's global development in the affective, social, cognitive, and motor aspects. Thus, the development of appropriate coping strategies is influenced by the quality of affective relationships, cohesion, safety, and organization. Such aspects favour the development of social skills and competencies and, consequently, cognitive stimulation (Carvalho, Ardores, and Castro). Yet this discourse results in another perception. The vulnerabilities generate a reality identified in many families that must support their children with intellectual disabilities.

The household's environment directly interferes with the developmental phases, and one of the main influencing factors can be described by the quality of these environments, which is offered to children, from birth to adulthood (Shonkoff and Meisels). In this context, we realized that although families cannot physically designate a specific space for teaching their children, they seek to provide a place for this moment to occur. Parents lack sufficient knowledge to implement and prepare such environments, which, properly designed, could be a place where children with intellectual disabilities could create and recreate knowledge, enabling new learning, which would certainly benefit cognitive development.

Besides offering an environment conducive to learning, adequate strategies and resources should be in place, which would allow the child to emerge per the desired level of development (Bossardi et al. 3). Appropriate stimuli—such as books, toys, games, and stimuli provided by play—enable the evolution of cognitive development (Avelar et al. 341).

Having the authority to know and understand their children and the responsibility and commitment to watch over their global development, households should offer minimum resources to produce home stimulation (Falbo et al. 152). Parents are not always aware of the resources required for cognitive stimulation.

Home was presented as the starting point, highlighting the desire to adapt the environment and correctly adopt a stimulus to learning. The term "learning" was aligned with the stimulus, as several factors are required for cognitive development (Reichenberger et al. 4), such as adequate and well-targeted resources to transform boring content into interesting and pleasurable activities (Ribeiro et al. 9). Thus, family members must be aware that these resources trigger significant learning and stimulate the construction of new knowledge with the development of new skills (Avelar et al. 348).

In this context, families are not aware of and do not understand the need to carry out the prior planning of a home activity. The family revealed the importance of the guidelines given by professionals, which direct the work to advance with the level of learning for children with intellectual disabilities (Fonseca et al. 13).

Before the problems and challenges faced by the family—the scarce support that favors effective directions for cognitive home stimulation, and shifting the responsibility in developing the autonomy of the disabled child to therapists and teachers—we noticed the difficulties of these family members in expressing their real anxieties related to children with intellectual difficulties. In this context, these family members are prevented from clearly expressing how they could help them during home learning.

Final Considerations

The results show us the need and urgency of a way to help these family members to act directly in their children's home learning, which could include involving the family in the home stimulation activities with their children through dialogue between the specialized institution and the school. In this way, the home becomes a space for the construction of practices conducive to learning.

Works Cited

Albuquerque, Maria S., et al. "Access to Healthcare for Children with Congenital Zika Syndrome in Brazil: Perspectives of Mothers and Health Professionals." *Health Policy and Planning*, vol. 34, no. 7, 2019, pp. 499-507.

American Psychiatric Association. *Diagnostic and Statistical Manual of Mental Disorders, Fifth Edition* (DSM-V). American Psychiatric Association, 2013.

Avelar, Kátia Santos, et al. "Estratégias de ensino-aprendizagem com alunos portadores de deficiência intelectual na disciplina de português." *Revista de Pesquisa Interdisciplinar*, vol. 2, no. 2, 2019, pp. 437-51.

Batista, Cristiane Elisa Ribas, and Santa Cecília Marques Herzog. *A família no contexto de ensino aprendizagem: perspectivas no contexto da pandemia do novo coronavirus*. UnC, 2020.

Benitez, Priscila, and Camila Domeniconi. "Capacitação de agentes educacionais: proposta de desenvolvimento de estratégias inclusivas." *Revista Brasileira de Educação Especial*, vol. 20, no. 3, 2014, pp. 371-86.

Bossardi, Carina Nunes, et al. "Funcionamento familiar e deficiência: um estudo com pessoas com deficiência física adquirida na região do vale do itajaí (SC)." *Psicologia: Ciência e Profissão*, vol. 41, no. 3, 2021, www.scielo.br/j/pcp/a/HHK5XJSPmpyLjMcV4BR6hDn/?lang=pt. Accessed 17 Feb. 2023.

Brasil. Ministério da Saúde. "Resolução nº 466, de 12 de dezembro de 2012." *Dispõe sobre diretrizes e normas regulamentadoras de pesquisas envolvendo seres humanos*. Ministério da Saúde, 2012, https://bit.ly/2UD9Dre. Accessed 17 Feb. 2023.

Camargo, Brígido V., and Ana M. Justo. "IRAMUTEQ: Um software gratuito para análise de dados textuais." *Temas em Psicologia*, vol. 21, no. 2, 2013, pp. 513-18.

Carvalho, Cláudia Lopes, Marilena Ardores, and Leila Regina de Castro. "Cuidadores familiares e o envelhecimento da pessoa com DI: implicações na prestação de cuidados." *Revista Kairós Gerontologia*, vol. 18, no. 3, 2015, pp. 333-52.

Falbo, Bruna Cristine Peres, et al. "Estímulo ao desenvolvimento infantil: produção do conhecimento em enfermagem." *Revista Brasileira de Enfermagem*, vol. 65, no. 1, 2012, pp. 148-54.

Fonseca, Sarah Cecílio, et al. "Investigação-ação com mães de pessoas com deficiência intelectual: a redução da sobrecarga como um projeto de vida." *Revista Educação Especial*, vol. 33, 2020, pp. 1-21.

Freitas, Patricia Martins de, and Denise Oliveira Ribeiro. "Neuroplasticidade na educação e reabilitação cognitiva da deficiência intellectual." *Revista Educação Especial*, vol. 32, 2019, pp. 1-20.

Gualda, Danielli Silva, et al. "Famílias de crianças com necessidades educacionais especiais: recursos e necessidades de apoio." *Revista Educação Especial*, vol. 26, no. 46, 2013, pp. 307-19.

Heilborn, Maria Luiza A, et al. "Tensões familiares em tempos de pandemia e confinamento: cuidadoras familiares." *Physis: Revista de Saúde Coletiva*, vol. 30, no. 2, 2020, www.scielo.br/j/physis/a/HZrBGxLgjTfdHXNPQM36CFM/?lang=pt. Accessed 17 Feb. 2023.

Reichenberger, Veronika, et al. "O desafio da inclusão de pessoas com deficiência na estratégia de enfrentamento à pandemia de COVID-19 no Brasil." *Epidemiologia e Serviços de Saúde*, vol. 29, no. 5, 2020, pp. 1-6.

Ribeiro, Everton, et al. "Novos arranjos familiares e homoparentalidade: uma apreciação do jogo da vida "famílias modernas". EccoS – Revista Científica, vol. 56, 2021, p. e11452.

Shonkoff, J. P., and S. J. Meisels. *Handbook of Early Childhood Intervention*. Cambridge University Press, 2000.

Tomaz, Rodrigo Victor Viana, et al. "Impacto da deficiência intelectual moderada na dinâmica e na qualidade de vida familiar: um estudo clínico-qualitativo". Cadernos de Saúde Pública, vol. 33, no. 11, 2017, www.scielo.br/j/csp/a/THGchgJ7SMGKPQK3w4DZ9Xt/?lang=pt. Accessed 17 Feb. 2023.

Chapter 3.

Attachment and the COVID-19 Pandemic

Brianne Coulombe, Bridget Cho, and Tuppett Yates

Attachment bonds between parents and children represent a core developmental system that supports adaptation to stress. A wealth of evidence suggests that secure attachment relationships are associated with greater psychological and physical wellbeing as well as with resilience in the wake of difficult life events (Darling Rasmussen et al.). At the same time, the family stress model (Masarik and Conger) emphasizes the negative influence of outside challenges on parent-child relationship quality and attachment. The COVID-19 pandemic has introduced numerous challenges for families, which both heighten the salience of attachment for child wellbeing and pose significant threats to its security.

In this chapter, we explore the role of attachment in children's experience of and adaptation to the COVID-19 pandemic. We focus on the development and impact of attachment security but also consider how the different forms of insecure attachment (i.e., avoidant, resistant, and disorganized) may influence these processes. Throughout, we emphasize the heightened significance of attachment in stressful contexts to explicate how attachment relationships have likely affected children's psychological responses (e.g., psychological distress and wellbeing), behavioural responses (e.g., prosocial behaviours to benefit others and health protective behaviours, such as masking and social distancing), and physiological responses (e.g., immune function) to the COVID-19 pandemic. We also consider how the security of parent-child attachments has likely been shaped by the changes and challenges introduced by the COVID-19 pandemic. We identify several factors, such as racial and ethnic disparities, facets of the family environment, and access to social support, which may further influence the relation between attachment and child adjustment within the COVID-19 context. We conclude by discussing how lessons learned in the context of the COVID-19 pandemic can be harnessed to support the ongoing negotiation and recovery of children and families in response to this crisis.

The Development and Adaptive Significance of Attachment Security

Psychological theorists and researchers have long centred the quality of the parent-child relationship in models of both health and illness. However, it was not until the 1950s that central features of this relationship were codified in John Bowlby and Mary Ainsworth's notions of attachment and sensitive caregiving. Bowlby coined the term "attachment" to describe a species-universal evolutionary process that encourages human survival by establishing and maintaining proximity to a sensitive and responsive caregiver. He posited that this behavioural system is activated by the introduction of environmental threats and reciprocally reinforced when caregivers manage or resolve the child's distress. In her direct observations of mother-infant interactions, Ainsworth demonstrated that repeated experiences of sensitive responding to children's attachment behaviours (e.g., crying, vocalizing, and clinging) contributed to the development of an organized regulatory system through which children manage the physical and psychological distance between themselves and their parent (Ainsworth et al.). Across development, children's trust in their relationship with their parent supports their exploration and interaction with their environment (i.e., secure base); they have confidence that they can find physical and emotional safety in the relationship should they become threatened (i.e., a safe haven; Ainsworth et al.). Together, these functions of secure base and safe haven comprise attachment security.

Over time, repeated exchanges in the caregiving relationship inform children's emergent beliefs and expectations, or mental representations, about the reliability and safety of others. In tandem, children develop a complementary representation of their own worth and competence (Bretherton and Munholland). Sensitive and responsive parents, and the resultant security of attachment, support children's understanding of the world as predictable and safe as well as their confidence in their capacity to overcome challenges with the help of their parent (Sroufe). Parents' sensitive modulation of children's emotional, behavioural, and physiological responses to contextual demands, or coregulation, offers critical support for children's emergent capacities to control their own responses in the interest of goal attainment through self-monitoring (i.e., self-regulation). Although attachment security develops across the infant and toddler years, its implications for adaptation are enduring, as it lays the foundation for the way individuals think about others, the self, and the self-with-others. These internal working models are informed by the quality of these early caregiving exchanges and remain relatively stable across time (Bretherton and Munholland).

Internal working models encompass individuals' beliefs and expectations of the self, others, and the self-in-relationship with others, which emerge from the quality of early caregiving exchanges. In the context of sensitive and responsive caregiving, children develop positive expectations for themselves and the social world. However, when caregiving sensitivity is compromised by rejecting or inconsistent parenting practises, children may develop insecure internal working models. In cases of a severe breakdown in parenting quality, such as when a parent is frightening and abusive or frightened and traumatized, the attachment system breaks down, resulting in a disorganized or disoriented attachment. In these cases, the parent either represents a source of fear, as in the case of a frightening or abusive parent, or communicates that the child is a source of fear, as in the case of a frightened or traumatized parent. Because the evolutionary function of attachment is to provide children with safety during times of vulnerability, the experience of frightening or frightened behaviour from their attachment figure evokes competing strategies for managing separation and challenge. In these instances, the attachment system becomes disorganized, as the child is compelled to both flee from the danger of the parent, as in avoidant attachment, and approach the safety of the parent, as in resistant attachment simultaneously.

Attachment security is positively associated with a range of adjustment indicators (Cassidy and Shaver). For example, children with secure attachments are better able to label and define emotions, which supports their capacity to manage and regulate them effectively. By engendering children's positive beliefs about the self and others, sensitive caregiving and ensuing attachment security also enhance the quality of children's social relationships. In the cognitive domain, attachment security is positively linked with children's executive functioning (e.g., working memory and attentional control) as well as academic achievement. Of particular relevance to children's navigation of the COVID-19 pandemic is the special significance of attachment relationships for understanding individual differences in adjusting to stressful contexts. Indeed, a wealth of literature points to the robust contribution of attachment security to positive adaptation in the face of adverse life events (Darling Rasmussen et al.).

Attachment Security and Adaptation to the COVID-19 Context

Given the role of attachment security in multiple domains of competence, and especially in coping with difficult life events, secure parent-child attachment relationships are an important source of support for children's and adolescents' successful navigation of the COVID-19 pandemic. Children have experienced a variety of stressful changes to their daily lives as a result of this pandemic, including the shift to remote schooling, limited access to extracurricular activities (e.g., sports and music groups), and reduced contact with extrafamilial social partners (e.g., friends, teachers, and extended family). For the more than 5.2 million children worldwide who have experienced the death of a parent due to COVID-19 (Unwin et al.)—and the countless others who have lost extended family members, particularly grandparents—these challenges are all the greater. In addition to direct stressors, children have witnessed changes in the physical, emotional, and economic stability of their families and communities that assuredly threaten their sense of safety and predictability in the world. For these reasons, parent-child attachment relationships have played an important role in children's psychological, behavioural, and biological adaptation to the COVID-19 pandemic.

Attachment and Psychological Adjustment to COVID-19

Among older children and adolescents, the quality of attachment relationships prior to the onset of the pandemic likely supported their psychological health during it, even amid contemporaneous changes in parenting stress or sensitivity. Children's confidence in the availability and sensitivity of their parents equips them with a wide repertoire of effective coping mechanisms to recruit when facing difficult life events, both in the presence and the absence of their attachment figure. As children gain experience coregulating difficult emotions with a supportive parent, they develop the skills to effectively regulate emotions independently, which decreases their risk for psychopathology. The COVID-19 pandemic precipitated worldwide spikes in anxiety, depression, and posttraumatic stress (Vindegaard and Benros). Thus, it is critical to understand and amplify the protective potential of attachment relationships to promote mental health.

A primary function of the attachment relationship is to mitigate the distress caused by difficult or stressful experiences. Thus, it is unsurprising that young children have demonstrated a significant increase in attachment-related behaviours, such as clinging to parents, since the start of the pandemic (Jiao et al.). Moreover, growing evidence demonstrates that parents' capacity to respond to these attachment-related demands appropriately promoted children's psychological wellbeing during the early phases of the pandemic (Neubauer et al.). Similarly, recent evidence suggests that relations between parents' and children's mental health problems during the pandemic were less pronounced in families with positive parent-child relationships (Bate et al.). That is, positive parent-child relationships protected children from the anxiety, depression, and behaviour problems that are typically associated with parental distress.

Adolescence represents a crucial transition period in attachment because youth turn towards peers and romantic partners as attachment figures of equal or greater value to parents (Cassidy and Shaver). COVID-19 lockdowns and school closures might have presented unique challenges for adolescents who experienced reduced contact with these emergent attachment relationships. For example, evidence suggests that attachment to peers was a stronger predictor of adolescents' posttraumatic stress symptoms during COVID-19 than attachment to parents (Tambelli et al.). The deleterious impact of COVID-19 restrictions might have been magnified for adolescents who depend on extrafamilial relationships for psychological support. For example, a study of Italian adolescents conducted at the height of the country-wide lockdown demonstrated that psychopathological outcomes were most pronounced among those high in attachment insecurity with both parents and peers (Muzi et al.). Notwithstanding the rising significance of extrafamilial relationships across development, parent-child attachment security continues to shape adolescents' psychological adjustment. Indeed, emerging evidence suggests that adolescents with secure attachment relationships prior to the pandemic evidenced fewer than expected mental health symptoms in response to the onset of the pandemic (Coulombe and Yates).

Attachment and Behavioural Adjustment to COVID-19

Attachment security supports children's prosocial behaviour, or behaviour intended to benefit others. Repeated experiences of successfully managing distress with the help of a sensitive parent gives children the confidence that they can be similarly effective in mitigating the distress of others (Cassidy et al.). Furthermore, as children effectively process their own distress, they gain the capacity to turn their attention to the needs of others (Williams and Berthelsen). Thus, secure attachments engender positive behaviours.

The containment of the COVID-19 pandemic relies heavily on our willingness and capability to behave prosocially. For example, although wearing a mask prevents the contraction of COVID-19, it mitigates the spread of the virus to others even more strongly. Likewise, COVID-19 vaccines not only enhance individual immunity but also reduce virus transmission rates and support herd immunity for the broader population. Thus, understanding how and why children may engage in these other-oriented behaviours is of critical importance to containing and ending the COVID-19 pandemic. Early longitudinal evidence suggests that secure attachment relationships in early adolescence promoted later psychological wellbeing during the onset of the COVID-19 pandemic and, as a result, engendered both prosocial and COVID-19 health-protective behaviours (Coulombe and Yates). However, even some instances of attachment insecurity, such as resistant attachment, might have contributed to positive health protective practices (Lozano and Fraley).

Attachment and Biological Adjustment to COVID-19

In addition to psychological and behavioural health outcomes, attachment security influences the development and operation of biological stress response systems (Gunnar et al.). Fundamental stress response systems, such as the hypothalamic-pituitary-adrenal (HPA) axis, are coregulated with parents. Over time, recurrent patterns of coregulation shape children's capacities to modulate their own biological responses to stressful experiences.

Although some level of physiological reactivity to stress is normative, absent, extreme, or prolonged (e.g., dysregulated), stress responses have markedly negative implications for physical health (Turner et al.). Stressful experiences, especially those occurring in childhood, are linked with a host of later health problems, including decreased immunity, cardiovascular disease, autoimmune disease, obesity, diabetes, and early mortality (Hughes et al.). Children with secure attachment relationships demonstrate adaptive HPA responsivity to and adequate recovery from stress (Gunnar et al.), which decreases their risk for subsequent health problems. Thus, attachment security has the potential to support children's navigation of pandemic-related stressors in ways that protect their physical health and may render them less vulnerable to disease contraction and progression.

The Development of Attachment Security during the COVID-19 Pandemic

The COVID-19 pandemic and the attendant restrictions placed on individuals and families changed the landscape in which attachment security develops. Families have encountered unprecedented economic and social stress, children have faced marked changes in their access to social partners, and together they have worried about and mourned the lost lives of loved ones. Against the backdrop of these disruptions, more than 3.5 million infants who were born in the United States (US) in 2020 are forming their primary attachments (Hamilton et al.). Theoretical and empirical findings suggest that COVID-19 has influenced attachment security and development across the lifespan.

Prenatal Attachment during the COVID-19 Pandemic

Prenatal attachment captures the unique relationship between an expectant parent and a developing fetus (Brandon et al.). During the prenatal period, parents think about their child-to-be, talk with others, prepare for delivery, and experience a host of feelings about their developing child. Expectant parents carry their own hopes and fears into this emerging relationship resulting in a set of beliefs and expectations (i.e., an internal working model) about their child-to-be that shapes the postnatal parent-infant relationship (Slade and Sadler).

In the best of times, pregnancy is accompanied by numerous worries, but the COVID-19 pandemic has magnified these uncertainties. Expectant parents face intensified worries about the quality and availability of their support networks amid social distancing requirements, potential insecurities in their finances and employment, and threats to the health and safety of their newborn in the absence of vaccination resources. Evidence from the first few months of the COVID-19 pandemic suggest that near-term pregnant women felt stressed and confused; half the sample were unsure as to whether breastfeeding would become unsafe, over a third frequently worried about becoming infected with COVID-19 while pregnant, and most worried that they or their baby may be infected during or right after delivery (Yassa et al.). Amid this heightened sense of uncertainty and vulnerability, parents may be more likely to question their capacity to adequately nurture and protect their child. In turn, these feelings of helplessness may undermine the development of prenatal attachment and subsequent self-efficacy in the caregiving role (George and Solomon). Recent findings indicate that the COVID-19 pandemic has negatively affected prenatal attachment for many women. For example, a spring 2020 survey of Italian pregnant women revealed negative relations between anxiety and important indicators of positive prenatal attachment, such as thinking about, planning for, and talking to the developing baby (Craig et al.). Other studies have documented negative associations between COVID-19 anxieties, such as fear of contracting the illness, and prenatal attachment (e.g., Karaca et al.). Since the COVID-19 pandemic began, pregnant women have consistently reported marked elevations in anxiety and depressive symptoms above prepandemic levels (e.g., King et al.). These escalations are of serious concern, since prior studies have shown that mothers' mental health difficulties undermine positive prenatal attachment (Alhusen et al.) with enduring implications for postnatal attachment security (Barnes and Theule).

Postnatal Attachment during the COVID-19 Pandemic

As with expectant parents, the COVID-19 pandemic has negatively affected parental wellbeing and attachment security in families with infants and children. As noted earlier, one mechanism by which the pandemic may have negatively affected postnatal attachment security is parental psychological distress, including parenting stress, anxiety, and depression. Parents struggling with mental health concerns may be "psychologically separated from their infants," making it difficult for them to be attuned and responsive, even when the parent and infant are physically together. The more psychological distress parents experience, the less secure their attachment relationships with their own infants and children tend to be (Barnes and Theule).

During the infant and toddler periods, postpartum depression (PPD), which is a clinical condition in which a parent experiences a major depressive episode within one month of delivery (American Psychiatric Association), may pose a particularly potent threat to parent-infant attachment security. Symptoms of PPD include low mood, lack of interest or pleasure, sleep disturbances, irritability, feelings of guilt and hopelessness, difficulty concentrating, and suicidality. PPD impairs parent-infant bonding, with parents suffering from the condition more likely to say that they feel irritated by their baby, trapped by parenthood, and that they lack closeness with their babies (Faisal-Cury et al.). Maternal depression, including PPD, consistently predicts insecure attachment (Barnes and Theule).

New parents are particularly vulnerable to PPD during community-wide catastrophic events due to the loss of psychosocial resources (Ehrlich et al.). Consistent with this prior literature, rates of PPD have increased during the COVID-19 pandemic. A study conducted in northeastern Italy, which was heavily affected by COVID-19 early in the pandemic, compared rates of PPD symptoms among women who gave birth between March and May of 2020 to a similar group of women who gave birth during the same time the previous year. The prevalence of PPD more than doubled during the pandemic; 12% of women reported clinically significant symptoms in 2019 compared to 26% in 2020 (Zanardo et al.). Similarly, in a Turkish study, twice as many women who gave birth in the spring of 2020 were at risk for PPD (14.7%), compared to a similar group of women surveyed at the same hospital prior to the pandemic (7.8%; Oskovi-Kaplan et al.). Maternal attachment security was also lower among mothers with high PPD symptoms in this sample.

In addition to PPD, the pandemic might have affected postnatal attachment via escalations of intimate partner conflict. Stressful life events negatively affect subjective perceptions of intimacy, support, and enjoyment in romantic relationships (Williams). Romantic partnerships have suffered during the pandemic amid increased stress and uncertainty (e.g., Agüero). These risks may be compounded in families with young children, as the postpartum period is associated with lower relationship and sexual satisfaction at the best of times (Leavitt et al.) Given that interparental relationships with high conflict, low communication, and poor satisfaction predict lower parent-child attachment security during early childhood (Howes and Markman), the pandemic might have undermined attachment security via these relational processes.

For many couples, the pandemic introduced elevated threats of violence in the home as global rates of intimate partner violence rose sharply following initial pandemic lockdowns. Given previous evidence that rates of intimate partner violence increase during the perinatal period (Bowen et al.), families with infants were at particularly significant risk during the pandemic. Following the tenets of emotional security theory (Cummings and Davies), intimate partner violence undermines the development of attachment security during infancy and childhood. In these settings, children's heightened fear, due to violence exposure, activates the attachment system at the very moment when parents are least equipped to restore the child's sense of trust and safety.

Moderators of the Association Between Pandemic Stressors and Attachment Security

Notwithstanding the adaptive significance of parent-child attachment security, as well as the aforementioned risks to its development during this pandemic, the experience of the COVID-19 pandemic has been far from uniform, even within the US. Numerous factors influenced how each family adapted to the pandemic, including prepandemic child, parent, and family characteristics; the extent to which the pandemic altered the family environment; and the degree to which the family's economic and social resources were affected. Thus, it is important to consider potential moderators of associations between attachment security and children's adaptation to the pandemic as well as between pandemic stressors and the development of attachment security.

Racial and Ethnic Disparities

The COVID-19 pandemic has been a uniquely traumatic experience for racial and ethnic minority families for several reasons. First, the coronavirus has disproportionately caused illness and death among people of colour (Holmes et al.). Second, racial and ethnic minority groups experienced greater economic and employment instability compared to white people (Dias). Finally, the COVID-19 pandemic coincided with increased anti-Asian violence and heightened exposure to anti-Black violence in the US, including highly publicized instances of police brutality and social backlash against protests calling for racial justice. Although psychological distress was widely experienced during the pandemic, racial and ethnic minority individuals were particularly hard hit (Gibbs et al.), especially those with prepandemic psychosocial risk factors such as financial strain (Adesogan et al.). Thus, both the significance of attachment security and threats to its development may have been heightened for racial and ethnic minority families.

Family Environment

The COVID-19 pandemic introduced shifts in the degree of contact between parents and children. In many cases, parents and children found themselves working and learning from home, with attendant increases in parent-child contact. For example, one study conducted in the spring of 2020 found that parents were spending more time with their children in a variety of activities compared to before the pandemic, including playing, eating meals, going for walks, reading books, and watching television together (Lee et al.). In cases of positive relationships, heightened proximity may have increased the relevance and security of attachment relationships. For example, one study evaluating the musical engagement of parents and children during the pandemic indicated that parents found many opportunities to help their children connect with music during the pandemic and parent-child musical engagement predicted attachment security (Steinberg et al.).

For other families, the heightened intensity of parent-child contact might have strained the attachment relationship. Results of the American Psychological Association's (2020) *Stress In America* poll found that parents were significantly more stressed than adults without children, and longitudinal studies documented increases in parents' depression, anxiety, and stress since before the pandemic began (Westrupp et al.). Being confined to the same living quarters without the possibility of the reprieve normally offered by out-of-home childcare and social engagements with friends and family may have rendered parents less patient and emotionally available to their children, with expected negative implications for parent-child relationship quality and child adaptation. Given that attachment behaviours are most relevant in stressful situations, reductions in parents' patience and emotional availability may have undermined children's successful navigation of COVID-19 and related stressors (Neubauer et al.).

Of note, a significant number of families experienced dramatic declines in the quantity and quality of time spent together. Many frontline workers isolated themselves from their families to avoid disease transmission or were temporarily separated from their families while they travelled to areas where their clinical services were needed (Schwartz). Although empirical data regarding the impact of family separation for frontline workers and their children have yet to emerge, prior studies showing that even temporary parent-child separations negatively affect children's attachment security point to the need for targeted research focussed on these families.

Economic Stressors

Variable experiences of economic and occupational stability throughout the pandemic likely shaped the significance and quality of parent-child attachment. Many parents experienced layoffs alongside increased childcare demands. More than 22 million Americans lost their jobs during the first month after the US declared COVID-19 a national emergency (Long). One quarter of adults reported that they or someone in their household was laid off or lost their job due to the pandemic, one quarter reported trouble paying their bills, and about one-in-six had borrowed money from others or visited a food bank to make ends meet (Parker et al.).

As noted earlier, the family stress model (Masarik and Conger) provides a theoretical framework for understanding how stress, particularly economic stress, adversely affects family functioning. In this view, economic hardship introduces several threats to positive child and adolescent development through its negative effects on parents' psychological functioning, relationship quality, and parenting behaviour. Consistent with this theory, pandemic mental health effects were more pronounced among lower-income parents compared to higher-income parents (Fong and Iarocci). Likewise, parental job loss was associated with increased conflict between parents and adolescents, which, in turn, predicted declines in adolescents' expression of positive emotions (Wang et al.).

Research has yet to be published regarding the effects of family economic insecurity on parent-infant relationships or the formation of attachment during COVID-19, but parental job loss and other economic and social stressors might have increased rates of child maltreatment (e.g., Griffith). Even parents who continued to work throughout the pandemic, though fortunate not to experience job loss, might have encountered childcare issues, raising the potential for supervisory neglect when parents were required to work outside the home despite school and daycare centre closures (Humphreys et al.)

Social Support

Social support promotes positive mental health outcomes and attenuates the impact of stress and adversity on mental health. Although emotional support from friends and family buffered the effects of COVID-19 stress on mental health difficulties (Szkody et al.), the lack of physical support instantiated by social distancing guidelines may have been particularly impactful for families with children. Amid childcare closures and travel restrictions, families may have lost access to previously available social support networks. Prior research demonstrates that parents' lack of contact with and assistance from friends and family members, such as grandparents, accounts for up to half the parenting stress that parents experience (Parkes et al.). Despite the availability of telecommunications, many parents found these to be an inadequate replacement for in-person social support and contact (Ollivier et al.), and these, too, were differentially accessible across economic and regional groups.

Concluding Thoughts and Future Directions of Research

Attachment theorists emphasize the contribution of sensitive and responsive caregiving to the development of children's trust in the parent-child relationship, regulatory competence, and successful navigation of difficult life events. The COVID-19 pandemic has introduced numerous challenges for both parents and children, but attachment security can help children survive and thrive during this period of marked uncertainty. Likewise, the COVID-19 pandemic has dramatically altered the landscape in which attachment relationships develop, which may have important implications for children's capacity to navigate future crises. As theory and research on the impact of COVID-19 become increasingly available, it is important to consider best practices for moving through and beyond this global crisis. At a time when so much about the COVID-19 pandemic is beyond our control, we can take comfort in knowing that active efforts on the part of parents, providers, and policymakers to protect and promote attachment security can equip children with effective tools to navigate this and future crises. Supporting parents during these challenging times will positively affect family and child functioning. At the same time, supporting children may help to reduce parenting stress during COVID-19.

Several evidence-based dyadic interventions have been developed to support secure attachment and enhance positive parenting of infants and young children, including Child Parent Psychotherapy (Lieberman et al.), Circle of Security (Coyne et al.), and Attachment and Biobehavioral Catch-up (ABC; Dozier and Bernard). These and other attachment-based interventions have been adapted for delivery via telehealth during the pandemic (Zayde et al.) and have shown positive empirical results regarding the feasibility and effectiveness of Circle of Security (Cook et al.) and ABC (Schein et al.). Provision of telehealth services has been facilitated by changes allowing Medicaid to reimburse telehealth therapy services, providing more people safe access to mental health services. Although many have argued for the continuation of this policy, additional support and funding will be needed to increase accessibility of telehealth services for marginalized communities (Ortega et al.), who may be most at risk for negative COVID-19 effects on attachment.

Emerging theory and research clearly indicate that attachment security was and continues to play a vital role in children's adaptation to and recovery from the COVID-19 pandemic. At the same time, pandemic-related stressors have threatened the development of attachment security. Importantly, associations between attachment and child outcomes are likely recursive in ways that have yet to be examined during this pandemic. For example, children with less secure attachments may have experienced greater emotional distress and behaviour problems in response to the pandemic which, in turn, may have further taxed the parent-child relationship and undermined attachment security in ways that contributed to ongoing escalations of child problems. As we work to understand whether and why children may realize adaptive or maladaptive outcomes during and following the COVID-19 pandemic, future research should examine bidirectional models that fully capture the interplay between attachment and child behaviour.

The consequences of COVID-19 are likely to reach beyond the pandemic's end, as the landscape in which children are developing has changed in significant and potentially enduring ways. Educational systems have shifted, with many schools continuing to vacillate between in-person and online educational modalities. Likewise, interactions with individuals living outside the home have become distanced and strained. Many families have exhausted their emergency savings and many parents, especially mothers, have faced career setbacks that could have long-term implications for their future economic and financial stability.

At the level of policy, we encourage ongoing efforts to provide financial assistance to low- and middle-income families with children (e.g., Child Tax Credits provided through President Biden's American Rescue Plan), especially given recent findings suggesting that cash payments and increases in the minimum wage have positive effects on infant brain development (Troller-Renfree et al.) and family well-being (Raissian and Bullinger). As children learn to navigate this and future crises, they will continue to rely heavily on their attachment figures for support and guidance. Thus, we must support both parents and children to promote positive outcomes now and for future generations.

Works Cited

Adesogan, Olutosin, et al. "COVID-19 Stress and the Health of Black Americans in the Rural South." *Clinical Psychological Science*, Oct. 2021, p. 21677026211049380. *SAGE Journals*, https://doi.org/10.1177/21677026211049379.

Agüero, Jorge M. "COVID-19 and the Rise of Intimate Partner Violence." *World Development*, vol. 137, 2021, p. 105217.

Ainsworth, Mary, D. Salter, et al. *Patterns of Attachment: A Psychological Study of the Strange Situation*. Psychology Press, 2015.

Alhusen, Jeanne L., et al. "The Role of Mental Health on Maternal Fetal

Attachment in Low Income Women." *Journal of Obstetric, Gynecologic & Neonatal Nursing*, vol. 41, no. 6, Nov. 2012, pp. E71-81.

American Psychiatric Association. *Diagnostic and Statistical Manual of Mental Disorders*. 5th ed. APA, 2013.

Barnes, Jennifer, and Jennifer Theule. "Maternal Depression and Infant Attachment Security: A Meta Analysis." *Infant Mental Health Journal*, vol. 40, no. 6, Nov. 2019, pp. 817-34.

Bate, Jordan, et al. "Be My Safe Haven: Parent-Child Relationships and Emotional Health During COVID-19." *Journal of Pediatric Psychology*, vol. 46, no. 6, 2021, pp. 624-34.

Bowen, Erica, et al. "Domestic Violence Risk during and after Pregnancy: Findings from a British Longitudinal Study." *BJOG: An International Journal of Obstetrics & Gynaecology*, vol. 112, no. 8, 2005, pp. 1083-89.

Bowlby, John. "The Nature of the Child's Tie to His Mother." *International Journal of Psycho-Analysis*, vol. 39, 1958, pp. 350-73.

Brandon, Anna R., et al. "A History of the Theory of Prenatal Attachment." *Journal of Prenatal & Perinatal Psychology & Health: APPPAH*, vol. 23, no. 4, 2009, pp. 201-22.

Bretherton, Inge, and Kristine A. Munholland. "Internal Working Models in Attachment Relationships: Elaborating a Central Construct in Attachment Theory." *Handbook of Attachment: Theory, Research, and Clinical Applications*, edited by J. Cassidy and P. R. Shaver, The Guilford Press, 2008, pp. 102-27.

Cassidy, Jude, et al. "Influences on Care for Others: Attachment Security, Personal Suffering, and Similarity between Helper and Care Recipient." *Personality and Social Psychology Bulletin*, vol. 44, no. 4, 2018, pp. 574-88.

Cassidy, Jude, and Phillip R. Shaver. *Handbook of Attachment: Theory, Research, and Clinical Applications*. Rough Guides, 2002.

Cook, Alison, et al. "Pivot to Telehealth: Narrative Reflections on Circle of Security Parenting Groups during COVID-19." *Australian and New Zealand Journal of Family Therapy*, vol. 42, no. 1, Mar. 2021, pp. 106-14.

Coulombe, Brianne R., and Tuppett M. Yates. "Attachment Security Predicts Adolescents' Prosocial and Health Protective Responses to the COVID-19 Pandemic." *Child Development*, vol. 93, no. 1, 2022, pp. 58-71.

Coyne, Joe, et al. "The Circle of Security." *Handbook of Infant Mental Health*, edited by Charles H. Zeanah, The Guilford Press, 2018, pp. 286-498.

Craig, Francesco, et al. "Effects of Maternal Psychological Distress and Perception of COVID-19 on Prenatal Attachment in a Large Sample of Italian Pregnant Women." *Journal of Affective Disorders*, vol. 295, 2021, pp. 665-72.

Cummings, E. Mark, and Patrick Davies. "Emotional Security as a Regulatory Process in Normal Development and the Development of Psychopathology." *Development and Psychopathology*, vol. 8, no. 1, 1996, pp. 123-39.

Darling Rasmussen, Pernille, et al. "Attachment as a Core Feature of Resilience: A Systematic Review and Meta-Analysis." *Psychological Reports*, vol. 122, no. 4, 2019, pp. 1259-96.

Dias, Felipe A. "The Racial Gap in Employment and Layoffs during COVID-19 in the United States: A Visualization." *Socius*, vol. 7, 2021, p. 2378023120988397.

Dozier, Mary, and Kristin Bernard. "Attachment and Biobehavioral Catch-Up." *Handbook of Infant Mental Health*, edited by Charles H. Zeanah, The Guilford Press, 2018, pp. 499-511.

Ehrlich, Matthew, et al. "Loss of Resources and Hurricane Experience as Predictors of Postpartum Depression among Women in Southern Louisiana." *Journal of Women's Health*, vol. 19, no. 5, May 2010, pp. 877-84.

Faisal-Cury, Alexandre, et al. "Postpartum Bonding at the Beginning of the Second Year of a Child's Life: The Role of Postpartum Depression and Early Bonding Impairment." *Journal of Psychosomatic Obstetrics & Gynecology*, vol. 41, no. 3, 2020, pp. 224-30.

Fong, Vanessa C., and Grace Iarocci. "Child and Family Outcomes Following Pandemics: A Systematic Review and Recommendations on COVID-19 Policies." *Journal of Pediatric Psychology*, vol. 45, no. 10, 2020, pp. 1124-43.

George, Carol, and Judith Solomon. "Caregiving Helplessness: The Development of a Screening Measure for Disorganized Maternal Caregiving." *Disorganized Attachment and Caregiving*, 2011, pp. 133-66, https://pascal-uscaiken.primo.exlibrisgroup.com. Accessed 18 Feb. 2023.

Gibbs, Tresha, et al. "Mental Health Disparities Among Black Americans During the COVID-19 Pandemic." *Psychiatric Times*, https://www.psychiatrictimes.com/view/mental-health-disparities-among-black-americans-during-covid-19-pandemic. Accessed 18 Feb. 2023.

Griffith, Annette K. "Parental Burnout and Child Maltreatment During the COVID-19 Pandemic." *Journal of Family Violence*, June 2020. *Springer Link*, https://doi.org/10.1007/s10896-020-00172-2.

Gunnar, Megan R., et al. "Stress Reactivity and Attachment Security." *Developmental Psychobiology*, vol. 29, no. 3, 1996, pp. 191-204.

Hamilton, Brady E., et al. *Births: Provisional Data for 2020*. CDC, 2021, www.cdc.gov/nchs/data/vsrr/vsrr012-508.pdf. Accessed 18 Feb. 2023.

Holmes, Laurens, et al. "Black–White Risk Differentials in COVID-19 (SARS-COV2) Transmission, Mortality and Case Fatality in the United States: Translational Epidemiologic Perspective and Challenges." *International Journal of Environmental Research and Public Health*, vol. 17, no. 12, Jan. 2020, p. 4322.

Howes, Paul, and Howard J. Markman. "Marital Quality and Child Functioning: A Longitudinal Investigation." *Child Development*, vol. 60, no. 5, Oct. 1989, pp. 1044-51.

Hughes, Karen, et al. "The Effect of Multiple Adverse Childhood Experiences on Health: A Systematic Review and Meta-Analysis." *The Lancet Public Health*, vol. 2, no. 8, 2017, pp. e356-66.

Humphreys, Kathryn L., et al. "Increased Risk for Family Violence During the COVID-19 Pandemic." *Pediatrics*, vol. 146, no. 1, 2020, p. e20200982.

Jiao, Wen Yan, et al. "Behavioral and Emotional Disorders in Children during the COVID-19 Epidemic." *The Journal of Pediatrics*, vol. 221, 2020, p. 264.

Karaca, Pelin Palas, et al. "The Relationship between Pregnant Women's Anxiety Levels about Coronavirus and Prenatal Attachment." *Archives of Psychiatric Nursing*, vol. 36, Feb. 2022, pp. 78-84.

Leavitt, Chelom E., et al. "Parenting Stress and Sexual Satisfaction among First-Time Parents: A Dyadic Approach." *Sex Roles*, vol. 76, no. 5, Mar. 2017, pp. 346-55.

Lee, Shawna J., et al. "Parenting Activities and the Transition to Home-Based Education during the COVID-19 Pandemic." *Children and Youth Services Review*, vol. 122, Mar. 2021, p. 105585.

Lieberman, Alicia, et al. "Child-Parent Psychotherapy." *Handbook of Infant Mental Health*, edited by Charles H. Zeanah, The Guilford Press, 2018, pp. 471-85.

Masarik, April S., and Rand D. Conger. "Stress and Child Development: A Review of the Family Stress Model." *Current Opinion in Psychology*, vol. 13, 2017, pp. 85-90.

Muzi, Stefania, et al. "What's Happened to Italian Adolescents during the COVID-19 Pandemic? A Preliminary Study on Symptoms, Problematic Social Media Usage, and Attachment: Relationships and Differences with Pre-Pandemic Peers." *Frontiers in Psychiatry*, vol. 12, 2021. www.frontiersin.org/articles/10.3389/fpsyt.2021.590543/full. Accessed 18 Feb. 2023.

Neubauer, Andreas B., et al. "A Little Autonomy Support Goes a Long Way: Daily Autonomy-Supportive Parenting, Child Well-Being, Parental Need Fulfillment, and Change in Child, Family, and Parent Adjustment Across the Adaptation to the COVID-19 Pandemic." *Child Development*, vol. 92, no. 5, 2021, pp. 1679-97.

Ollivier, Rachel, et al. "Mental Health & Parental Concerns during COVID-19: The Experiences of New Mothers Amidst Social Isolation." *Midwifery*, vol. 94, Mar. 2021, p. 102902.

Ortega, Gezzer, et al. "Telemedicine, COVID-19, and Disparities: Policy Implications." *Health Policy and Technology*, vol. 9, no. 3, Sept. 2020, pp. 368-71.

Oskovi-Kaplan, Z., Asli, et al. "The Effect of Covid-19 Pandemic and Social Restrictions on Depression Rates and Maternal Attachment in Immediate Postpartum Women: A Preliminary Study." *Psychiatric Quarterly*, Sept. 2020. 2020-67581-001, *EBSCOhost*, https://doi.org/10.1007/s11126-020-09843-1.

Parker, Kim, et al. "Economic Fallout From COVID-19 Continues To Hit Lower-Income Americans the Hardest." *Pew Research Center's Social & Demographic Trends Project*, 24 Sept. 2020, https://www.

pewresearch.org/social-trends/2020/09/24/economic-fallout-from-covid-19-continues-to-hit-lower-income-americans-the-hardest/. Accessed 18 Feb. 2023.

Parkes, Alison, et al. "Parenting Stress and Parent Support among Mothers with High and Low Education." *Journal of Family Psychology*, vol. 29, no. 6, 2015, p. 907.

Raissian, Kerri M., and Lindsey Rose Bullinger. "Money Matters: Does the Minimum Wage Affect Child Maltreatment Rates?" *Children and Youth Services Review*, vol. 72, 2017, pp. 60-70.

Schein, Stevie S., et al. "Assessing Changes in Parent Sensitivity in Telehealth and Hybrid Implementation of Attachment and Biobehavioral Catch-Up During the COVID-19 Pandemic." *Child Maltreatment*, Jan. 2022, p. 10775595211072516. *PubMed*, https://doi.org/10.1177/10775595211072516.

Schwartz, Susan. "Front-Line Health Care Workers Reunite with Children after Months Fighting COVID-19." *ABC News*, https://abcnews.go.com/Health/front-line-health-care-workers-reunite-children-months/story?id=71521151. Accessed 18 Feb. 2023.

Slade, Arietta, and Lois Sadler. "Pregnancy and Infant Mental Health." *Handbook of Infant Mental Health*, edited by Charles H. Zeanah, The Guilford Press, 2018, pp. 25-40.

Sroufe, L. Alan. "Relationships, Self, and Individual Adaptation." *Relationship Disturbances in Early Childhood: A Developmental Approach*, edited by J. A. Sameroff and R. N. Emde, Basic Books, 1989, pp. 70-94.

Steinberg, Selena, et al. "Musical Engagement and Parent-Child Attachment in Families With Young Children During the Covid-19 Pandemic." *Frontiers in Psychology*, vol. 12, 2021. *Frontiers*, https://www.frontiersin.org/article/10.3389/fpsyg.2021.641733. Accessed 18 Feb. 2023.

Szkody, Erica, et al. "Stress-Buffering Role of Social Support during COVID-19." *Family Process*, vol. 60, no. 3, 2021, pp. 1002-15.

Tambelli, Renata, et al. "Late Adolescents' Attachment to Parents and Peers and Psychological Distress Resulting from COVID-19. A Study on the Mediation Role of Alexithymia." *International Journal of Environmental Research and Public Health*, vol. 18, no. 20, 2021, p. 10649.

Troller-Renfree, Sonya V., et al. "The Impact of a Poverty Reduction Intervention on Infant Brain Activity." *Proceedings of the National Academy of Sciences*, vol. 119, no. 5, Feb. 2022. https://doi.org/10.1073/pnas.2115649119.

Turner, Anne I., et al. "Psychological Stress Reactivity and Future Health and Disease Outcomes: A Systematic Review of Prospective Evidence." *Psychoneuroendocrinology*, vol. 114, 2020, p. 104599.

Unwin, H. Juliette T., et al. "Global, Regional, and National Minimum Estimates of Children Affected by COVID-19-Associated Orphanhood and Caregiver Death, by Age and Family Circumstance up to Oct 31, 2021: An Updated Modelling Study." *The Lancet Child & Adolescent Health*, vol. 6, no. 4, pp. 249-59.

Vindegaard, Nina, and Michael Eriksen Benros. "COVID-19 Pandemic and Mental Health Consequences: Systematic Review of the Current Evidence." *Brain, Behavior, and Immunity*, vol. 89, 2020, pp. 531-42.

Wang, Ming-Te, et al. "COVID-19 Employment Status, Dyadic Family Relationships, and Child Psychological Well-Being." *Journal of Adolescent Health*, vol. 69, no. 5, Nov. 2021, pp. 705-12.

Westrupp, E. M., et al. "Child, Parent, and Family Mental Health and Functioning in Australia during COVID-19: Comparison to Pre-Pandemic Data." *European Child & Adolescent Psychiatry*, Aug. 2021. *Springer Link*, https://doi.org/10.1007/s00787-021-01861-z.

Williams, Kate, and Donna Berthelsen. "The Development of Prosocial Behaviour in Early Childhood: Contributions of Early Parenting and Self-Regulation." *International Journal of Early Childhood*, vol. 49, no. 1, 2017, pp. 73-94.

Williams, Lee M. "Associations of Stressful Life Events and Marital Quality." *Psychological Reports*, vol. 76, no. 3_suppl, June 1995, pp. 1115-22.

Yassa, Murat, et al. "Near-Term Pregnant Women's Attitude toward, Concern about and Knowledge of the COVID-19 Pandemic." *The Journal of Maternal-Fetal & Neonatal Medicine*, vol. 33, no. 22, Nov. 2020, pp. 3827-34.

Zanardo, Vincenzo, et al. "Psychological Impact of COVID-19 Quarantine Measures in Northeastern Italy on Mothers in the Immediate Postpartum Period." *International Journal of Gynecology & Obstetrics*, vol. 150, no. 2, 2020, pp. 184-88.

Zayde, Amanda, et al. "Connection During COVID-19: Pilot Study of a Telehealth Group Parenting Intervention." *American Journal of Psychotherapy*, 2021, https://psychotherapy.psychiatryonline.org/doi/10.1176/appi.psychotherapy.20210005. Accessed 18 Feb. 2023.

Chapter 4.

Taking Care of Children and Preadolescents in the Restrictive Home Stay: Caregivers' Actions during the Early Months of the Pandemic

Eny Dórea Paiva, Karina Rangel da Silva Garcia, Luciana Rodrigues da Silva, Maria Estela Diniz Machado, Paloma Gonçalves Martins Acioly, and Rosane Cordeiro Burla de Aguiar

By November 2021, COVID-19 had caused more than 22 million confirmed cases and 615,000 deaths in Brazil. Since the beginning of the pandemic, various strategies have been used worldwide to suppress the transmission of the disease. Per Law No. 13,979, enacted on February 6, 2020, which provides for measures to fight the COVID-19 pandemic, Brazil implemented actions, such as social distancing by closing schools and modifying the school routine of all children. Thus, some schools organized their activities and adopted online classes, while others remained without classes (Brazil, Presidency of the Republic).

To control the pandemic worldwide, vaccines have been prioritized, and, in Brazil, the beginning of vaccination started in January 2021 with priority groups: health workers, institutionalized people (those who reside in nursing homes) aged sixty years or more, institutionalized people with disabilities, and the Indigenous population (Agência Brasil 2021).

Even with vaccination in process, school classes have not yet returned in the same way as before the pandemic, especially because schools need to respect protocols imposed by health surveillance bodies.

The suspension of school activities and confinement of children and adolescents in their homes during the pandemic has affected their mental health (Aydogdu). Florence Bauer, the representative of the United Nations International Children's Emergency Fund (UNICEF) in Brazil, states that school closings and social isolation have profoundly affected the mental health of children and adolescents (UNICEF).

One Brazilian study examined child behaviour and described the routine activities performed by children aged six to twelve during social distancing in the face of the COVID-19 pandemic. It concluded that anxiety had increased among children and was significantly associated with changes in sleep and appetite (Paiva et al.). In this context, the authors suggest that health professionals and institutions need to be prepared to help this population overcome the obstacles and problems generated by the pandemic (Liu et al.).

Despite the importance of social distancing to control the pandemic, it is also important to prevent physical, mental and social disorders related to this situation. Understanding the challenges children and preadolescents have experienced during social distancing allows health professionals to promote actions aimed at supporting and helping guardians and children overcome such challenges.

Given this context, the following research question emerged: What precautions were implemented by guardians of children during the first months of the COVID-19 pandemic to alleviate the effects of social distancing? Thus, this study aimed to analyze the care implemented by guardians of children aged six to twelve during social distancing in the first months of the COVID-19 pandemic.

Ethical Considerations

The research was developed considering Resolution n° 466/2012 of the Brazilian National Health Council and was approved by the Ethics Committee of the Faculty of Medicine at the Universidade Federal Fluminense (FMUFF) under the protocol CAAE: 30992420.0.0000.5243.

Methods

A quantitative exploratory study (Polit and Beck) was carried out through online surveys using Google Forms and included participants from all regions of Brazil. Quantitative information is analyzed through statistical procedure. It covers a broad range of techniques, and researchers use statistical procedure to organize, interpret, and communicate numeric information (Polit and Beck).

The population consisted of 548 guardians of children aged between six and twelve. The sample was calculated based on the number of Brazilian children nationally in the age group in 2018. A nonprobabilistic convenience sampling method was used (Polit and Beck); the inclusion criterion was being a parent or guardian of a Brazilian child aged six to twelve. Convenience sampling is a nonprobabilistic sampling technique in which samples are selected from the population because they are conveniently available to researchers—that is, the sample is taken from a group of people that are easy to contact or reach (Polit and Beck). This nonprobabilistic sample, from 2018, corresponded to approximately 0.004 per cent of the population of twelve million children between six and twelve years old enrolled in elementary education, in public or private schools, and in urban areas of Brazil (QEdu). Data collection took place in April 2020.

The data collection instrument was a form filled out online, via Google Forms, built by the researchers, containing closed questions to characterize the children, including the region of residence, gender, and age, and one open question directed to responsible guardians: "Have you been doing anything to help your child, in this period of social distancing, the result of which you consider positive?"

The dissemination of the research was done through the WhatsApp application, e-mail, and Facebook, and disclosure was restricted to family members, family friends, and acquaintances of the researchers.

A total of 548 forms filled out online with complete responses were included by guardians of Brazilian children aged six to twelve years living in Brazil. Within twenty-four hours of disclosing the form, the sample number calculated for the study had already been exceeded, and the data collection was then interrupted.

The answers from the forms constituted the textual corpus submitted to lexicographical analysis, using the Interface de R pour les Analyses Multidimensionnelles de Textes et de Questionnaires (IRAMuTeQ) software, by descending hierarchical classification (DHC) and word cloud (Souza et al.). The open question was also analyzed using IRAMuTeQ. This software presents statistical rigour, allowing researchers to use different technical resources of lexical analysis, from the simplest ones, such as basic lexicography, to multivariate analysis techniques, such as DHC and word cloud (Camargo and Justo 2013).

This study used DHC analysis, Reinert, and word cloud. The DHC analysis aims to obtain classes of elementary context units (ECUs), which at the same time have similar vocabulary among themselves and different vocabulary from other classes (Camargo and Justo). The cloud method groups words graphically and organizes them according to their frequency (Camargo and Justo). Within the cloud method, words are randomly positioned so that the most frequent ones appear larger than the others, thus demonstrating their prominence in the analysis's corpus (Kami et al.).

The children's characterization data (gender and age) were tabulated using Microsoft Excel 2016. The authors used descriptive statistics (relative and absolute frequency) and arranged the information in a table.

Results and Discussion

Data from 548 forms were analyzed; 313 (57 per cent) guardians reported that they implemented actions to help the child during social distancing in the first months of the pandemic. Of these, 275 (50.2 per cent) were responsible for female children, and most children were six years old (100, 18.2 per cent), as shown in Table 1.

Age (years)	N	%
6	100	18.2%
7	83	15.1%
8	97	17.7%
9	88	16.1%
10	70	12.8%
11	56	10.2%
12	51	9.3%
Not informed	3	0.5%
Total	**548**	**100%**

Gender	N	%
Female	275	50.2%
Male	272	49.6%
Not informed	1	0.2%
Total	**548**	**100%**

Table 1. Age and gender of children aged six to twelve years during social distancing in the first months of the COVID-19 pandemic (Brazil, Presidency of the Republic).

After data input from the DHC analysis, the software indicated a total corpus consisting of 454 texts, separated by a total of 456 text segments (TSs), of which 390 TSs (85.33 per cent) were used. In total, 4,577 occurrences emerged (words, forms, or word elements), with 918 different words (number of forms) and 501 had a single occurrence (number of hapaxes).

The analyzed content was categorized into three classes, distributed as follows: class 1 with 157 TSs (40.26 per.cent); class 2 with 158 TSs (40.51 per cent); and class 3 with 75 TSs (19.23 per cent). (Figure 1).

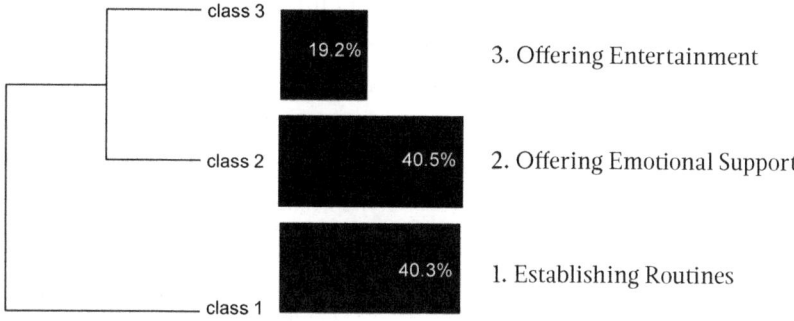

Figure 1. Dendrogram depicting the Descending Hierarchical Classification of text segments related to care implemented by guardians of children aged 6 to 12 years during social distancing in the first months of the COVID-19 pandemic. Brazil, 2021.

The first class of words was characterized by care actions related to establishing routines and carrying out activities with children in different contexts, forming the first category called "establishing routines." The second class of words formed the second category, called "offering emotional support," and was characterized by care actions related to the emotional support offered to children. The third class of words constituted the third category, called "offering entertainment," and was based on entertainment-related actions during social distancing.

Establishing Routines

The first class encompassed the second largest quantity of text segments, and the active forms that showed statistical significance were the verb "maintain" and the nouns "routine" and "activity."

These first terms indicate the clear decision of parents or caregivers regarding the establishment of a new domestic routine during the period of confinement. It is important to emphasize that social distancing, though necessary, can compromise mental health. An international study found that among the various negative psychological effects related to social distancing and quarantine by COVID-19, symptoms of post-traumatic stress disorder, confusion, and anger stood out (Brooks et al.).

As for the child population, the impact of social distancing on their psychological development remains undetermined, as many of these outcomes will only be identified over time (Linhares and Enumo). However, its impact on the mental health of children and adolescents is already clear (Meherali et al.). Social distancing can result in high-stress levels for long periods among children. The Brazilian Society of Paediatrics has warned that the increase in stress hormones in childhood, such as cortisol and adrenaline, results in an overload of the cardiovascular system and risks the healthy construction of children's brain architecture.

The quality and magnitude of the impact of social distancing on the child population are determined by several factors, such as age, education, preexisting mental health conditions, socioeconomic conditions, and fear of being infected (Singh et al.). Empirically, there was a need to reorganize family dynamics in this context. The home environment became a fragmented space for activities in an environment common to the whole family, where each activity was shared by its members. If, on the one hand, there is a positive aspect of interaction, on the other, there were overlapping roles and an overload of work and demands in the family environment with the absence or weakening of the family support network (Paiva et al.).

The creation of a new routine for children may have helped parents to control their stress, which initially arose over their concern of their children becoming infected (Araújo et al.).

Although it was essential to establish a family routine, it is important to emphasize that there is no standard one for all family contexts because each one faces particular realities. However, following good nutritional practices, having periods of the day for moments of leisure and interaction with the children, and getting enough sleep are essential for the mental health of all family members (Fava et al.).

In this sense, the parents mentioned the creation of a routine that included varied activities, as they tried to build a structure that would meet the needs of everyday life but without disregarding leisure. Household activities—such as preparing meals with the children, teaching them how to cook, and involvement in household activities—were identified. Regular participation in household chores enables children to develop important skills to have more independence in daily life and the community. In addition, it can provide important moments of affection and care among family members (PUC Psychology Service-School 2021).

Other activities, such as researching the coronavirus or studying art and science in general, were mentioned. Talking more, being together, and even getting a new pet were also mentioned. When starting online learning, parents tried to keep these classes at the same time as when the child used to go to school. It is worth highlighting the importance of maintaining regular habits to create a sense of a school atmosphere at home (PUC Psychology Service-School).

Some parents proposed more physical activities at home or outdoors and encouraged playful activities, reading, and games that the whole family could participate in, such as board games, dancing, listening to music, and watching movies. In general, doing physical activities, even indoors, is essential. In addition to the benefits that physical exercise already brings, it can be a powerful tool in adapting to the new reality imposed by the pandemic, reducing stress and anxiety, and increasing the sense of wellbeing (PUC Psychology Service-School).

Many parents reported that the activities of this new routine were implemented as a way not only to occupy the children but also to reduce screen time and to better control feelings of anxiety, fear, frustration, and boredom. These results are in line with what the Brazilian Society of Paediatrics (2020) recommends—that even though parents encounter difficulties in reconciling their various daily demands, especially during the pandemic, it is essential to limit and supervise the use of screens by children, preventing damage to the child's development.

Overusing screens can result in many negative health issues among children. These can include irritability, anxiety, and depression; attention deficit hyperactivity disorder; sleep disorders; eating disorders, such as for overweight/obesity and anorexia/bulimia; a sedentary lifestyle; and lack of exercise. The Brazilian Society of Paediatrics (2019) recommends the use of screens between one to two hours daily for children aged six to twelve years old.

Parents and caregivers acted positively by establishing a new home routine to serve the entire family. However, it is noteworthy that it may not have been enough to ensure their children's development, whether physical, emotional, or mental. Health professionals need to prepare for the consequences of this period, which will be relevant for the coming years.

Offering Emotional Support

This second class encompassed the largest amount of TSs and the first active form that showed statistical significance was the verb "to talk." Parents play an important role in regulating their children's behaviour and emotions. Providing a healthy and safe environment, however, became a challenge during the pandemic amid its uncertainties (Rodrigues and Lins). In this context, J. V. Rodrigues and Ana Lins suggest that parents must provide emotional support to mitigate the negative affects on the child's mental and physical health during social distancing when the child needed to stay home and away from others as much as possible to help prevent the spread of COVID-19. In the postpandemic period, returning to daily activities can also generate insecurities, contributing to increased anxiety (Paiva et al.).

One study showed that children's emotional fragility was accentuated during the pandemic, as children were less listened to because their caregivers were worried about dealing with the situation, and they did not give children the attention they needed. The authors observed feelings of discouragement, stress, sadness, and lack of emotional ability to deal with conflicts in children and their caregivers (Cabana et al.). Another study pointed out the need for parents or guardians to recognize the signs of changes in their children's behaviour and encourage moments for children to express themselves so as not to minimize their feelings (Paiva et al.). It is essential that adults, especially those who live with and have the confidence of children, learn to listen empathically and to amplify their children's voices in order to meet the challenges of a post-COVID-19 world (Cabana et al.).

With changes in parental routines, who also experience insecurity and fear, both caregivers and children needed to adapt, and conversations became crucial for the new health rules to be practised responsibly and peacefully by the whole family (Rodrigues and Lins).

Offering Entertainment

This class encompassed the smallest quantity of TSs, and the first active form that showed statistical significance was the verb "to play." Among the entertainment activities reported by guardians and parents were games, family activities, outdoor hiking, cycling, and the use of screens for watching movies or playing video games. Interacting with other people in the family and friends through screens was also reported.

The parents' reports are in line with the guidelines of the Brazilian Society of Paediatrics, which points out that it is important to plan and organize daily activities and maintain a routine that involves playing, studying, reading, listening to music, doing physical activity, sleeping, and using screens; the organization also recommends implementing creative leisure breaks for the child to reflect and play. Such activities can contribute to preserving the physical and mental health of children during periods of social isolation, which can minimize damage to their growth and development (Brazilian Society of Paediatrics).

Studies show the relevance of having a structured routine, carrying out activities together with parents and children, whenever possible, outside, including walks and bicycle rides. Those are practical and easily accessible strategies that can promote greater wellbeing for children and adolescents during the COVID-19 pandemic (Brazilian Society of Paediatrics; Rosen et al.).

A study aiming to show the hidden impact of COVID-19 on child protection and wellbeing found that children who did not particpate in family activities felt less happy, less hopeful, and less secure. Efforts to guarantee children's rights and protect them and their physical and mental wellbeing are essential to avoid the negative impacts of

COVID-19 on child development (Rits et al.).

Importantly, technology was widely used during this period of social isolation. Some studies highlight the postitive aspects of technology as a positive factor, insofar as it allows for children to continue their school activities, for children to maintain contact with friends and family, and for children to enjoy some entertainment. The use of technology, however, must be done under supervision, according to the age group, so that children do not access inappropriate content or overuse it (Rosen et al.; Silva et al.).

Finally, in the present research, when analyzing the responses of parents or guardians with the cloud method, the most cited words in the speeches concerning what they did with their children during social distancing due to the pandemic were "activity," "routine," "chat," and "play." The conjunction "and" at the centre of the word cloud denotes that those responsible did not just do one action; they always reported an "and" plus one activity (see Appendix: Word Cloud).

A study carried out in thirty-seven countries to describe the impact of the pandemic on the safety, protection, and wellbeing of children and adolescents suggests the organization of the sectors of health, education, and social assistance at different levels of society from the individual to the national, ensuring a safe environment in all respects (Ritz et al.). Thus, the family plays an important role in providing a safe and welcoming environment to prevent children from suffering even more from the negative effects of the pandemic.

Conclusion

The caregivers of children aged between six and twelve implemented some actions during the early months of pandemic. The attempt to establish a routine in children's lives, in parallel with the great effort to talk to their children to clarify the situation of the pandemic, was reported by most respondents. During the pandemic, the search for new ways to entertain children was extremely important to overcome difficult moments due to social distance during the first months of the pandemic.

Given the changes to people's routines the pandemic has caused, it is recommended that health professionals establish evidence-based guidelines and simpler operational strategies to deal with health problems related to the COVID-19 pandemic in children. These results highlight the importance of home educational interventions by caregivers. Further research needs to be carried out to produce additional knowledge about appropriate care interventions during the pandemic. It is up to the scientific and academic community and managers to guarantee resources for this purpose.

Health professionals must learn to adapt to new circumstances and be prepared for the consequences of the COVID-19 pandemic and its impact on child development. Experiences lived during the pandemic have clearly shown the need for greater and continuous investments in science, education, technology, and health worldwide.

Appendix: Word Cloud

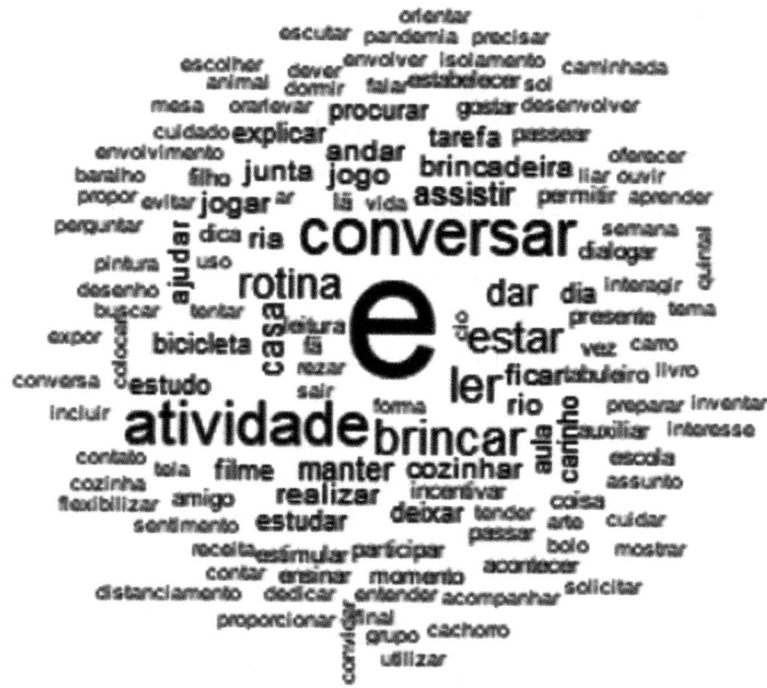

The word cloud highlights the care actions implemented by guardians of children aged six to twelve years during social distancing in the first months of the COVID-19 pandemic in Brazil.

The word cloud, depicted, presents the words in Brazilian Portuguese, as the interviews were conducted in this language. However, the results presentation and discussion were written in English.

Works Cited

Agência Brasil. "Vacinação contra a covid-19 começa em todo o país, 19/01/2021." *Agência Brasil*, 28 Nov 2021, agenciabrasil.ebc.com.br/saude/noticia/2021-01/vacinacao-contra-covid-19-começa-em-todo-o-pais. Accesed 19 Feb. 2023.

Araújo, L. A., et al. "The Potential Impact of the COVID-19 Pandemic on Child Growth and Development: A Systematic Review." *Jornal de Pediatria*, vol. 97, no. 4, 2021, pp. 369-77.

Aydogdu, A. L. F. "Saúde mental das crianças durante a pandemia causada pelo novo coronavírus: revisão integrativa." *Journal Health NPEPS*, vol. 5, no. 2, 2020, periodicos.unemat.br/index.php/jhnpeps/article/view/4891. Accessed 19 Feb. 2023.

Brazil. Presidency of the Republic. "Medida Provisória No 934, de lo de abril de 2020. Estabelece normas excepcionais sobre o ano letivo da educação básica e do ensino superior decorrentes das medidas para enfrentamento da situação de emergência de saúde pública de que trata a Lei no 13.979, de 6 de fevereiro de 2020." *Presidency of the Republic of Brazil*, 8 Nov 2020, www.in.gov.br/en/web/dou/-/medida-provisoria-n-934-de-1-de-abril-de-2020-250710591. Accessed 19 Feb. 2023.

Brazil. Presidency of the Republic. "Lei No 13.979 de 6 de fevereiro de 2020. Dispõe sobre as medidas para enfrentamento da emergência de saúde pública de importância internacional decorrente do coronavírus responsável pelo surto de 2019." *Presidency of the Republic of Brazil*, 2020, www.planalto.gov.br/ccivil_03/_ato2019-2022/2020/lei/L13979.htm. Accessed 19 Feb. 2023.

Brazilian Society of Paediatrics. "Pais e filhos em confinamento durante a pandemia de Covid-19." *Brazilian Society of Paediatrics*, 2020, www.sbp.com.br/imprensa/detalhe/nid/pais-e-filhos-em-confinamento-durante-a-pandemia-de-covid-19/. Accessed 19 Feb. 2023.

Brooks, S. K., et al. "The Psychological Impact of Quarantine and How to Reduce It: Rapid Review of the Evidence." *The Lancet*, vol. 395,

2020, pp. 912-20.

Cabana, J. L., et al. "Percepciones y sentimientos de niños argentinos frente a la cuarentena COVID-19." *Archivos Argentinos de Pediatría*, vol. 119, no. 4, 2021, pp. S107-S122.

Camargo, B. V., and Ana M. Justo. "IRAMUTEQ: um software gratuito para análisede dados textuais." *Temas em Psicologia*, vol. 21, no. 2, 2013, pp. 513-18.

Fava, D. C., et al. *Orientação para pais. O que é preciso saber para cuidar de um filho*. Artesã, 2018.

Kami, M. T. M., et al. "Trabalho no consultório na rua: Uso do software Iramuteq no apoio à pesquisa qualitative." *Escola Anna Nery*, vol. 20, no. 3, 2016, pp. 1-5.

Linhares, M. B. M., and Sônia R. F. Enumo. "Reflexões baseadas na Psicologia sobre efeitos da pandemia COVID-19 no desenvolvimento infantil." *Estudos de Psicologia*, vol. 37, 2020, p. e200089.

Liu, J. J., et al. "Mental Health Considerations for Children Quarantined Because of COVID-19." *Lancet Child Adolesc Health*, vol. 4, no. 5, 2020, pp. 347-49.

Meherali, S., et al. "Mental Health of Children and Adolescents amidst Covid-19 and Past Pandemics: A Rapid Systematic Review." *International Journal of Environmental Research and Public Health*, vol. 18, no. 7, 2021, p. 3432.

Paiva, E. D., et al. "Child Behavior during the Social Distancing in the COVID-19 Pandemic." *Revista Brasileira de Enfermagem*, vol. 74, n. Suppl 1, 2021, p. e20200762.

Polit, D. F., and T. C. Beck. *Fundamentos de pesquisa em enfermagem: avaliação de evidências para a prática da enfermagem*. Artmed, 2019.

PUC Psychology Service-School. "A rotina em tempos de pandemia. Cartilha. Escola de Psicologia-PUC/Campinas." PUC Psychology Service-School, 2021, www.puc-campinas.edu.br/wp-content/uploads/2021/02/Cartilha_Educacao-Rotina.pdf. Accessed 19 Feb. 2023.

QEdu. "Censo Escolar/INEP 2018." *QEdu*, 23 Apr 2020, www.qedu.org.br/brasil/censo-escolar?year=2018&dependence=0&localization=0&education_stage=0&item=. Accessed 19 Feb. 2023.

Ritz, D., et al. "The Hidden Impact of COVID-19 on Child Protection and Wellbeing." *Save the Children International*, 28 Nov 2021, resourcecentre.savethechildren.net/pdf/the_hidden_impact_of_covid-19_on_child_protection_and_wellbeing.pdf. Accessed 19 Feb. 2023.

Rodrigues, J. V. dos S., and Ana C. A. de A. Lins. "Possible Impacts Caused by the COVID-19 Pandemic on Children's Mental Health and the Role of Parents in this Scenario." *Research, Society and Development*, vol. 9, no. 8, July 2020, p. e793986533,

Rosen, M. L., et al. "Promoting Youth Mental Health during the COVID- 19 Pandemic: A Longitudinal Study." *PLoS ONE*, vol. 16, no. 8, 2021, p. e0255294.

Silva, A. C. P. da, et al. "Effects of the COVID-19 Pandemic and Its Repercussions on Child Development: An Integrative Review." *Research, Society and Development*, vol. 10, no. 4, Apr. 2021, p. e50810414320.

Singh, S., et al. "Impact of COVID-19 and Lockdown on Mental Health of Children and Adolescents: A narrative Review with Recommendations." *Psychiatry Research*, vol. 293, 2020, p. 113429.

Souza, M. A. R., et al. "The Use of IRAMUTEQ Software for Data Analysis in Qualitative Research." *Revista da Escola de Enfermagem da USP*, vol. 52, 2018, p. e03353.

United Nations International Children's Emergency Fund (UNICEF). "UNICEF alerta: situação de crianças e adolescentes se agravou consideravelmente após nove meses de pandemia." *UNICEF*, 2020, www.unicef.org/brazil/comunicados-de-imprensa/unicef-alerta-situacao-de-criancas-e-adolescentes-se-agravou-consideravelmente-apos- nove-meses-pandemia. Accessed 19 Feb. 2023.

Chapter 5.

An Upside of Separation and Divorce: Mothering and Coparenting in the Pandemic

Rebecca Jaremko Bromwich

I am writing this on January 5, 2022, as the province in which I live, Ontario, enters yet another lockdown, and COVID-19 numbers surge to unprecedented levels, two years into a devastating global pandemic. Like the rest of us, no doubt, I am, in this moment, working through a dizzying haze of rage and grief. The pandemic was destabilizing in many ways for societies and economies across the world, and for human relationships within them. Like many other marriages in what has been characterized as a divorce boom, mine did not survive the COVID-19 pandemic. After twenty years of cohabitation and the births of four children, we split a few months into the first lockdown.

A perhaps not so strange thing then happened. My experience as a professionally employed mother engaged in full-time paid work during the first lockdown was almost unbearable, resulting in mental health issues for me and my four children. However, once I separated from my husband and we arrived at a fifty-fifty shared parenting arrangement, my unpaid workload in terms of caregiving and childrearing for children, who had no childcare and were to be homeschooled during the pandemic, was suddenly far more manageable. None of this, especially, surprised me. I had, ironically, in 2019, coedited an anthology about wives. Spoiler: A major theme in that collection was how women disproportionately bear unpaid labour burdens in the context of heterosexual marriages around the world (O'Brien Hallstein and Bromwich). In fact, once I had fifty-fifty custody of my kids, I was able to not only work full time but start and complete my MBA in what was suddenly my spare time.

In this chapter, I examine the ways that my personal experience is reflective of broader political trends, whereby it is now often more advantageous for mothers to be divorced or separated than to continue in relationships with their male partners. Specifically, I suggest that mothers engaged in shared parenting after separation or divorce fared better than those in intact heterosexual conjugal relationships or marriages during the COVID-19 pandemic. I contend that the better situation of divorced or separated mothers during the pandemic, relative to their married or cohabiting counterparts, is underscored by the context of the pandemic, but as shared parenting becomes the norm, it is increasingly more advantageous for mothers, in terms of workload, to be separated or divorced.

In short, this evidence shows that despite being culturally valorized as a family form, marriage as currently culturally constituted in mainstream North America is in fact a family form less conducive to the best interests of children and the thriving of women than shared parenting after separation or divorce. Women and children in homes that are broken, it would seem, have in at least some circumstances broken free of oppressive and unequal gender relations, which are harmful to all.

Marriage, Unpaid Labour, and Gender Inequality

Marriage has long been culturally understood as the optimal context for childrearing in the West (Howell). Although a diversity of family forms is now widely accepted in North America and Europe, marriage remains valorized, and dominance by men over women within marriage under the cloak of privacy remains culturally affirmed even where formal laws provide for gender equality (Siegal). Furthermore, an ideology of intensive motherhood dominates, in which a mother is expected to be singularly focussed on childrearing all the time (O'Reilly). She was not the first, nor will she be the last to say it, but blogger Zawn Villines struck a chord and went viral when she wrote a Facebook post in 2019 called "divorce his ass," encouraging women everywhere to leave their husbands if they did not bear their share of the load of unpaid work in parenting and housekeeping domestically. Villines wrote: "Knowingly harming another person and causing them to suffer so that you can get more sleep or free time is pretty much the dictionary definition of abuse" (qtd. in Abrahamson).

While understanding these unequal gender conditions as abusive, it is generally unfair to assume this is intentional wrongdoing on men's part. Perhaps sadly, men as well as women in these marriages or conjugal unions often have normalized inequalities in terms of domestic and childrearing labour, so much so that the men are, in fact, not knowingly harming the women concerned. Men are easily rendered oblivious by social norms and expectations that permit them the luxury of not noticing or concerning themselves with the discrepancies in the quality of life they enjoy as compared to that of the mother of their children. Indeed, women are often complicit in their own oppression; they adopt hegemonic views about their roles and duties that result in their own subjugation, and embrace intensive motherhood, which mandates their self-abnegation (O'Reilly). On a personal level, despite my own years of education and writing about gender inequalities, I was certainly an accomplice in my own oppression in the context of my marriage. Cultural ideas about what constitutes a good wife or good mother are very difficult to resist.

Understood as a form of abuse, women's subordination in the domestic sphere, even when they have paid roles in the public sphere (McClain), and the rendering invisible of mothers' unpaid labour (Waring) have been exacerbated during the COVID-19 pandemic. Supports, such as childcare and in-person schooling, which allow mothers to offload some caregiving responsibilities to third parties were removed (Green and O'Reilly). When women were in legally imposed shared-parenting arrangements, they were spared from disproportionately taking the burden of care for children resulting from the COVID-19 lockdowns. As a result, separated or divorced mothers with shared-parenting arrangements were spared some of the harshest gendered consequences of the pandemic.

The cultural ideal in heteronormative Western societies remains the two-parent family, with a male father and female mother caring for the children together (Johnson). Women have been told for generations that this is the optimal arrangement. Yet 90 per cent of divorces that involve postsecondary educated women are initiated by the women. Separated mothers who are parties to fifty-fifty or otherwise shared-parenting arrangements have fared significantly better in the context of the pandemic than mothers who are in intact families. The pandemic provides evidence that the cultural ideal of marriage may in fact be the converse of what is beneficial for women as a context in which to mother children. Perhaps, sadly, many men will only do their fair share of unpaid labour with respect to parenting once court ordered to do so. In any case, the pandemic shows stark evidence that women who are divorced and in shared-parenting contexts thrive much better, by and large, than women who are still in relationships with the children's fathers.

Family Law Shifts

Formerly focussed on authority and male ownership of women and children, family law in the liberal West has shifted in the past few decades into an area of law focussed on fostering clean breaks that are framed in gender neutral terms (Boyd), amicable divorces and separations, and the best interests of children (Kronby). Now, rather than considering factors that were once at issue in family law, like hierarchy of the male spouse over his wife, the gender of children as determinative of custody, or matrimonial misconduct, an agreement about parenting arrangements after a separation must only consider the child's best interests. Parenting orders too must consider the child's best interests, with an understanding that maximum contact with both parents is generally strongly in the child's best interests (Shaffer).

The "best interests of the child" is a phrase used to refer expansively to what would best protect and nurture a child's physical, psychological, and emotional safety as well as their security and well-being. To legally determine what is in the child's best interests when making parenting arrangements, courts, lawyers, parents, and others are to consider other factors: the child's emotional health and wellbeing; the child's views (to be considered in an age-appropriate manner) (Joyal); the child's relationships with their parents, guardians, and other important people in their life; the history of care the child has experienced; and the impact of any family violence and conflict between the parents (Zermatten).

In the Supreme Court of Canada case of *Young v. Young* 1993, Justice L'Heureux-Dubé held that the best interests of the child is meant to be an individualized, child-centric analysis. She wrote that it "is the positive right [of the child] to the best possible arrangements in the circumstances of the parties." (at 35) She went on to say that courts should not focus only on harm to a child in this determination, although the presence or absence of harm may be an important factor. The "best interests" test is contextual, and it is future focussed, encompassing many considerations. It is individual in that it is "person-oriented" rather than "act-oriented" and thus requires consideration of the "whole person viewed as a social being" (para 71).

Through the understanding that more contact with both parents is good for children (Schwartz and Finley), the legal landscape for parenting after divorce in Canada has shifted over the past twenty years, both demographically and legislatively, away from solo parenting by one parent, with access to the children by the other upon separation, to shared parenting as the assumed norm (Bala). After separation or divorce, most parents now split time with their children. There is a general increase in shared parenting after separation or divorce. Under Canada's Divorce Act, a general concept of "parenting" now replaces the concepts of "custody" and "access." Under this law, a court may make a parenting order about the exercise of parenting time or decision-making responsibility for each child. Either or both former spouses, along with certain enumerated nonspouses, can apply for a parenting order under the Act. Canadian law thus presumes that parents will share in parenting after they separate and divorce. The Act no longer deploys an approach based on "custody" and "access" but instead focuses on "parenting time" and "decision-making responsibility," which may be allocated in a variety of ways through a parenting order. Children are reconceptualized, not as property to be split, but as ongoing obligations of both spouses. Unlike "custody" and "access," terms commonly associated with property ownership, the new "parenting" language encourages parents to focus together on the needs of their children.

Where separation takes place outside of a divorce application, Alberta, British Columbia, several American states, the United Kingdom and Australia, have also moved away from the concepts of "custody" and "access," and many Canadian judges and mediators no longer use these terms in their discussions and agreements. Parenting orders are written as intended to allocate responsibilities between people who take on responsibilities for the care and upbringing of a child.

Unpaid Labour and Mothers during the COVID-19 Pandemic

Without question, COVID-19 has had devastating consequences to public health; it has killed over five million people globally at the time of writing and has infected millions more. The economic impact of COVID-19 has also been enormous. This economic impact has been gendered. The pandemic has had a devastating impact on women's, and in particular, mothers' equality. Decades of progress towards shoring up women's ability to meaningfully participate in paid employment through the establishment of childcare, as well as the regularization of school systems, were suddenly erased with the announcement of the shutdowns in March 2020. The pandemic also had detrimental effects on the position of women in the paid workforce, on mothers' mental health, and the mental health of children and teens. School closures in 138 countries isolated children and youth, leading to mental health crises (Phelps and Sparry). Teens in particular, peer oriented and focussed on their futures, have suffered a great deal from the school closure and lockdowns, resulting in shadow pandemics of depression, self-harm, substance abuse, and even suicide (Vaillancourt et al.). Although the isolation of the lockdowns was problematic, it was exacerbated for teens when there was conflict and disruption in homes from which they could not escape.

In the United States, by September of 2020, and due to the pandemic, a million women had left their paid jobs to care for children who had no school or childcare to go to (Gender Differences). Women disproportionately shouldered the care and domestic labour burdens of caring for children, the elderly, and those with disabilities (O'Reilly and Green). The invisibility of unpaid labour to the economy and society more broadly contributed to a lack of due consideration for how mothers could possibly function as workers and caregivers in the COVID-19 context.

The pandemic also caused a boom in divorce rates (Savage). Rates of applications for divorce and legal separations climbed by more than 30 per cent across Western nations within the first few months of the pandemic (Savage). In this context, those women who were spared some of the blunt impact of the COVID-19 lockdowns on their careers and mental health had custody arrangements in which their children were legally ordered to be elsewhere at least some of the time. Mothers in shared custody situations, therefore, were sheltered from some of the impact of the shutdowns. The availability of caregiving labour is a benefit separate and apart from any domestic violence or other forms of abuse, whether emotional, financial or otherwise, to which women might disproportionately be subject in the context of those marriages.

Conclusion

Over the past decade in Canada, there has been a shift away from lone parenting after divorce or separation, predominantly by single mothers, to coparenting in joint legal custody arrangements. Changes to the Divorce Act, which took effect in 2021, assume parents will both continue to be involved in the lives of their children after separation; the Act replaces the terms "custody" and "access" with "decision-making," "parenting time," and "contact"—a legal change that mirrors and reinforces social change across the country. This chapter has discussed this emerging new legal and social context of coparenting in Canada from a feminist perspective. It argues that mothers who were separated or divorced largely fared better than their counterparts who were married or otherwise partnered with the fathers of their children with respect to the unpaid labour burdens imposed by the lockdowns and childcare deprivations affected by the COVID-19 pandemic. This argument counters long-held cultural assumptions that women and children are in a better situation in intact two-parent heteronormative families, since the emerging family law regime compels men to do their share of unpaid work post-separation or divorce.

Much research indicates that having a strong relationship with both parents, or really with several committed adults (Bala), as opposed to only an isolated and overstressed mother alone, is in the best interests of children. The pandemic has underscored that the best contemporary way to ensure that children are cared for equitably and to ensure engagement by fathers in their care is for women to get divorced. This is, unfortunately, on its face an unromantic finding. However, if conjugal relationships are predicated on exploitation of women's labour, they do not seem so romantic in the first place.

The findings of this analysis of coparenting after divorce or separation in the pandemic contradict cultural assumptions about parenting. Simply put, growing numbers of mothers and children are better off after divorce or separation. "Broken homes," traditionally conceptualized as spaces of dysfunction, seem to be, at least for some, places where women and children have escaped traditional gender inequalities. This was certainly the case for me.

However, my argument that men, women, and children are better served outside of marriage than within it in the current context is not to suggest that conjugal partnerships and marriages are places where more equal gender relations are not possible. In contrast, the destabilizing impact of the pandemic offers a new chance to rebuild. Indeed, if a court order or legal arrangement can create more equal sharing of unpaid and caregiving labour, more equal forms of caregiving can be realized without such legal agreements. If we can share in parenting more equally when separated, we can learn to do it in the context of intact relationships. Perhaps a first step towards better marriages and conjugal partnerships that can withstand pressures is understanding that everyone, and not least children, benefits from movement towards equality. For instance, Lynn O'Brien Hallstein provides an experiential roadmap towards how couples choose to share parenting more equally during marriage, primarily by having explicit conversations about their values and intended labour sharing in the context of coparenting. Hallstein notes that these conversations may preemptively prevent some couples from having children together in the first place (Ennis), which, ultimately, may not be a bad thing.

Works Cited

Abrahamson, Rachel Paula. "Writer Has a Suggestion for Moms with Lazy Husbands: Divorce Them." *Today*, 18 Sept. 2019, www.today.com/parents/zawn-villines-say-moms-should-divorce-their-lazy-husbands-tl62824. Accessed 3 Mar. 2023.

Bala, Nicholas, et al. "Shared Parenting in Canada: Increasing Use but Continued Controversy." *Family Court Review*, vol. 55, no. 4, 2017, pp. 513-30.

Divorce Act R.S.C., 1985, c. 3 (2nd Supp.)

Ennis, Linda. *After the Happily Ever After: Empowering Women and Mothers in Relationships*. Demeter Press, 2017.

Howell, Martha C. "Marriage, Property, and Patriarchy: Recent Contributions to a Literature." *Feminist Studies*, vol. 13, no. 1, *Feminist Studies, Inc.*, 1987, pp. 203-24.

Joyal, Renee, and Anne Quéniart. "Enhancing the Child's Point of View in Custody and Access Cases in Québec: Preliminary Results of a Study Conducted in Québec." *Can. J. Fam. L.*, vol. 19, 2002, p. 173.

Kronby, Malcolm C. *Canadian Family Law*. Wiley, 2010.

McClain, Linda "Atomistic Man; Revisited: Liberalism, Connection, and Feminist Jurisprudence." *Southern California Law Review*, vol. 64, no. 1171, 1992, pp. 1196-1202.

O'Brien Hallstein, Lynn, and Rebecca Jaremko Bromwich. *Critical Perspectives on Wives: Roles, Representations, Identities, Work*. Demeter Press, 2019.

O'Reilly, Andrea, and Fiona Green. *Mothers Mothering and COVID 19: Dispatches from the Pandemic*. Demeter Press, 2021.

O'Reilly, Andrea. *Maternal Theory: Essential Readings*. Demeter Press, 2007.

Phelps C., and L. L. Sperry. "Children and the COVID-19 Pandemic." *Psychological Trauma: Theory, Research, Practice, and Policy*, vol. 12, no. S1, 2020, pp. S73-S75.

Savage, Maddy. "Why the Pandemic Is causing Spikes in Break-Ups and Divorces." *BBC*, 6 Dec. 2020, www.bbc.com/worklife/article/20201203-why-the-pandemic-is-causing-spikes-in-break-ups-and-divorces. Accessed 3 Mar. 2022.

Schwartz, Seth, and Gordon Finley. "Mothering, Fathering, and Divorce: The Influence of Divorce on Reports of and Desires for Maternal and Paternal Involvement." *Family Court Review*, vol. 47, no. 3, 2009, pp. 506-22.

Shaffer, Martha. *Contemporary Issues in Family Law: Engaging in the Legacy of James G. McLeod*. Thomson Carswell, 2007.

Siegal, Riva. "Why Equal Protection No Longer Protects: The Evolving Forms of Status-Enforcing State Action." *Stanford Law Review*, vol. 49, no. 1111, 1997, pp. 1115-16.

Vaillancourt, T., et al. "Canada Is Failing When It Comes to the Mental Well-Being of Children." *Royal Society of Canada COVID-19 Series*, 2020, rsc-src.ca/en/voices/canada-is-failing-when-it-comes-to-mental-well-being-children. Accessed 3 Mar. 2023.

Waring, Marilyn. *If Women Counted: A New Feminist Economics*. Harper Collins, 1988.

Young v. Young 1993 CanLII 34 (SCC), [1993] S.C.J. No. 112 (Q.L.)

Zermatten, Jean. "The Best Interests of the Child Principle: Literal Analysis and Function." *International Journal of Children's Rights*, vol. 18, no. 4, 2010, pp. 483-99.

Part II.
How Children and Their Families Felt

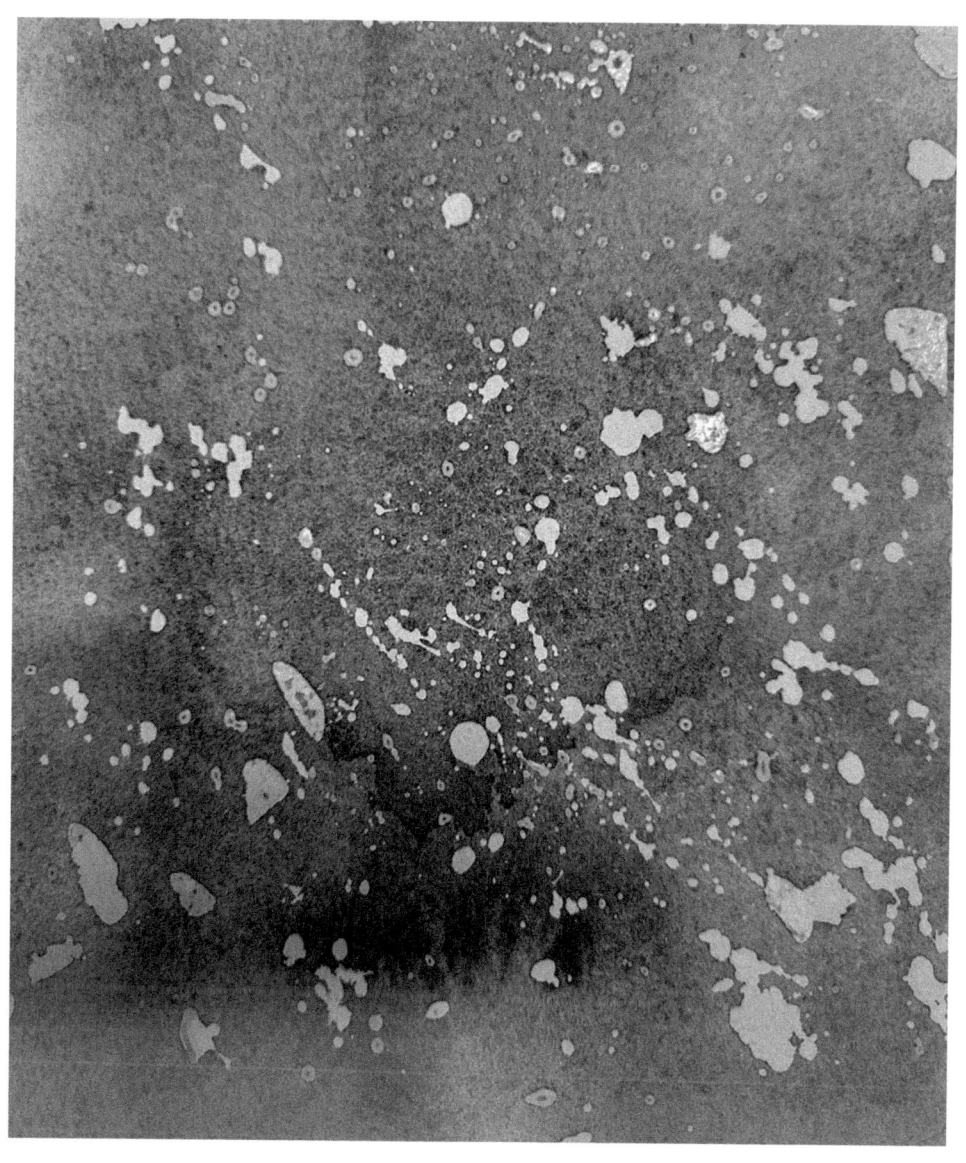

Chapter 6.

Grandparents: Overlooked, Missing Links

Jacqueline Kolosov

When I think back on my own childhood, my St. Petersburg-born grandmother is at the centre, second in importance only to my own parents. She cared for me in the weeks after my sister's birth and when my parents vacationed. My mother returned to work when I was nine and my sister just six, and our grandmother, who lived nearby, began to take on more consistent responsibilities. She took us to the dentist and much, much later drove and then picked me up from the appointment where I had my wisdom teeth out. Later, we laughed about her memory of guiding an eighteen-year-old, who stood half a foot taller than she did, down the hall to the elevator and then outside and back to her waiting car. Two decades have passed since she died at ninety-one, yet my memories of the meals she made and the impromptu dance performances she applauded in her living room remain as present as the diamond wedding ring I now wear—a ring that once graced her own hand.

Given my grandmother's centrality in my life, I have always been interested in grandparents and their grandchildren. Once the pandemic took hold, I became increasingly aware of the number of grandparents accompanying younger children to the neighbourhood park. Little wonder, given that the number of grandparents in the United States has now reached seventy million (David and Nelson-Kakulla). This is the largest it has been in the nation's history. With increased life expectancies and parents having fewer children, grandparents can play fundamental and impactful roles in their grandchildren's lives. These relationships benefit everyone. Adult grandchildren who possess strong ties to their grandparents are less likely to develop symptoms of depression. Grandparents who care for a grandchild on a regular basis have longer life expectancies. Researchers in one prepandemic study of children, ages ten to fourteen, from single- and two-parent households anticipated that the number of parents in a household would significantly affect their children's social and academic performance. Instead, the study revealed that children who interacted regularly with their grandparents were more empathetic and compassionate, and they tended to be more successful at school (Smith).

Grandparents, unlike parents, are not immersed in the pressures of daily parenting and can therefore approach learning and development more playfully, in the process of communicating social values, life lessons, and other forms of advice and wisdom. They can become companions and confidants, provide emotional support during times of change and family stress, and serve as role models for ageing as well as alternative parenting styles. They can be teachers of the family's heritage, traditions, and ancestral language. By sharing experiences from their own childhood and coming of age, they can lessen the distance and even enable perspective for older grandchildren that they can revisit throughout their lives. Often, they can and do provide financial support by supporting a particular activity, paying school tuition, or establishing a college fund. The ways in which they lessen the financial burdens of their adult children's families via childcare is a fundamental part of this chapter.

According to www.etymology.com, the first record of the word "grandparent" dates from around 1800. The origin of the word first appears around 1200; the special use of "grand" (adj.) in genealogical compounds means "a generation older than." "Elder" was the word commonly used and speaks less to kinship and more to the person's "authority in the community." "Elder" gave way to "parent" around 1500 and means "a mother or father; a forbear, ancestor." It helps to unpack the respect and power that the Bible gives to the word "elder" in these lines from 4.4 of the *New Oxford Annotated Bible Revelations*:

> Round the throne were twenty-four thrones, and seated on the thrones were twenty-four elders, clad in white garments, with golden crowns upon their heads.

> And whenever the living creatures give glory and honor and thanks to him who is seated on the throne, who lives for ever and ever, the twenty-four elders fall down before him and worship him who lives for ever and ever; they cast their crowns before the throne, singing, "Worthy art thou, our Lord and God, to receive glory and honor and power, for thou didst create all things, and by they will they existed and were created." (4:9-11)

The replacement of the word "elder" with "parent" and ultimately with grandparent speaks to the inaccurate slippages of status and the role of grandparents in modern, and for our purposes in contemporary society, inaccuracies the pandemic has served both to amplify and exacerbate. "Elder" carries with it honor and dignity, as well as an authority that disappears from the role grandparents have been reduced to in contemporary society. Additionally, "elder" is attached to a much more hierarchical but also interconnected familial and societal structure.

Sarah Stoller's article "The Transformation of Grandparenthood" focusses on carework, gender, and motherhood:

> While our perceptions of grandparents have remained static, we've asked them to do a lot more.... While some have been separated from their children and grand-children because of shutdowns and health concerns, others have become members, or near members, of the households of their children and grandchildren. Growing parental desperation due to a lack of affordable childcare, dramatized by the pandemic, has placed new pressures on grandparents to support their children's families.

Stoller highlights numerous ways in which grandparents remain wrongfully "overlooked as essential members of our communities." She outlines the historic reasons for the existing inaccurate perceptions surrounding grandparents, who are represented as sources of entertainment and pleasure, despite their increased presence in the day-to-day realities of their grandchildren's lives. Stoller traces this shift to industrialization and the decline in agricultural labour, which caused adult children to move away for employment and marriage and in the process made economic help from the extended family less central. Grandparents became distanced both physically and emotionally from the household routines of their children and grandchildren. And with these changes, grandparents, like the storied elders of the bible, began to lose their status as vital sources of wisdom and support in raising children. One 1940s poll revealed that most Americans believed that they should raise their children differently from the manner in which they themselves had been raised (Stoller). This brief sketch of the impact of the shift from agrarian life, supplemented by additional trades, towards industrialization helps contextualize, at least a little, how and why grandparents came to be seen as only providers of entertainment, special treats, and other privileges for their grandchildren.

Contemporary reality tells a dramatically different story: Grandparents have played a vital, if underappreciated, role long before social distancing. Throughout the period from the 1970s to the present, within immigrant families and communities of colour, grandparents have remained consistent in their roles as essential members of immediate families. In many of these cases, the grandparents are the young children's primary caregivers. According to *The Herald Tribune*, one prepandemic survey in the United States (US) revealed that grandparents were caring for one out of four children under the age of five, roughly the same number of children in licensed childcare (Doleatto, "Study").

Grandparents supported their adult children and grandchildren throughout the financial crises of the early 2000s and stepped in again during the pandemic. In 1980, only 12 per cent of American households were multigenerational, which was the overwhelming norm of the previous century. Forty years later, in 2020, 20 per cent of Americans found themselves living in multigenerational settings. Beyond financial benefits, involved grandparents lessen the stress of grandchildren in the household and build connections to the family's cultural history, thereby enabling children to build a healthy self-understanding. Underlying all of this, engaged grandparents bring more people into the community of those who love today's children and young adults.

A 2014 study of employed grandmothers demonstrated that 83 per cent of these women provided more care to their grandchildren than the parents of the children (Meyer and Candic). These numbers coincide with the increasing number of mothers who have become involved in paid work since the 1970s, resulting in the crisis of inadequate and unaffordable childcare. With longer life expectancies, grandparents are increasingly available to take on more significant caretaking roles. At the same time, marriage rates have declined from more than eight marriages per one thousand people at the start of the twenty-first century to six marriages, the lowest since the US government began keeping marriage records in 1867. As of January 28, 2022, the proportion of US births to unmarried mothers is roughly 40 per cent, double the percentage of 1980 (Wildsmith, Manlove, and Cook).

The dramatic changes in family structure have intensified the burdens surrounding work and childcare that families face and help to explain why the pandemic brought to the forefront the amorphous and tenuous place of grandparents in terms of societal as well as economic recognition and support. According to Rebecca Parlakian, senior director of programs at Zero to Three, a national nonprofit focussed on enabling childcare: "Grandparents are filling a gap in a broken child care system.... We've left them out because they're not attached to a system and not making the choices. They're performing a keystone role but doing it outside of systems that focus on parents" (qtd in Doleatto, "Study").

Grandparents on the Front Lines of Their Grandchildren's Lives

Grandparents who are the primary caregivers for their grandchildren now comprise 2.3 million Americans, a number that has doubled since 1970. The dramatic rise in numbers is multi-faceted, stemming from factors including a rise in multi-generational households, caregiver substance abuse and drug addiction, child abuse and neglect, and mental health problems (Choi, Sprang, and Esprenger). Alongside higher numbers of single parents are rising poverty levels and the staggering growth of the prison population. According to an October 2021 study by the ACLU, the US constitutes only 5 per cent of the global population while possessing more than 20 per cent of the world's prison population; the numbers of those incarcerated having increased by 500 per cent since 1970. Two million people are in jail and prison today in the US—numbers that are far, far ahead of population and crime growth. Women have the fastest growing numbers of the prison population in the US according to the ACLU, growing at twice the pace of men, which has had a profound impact on their children and families. These statistics on incarceration—and all that they imply—as well as the realities of mental illness, substance abuse and joblessness, and the high numbers of military servicepersons being deployed, are all central to the reason why 2.3 million grandparents now serve as their grandchildren's primary caregivers in the US.

Throughout the pandemic, these grandparents found themselves in unimaginably difficult situations. Not only has the coronavirus pandemic caused constant changes, but with its onset people also began to see the world as both disorienting and dangerous. Grandparents raising their grandchildren faced long stretches of isolation while remaining aware of the fact that they constituted the population most at risk, especially if they had underlying conditions. If they were to become ill, how would their grandchildren fare? What if they were to die? The implications of these questions extend beyond the focus of this chapter, though a valuable resource for further understanding here is a July 21, 2021, article in *Scientific American* entitled "At Least Two Million Children Have Lost a Parent or Grandparent Caregiver to Covid." Within the US, alone, by July 2021, at least 1.5 million children had lost a parent and two million had lost a parent, grandparent, or relative who had lived with them and helped to care for them.

Along with health risks and emotional stress, the grandparents faced increased financial concerns, as they assumed more responsibilities and costs. With their grandchildren often learning from home, some of them had to choose between their own employment and caregiving. Financial strain often came in the form of meals formerly provided by the school, along with the challenge of helping their grandchildren connect to technology and helping them with schoolwork. In a February 23, 2021, segment of the *PBSNewsHour*, Stephanie Sy pointed out that since the pandemic 40 per cent of "grandfamilies" had difficulty paying for housing and thirty per cent were struggling to provide food. "It's like, I'm hungry, I'm hungry," Lisa Banks, a grandmother raising her three grandchildren said: "You hear it all day, so it's breakfast, it's snack, it's lunch, it's snack, it's dinner, it's snack. You're spending more in utilities because they're using more electricity. Everything goes up" (qtd. in Sy).

For grandparents who do not possess legal custody or guardianship, at times because of eligibility requirements, there are major hurdles towards accessing government support services. Other grandparents may have been laid off or are no longer receiving income from family members. These situations can have devastating consequences. So many of the grandchildren in these situations have experienced a great deal of trauma, so their mental health has already been jeopardized. Remote education also introduces new challenges and compounds the ones already there. As one grandmother in Sy's report said: "The thing of the kids going to school on the computer and not having a social life just exacerbates the problem" (qtd. in Sy).

One sixty-three-year-old grandmother who had spent the last nine years raising her fourteen-year-old granddaughter confessed that the weeks of isolation proved exhausting, and she was afraid of becoming depressed: "I had the impression that the whole world has fallen on my head in an instant. Well, because when you are left alone with all of this, you start to panic. But I am doing better now. I had to figure it out somehow" (qt. in Sy).

Grandparents and the Pandemic

"Working with older adults, I'm seeing a lot of depression, a lot of increases in loneliness," Nich Nicholson, a nursing professor and researcher on aging at Connecticut's Quinnipiac University, told the Associated Press (qtd. in Sewell). "It's been really difficult ... the anxiety, the despair, the social isolation. Over time, there are so many adverse effects. The sooner we expand the bubble, the better, so people can start healing together" (qtd. in Sewell). "Expanding the bubble," as Nicholson calls it, began with vaccination. As of mid-March 2021, some 60 per cent of people sixty-five and older had gotten at least one dose with the Centers for Disease Control stating that only 10 per cent of the whole population had been fully vaccinated (qtd. in Sewell).

In the article "Grandparents Face Separation Anxiety during the Coronavirus," Ronda Kaysen highlights the separation anxiety experienced by some grandparents who could not see their grandchildren because of stay-at-home orders during the pandemic. Gloria Warnicki has four adult children in the Chicago area and used to spend most weekends with any number of her ten grandchildren in her home. COVID-19 put an end to weekend sleepovers, trips to Barnes & Noble, and ice cream shop visits. They were now forced to meet over Zoom. As Warnicki explains, "I miss feeling them, holding those little hands.... I don't want them to lose that feeling of wanting to be with me and wanting to spend time with me" (qtd. in Kaysen). The need for a meaningful relationship is urgent for many grandparents, who are keenly aware of their limited time and the need to make an impact. A yearlong separation can be more agonizing for a person of seventy-five—for whom one year constitutes a much larger span of her remaining lifetime—than their forty-year-old daughter.

Dr. Dimitri Christakis, Director of the Center for Child Health, Behavior and Development at Seattle Children's Research Institute, emphasized the resilience and adaptability of children in this context: "If a child is being reintroduced to grandparents after a year apart, they will still have a very important place in that child's life" (qtd. in Kaysen). Child psychiatry identifies grandparents as "enormously important attachment figures" (qtd. in Kaysen). Such a sentiment is meant to buttress the belief that physical separation will not weaken the bond between grandparents and their grandchildren on the grounds that "children are not going to forget loving grandparents" (qtd. in Kaysen). Still, although the bond may continue, children are growing up faster than ever.

Many grandparents remained determined to maintain their connections to their children and grandchildren. Many increased their use of phone calling, text messaging, and video chatting to keep in touch. A recent survey showed that half of the grandparents who participated stated that they communicated with their adult children and/or grandchildren more frequently than before COVID-19, and new technologies played a fundamental if not central role. Grandparents began using FaceTime and started text messaging; social media channels were the least popular among them. Grandchildren frequently assumed the role of tech teachers to their grandparents (David and Nelson-Kakulla). "Tech is playing an important role in maintaining those grandparent and grandchild relationships," Rebecca Parlakian, senior director of programs at Zero to Three, told *The Herald Tribune* as early as May 2020 (qtd. in Doleatto, "Grandparents"). She continued: "Even infants can form a relationship with someone they see on video chat. There are things parents can do to facilitate that like encouraging toddlers to show their grandparent a toy, pretend to feed their grandparent on the screen, or sing together" (qtd. in Doleatto, "Grandparents").

The October 30, 2020, edition of *The New York Times* features an article titled "Pandemic Grandparenting, Beyond the Dreary Video Calls." One of the grandparents featured, Sally-Ann Roberts, is a veteran television journalist who covered ten mayoral races for New Orleans and Hurricane Katrina in 2005. Despite forty years of experience reporting and anchoring the news, Roberts confessed that she "met her match'" as a grandparent once COVID-19 hit: "I am not doing the job I should be doing.... Before Covid, we'd have the five grandkids over for Sunday Time, from the afternoon until after dark. I'd usually have time to take each one of them aside. Give them each undivided attention. Now, that's ended. Now, that special time is rare. Now, when we get together, we can't even sit at the same table" (qtd. in Gilbert). Clear goals of her role as a grandmother defined Roberts's experience after her 2018 retirement. At the start of the pandemic, she decided that for the mutual safety of all, she would keep her distance, and she reduced her weekly visits to once a month. However, the need to wear masks and maintain physical distance "changed the quality of her interactions ... making conversations with her grandchildren more 'transactional' and less meaningful" (qtd. in Gilbert). Instead of their regular talks about faith, which she still hopes for in the future, her conversations with the oldest boys, aged five and twelve, focussed more on their schedules and grades.

Chuck Kalish, a cognitive and developmental psychologist and senior adviser for science at the Society for Research in Child Development, however, emphasizes that meaningful relationships are defined by "a set of transactional relationships," which ensure that the grandparent is "a resource in the child's life" (qtd. in Gilbert). What is important is to be part of the child's routine, even if remotely, as is the case of grandparents like Dr. Arthur Lanvin, a pediatrician and chairman of the American Academy of Pediatrics. He and his wife have a school-aged granddaughter in Hong Kong. "We see her lessons and we can comment on them. It's actually strengthened our connection," he said (qtd.in Gilbert).

A grandparent need not be technologically savvy or economically privileged to become part of a grandchild's daily routine. Buying two copies of the same book and mailing the other one to the grandchild to read together over a video or phone call, is a more accessible option. "That could be Grandma's job every night before the child goes to bed," advised The American Association of Retired Person's family and caregiving expert, Amy Goyer (qtd. in David and Nelson-Kakulla). "That establishes a routine. It's their special thing. And it gives the parents a break" (qtd. in David and Nelson-Kakulla). Grandparents can also share family history, traditions, and culture during "real-time cooking lessons" with recipes unfolding in step-by-step instructions—even communicated in their native language (qtd. in David and Nelson-

Kakulla). Through technology, grandparents can take an active interest in their grandchildren's hobbies, which may very well include online gaming—an activity at which the grandchildren will likely excel, which help build their confidence.

For those who do not want to rely on technology, letters allow grandparents to be present, even when they are not with their grandchildren. Letters can also be saved, which creates an opportunity for grandchildren to reread them in the future with an understanding that they did not possess at the time. Sending packages is also an immense pleasure, although this can require a grandparent to have access to the post office or UPS.

Yet remote experience cannot replace the intimacy that physical experiences can provide. Tashel Bordere, an assistant professor of human development and family science at the University of Missouri, and her wife, Dr. Kate Grossman, and their fourteen- and three-year-old daughters, visited or hosted one set of grandparents every other month: "Grandparents are essential for us because they give our children another set of people who reinforce their beauty and value," Dr. Bordere said (qtd. in Gilbert). "That's harder to do on Zoom or FaceTime. The quality of our conversations has shifted," she said, and although all of them have been trying, "the girls are missing out" (qtd. in Gilbert).

Despite the challenges the pandemic created, a range of experts came together to devise strategies for enabling grandparents and their grandchildren to create meaningful experiences. Two years before the pandemic, a research paper from *Contemporary Social Science* revealed that grandparent-grandchild relationships bring numerous positive benefits to grandchildren, making them less likely to have emotional and behavioral problems, along with better cognitive and social abilities (Cartusciello). By the 2030s, for the first time in history, one of every five people in the United States will be over sixty-five. U.S. Census Bureau demographers Jonathan Vespa, David M. Armstrong and Lauren Medina report that "...by 2035... older adults will outnumber children for the first time in U.S. history" (Jefferson). James Bates, an associate professor of family wellness, published a study exploring COVID-19's impact on grandparents and their relationships with their grandchildren. "Grandparents have had a lifetime of hard things happening," Bates told *The Columbus Dispatch* (qtd. in Ward). "They think, I've been through hard times and I can do this again. They shift into a different gear—a resiliency gear—and that shows grandchildren that they, too, can be resilient. If Grandma and Grandpa can do this, so can I" (qtd. in Ward). Mutually encouraging the wellbeing of grandparents and their grandchildren could, therefore, become one unexpected learning experience for some that the pandemic helped to realize.

Works Cited

ACLU. "Mass Incarceration." *ACLU*, 2022, www.aclu.org/issues/smart-justice/mass-incarceration. Accessed 5 Mar. 2022.

Buchanan, Ann, and Anna Rotkirch. "Twenty-First-Century Grandparents: Global Perspectives on Changing Roles and Consequences." *Contemporary Social Science*, vol. 13, no. 2, pp. 131-44.

Cartusciello, Jenna. "3 Ways Your Grandchildren Can Benefit from a Close Relationship with You." *Woman's World*, 1 December 2021, www.womansworld.com/posts/grandchildren/grandparent-grandchild-relationship. Accessed 5 Mar. 2023.

Choi, Moon, Ginny Sprang, and Jessica G. Eslinger. "Grandparents Raising Grandchildren: A Synthetic Review and Theoretical Model for Interventions." *Family and Community Health,* Vol. 39, No. 2 (April-June 2016), pp. 120-128. Accessed on 5 Mar. 2023.

David, Patty, and Brittne Nelson-Kakulla, "Grandparents Embrace Changing Attitudes and Technology." *AARP Research.* April 2019, www.aarp.org/research/topics/life/info-2019/aarp-grandparenting-study. Accessed 21 Feb. 2023.

Doleatto, Kim. "Study Points to Importance of Grandparents as Early Childhood Caregivers." *The Herald Tribune*, 23 Sep. 2019, www.heraldtribune.com/story/news/education/grade-level-reading/2019/09/23study-points-to-importance-of-grandparents-as-early-childhood-caregivers/272073800. Accessed 21 Feb. 2023.

Doleatto, Kim. "Grandparents Maintain Communication during Pandemic." *The Herald Tribune*, 5. Nov. 2020, www.heraldtribune.com/story/news/local/aspirations-journalism/2020/05/11/grandparents-maintain-communication-during-pandemic/112580144/. Accessed 21 Feb. 2023.

Gilbert, Allison. "Pandemic Grandparenting, Beyond the Dreary Video Calls." *The New York Times,* 10 Oct. 2020, www.nytimes.com/

2020/10/30/well/family/pandemic-grandparents-grandchildren-connection. Accessed 21 Feb. 2023.

"Grandparent." *Etymonline*, www.etymonline.com/word/grandparent. Accessed 5 Mar. 2023.

Herbert G. May and Bruce M. Metzger. Eds. *The New Oxford Annotated Bible*. New York: Oxford University Press, 1973.

Jefferson, Robin Seaton. "Older Adults Projected to Outnumber Children for First Time In U.S. History." *Forbes*, 19 Mar. 2018. www.forbes.com/sites/robinseatonjefferson/2018/03/19/older-adults-projected-to-outnumber-children-for-first-time-in-u-s-history/?sh=-282051f65ab2. Accessed 5 Mar. 2023.

Kaysen, Ronda. "Grandparents Face Separation Anxiety During Coronavirus Pandemic." *AARP*, 22 June 2020, www.aarp.org/home-family/friends-family/info-2020/grandparents-anxiety-coronavirus. Accessed 21 Feb. 2023.

Meyer, Madonna Herrington and Amra Kandic. "Grandparenting in the United States." *Innovation in Aging*, 30 Oct. 2017, www.ncbi.nlm.nih.gov/pmc/articles/PMC6177109. Accessed 5 Mar. 2023.

Sewell, Dan. "Grandparents in the Pandemic, a Lost Year but Now Some Hope." *AP News*, 21 Mar. 2021, www.apnews.com/article/lifestyle-sports-health-pandemics-coronavirus-pandemic- 8811d0cdef3fa0334861dff0e869c1c3. Accessed 21 Feb. 2023.

Smith, Peter K. "Grandparents and Grandchildren." The British Psychological Society. November 2005, www.thepsychologist.bps.org.uk. Accessed 21 Feb. 2023.

Stoller, Sarah. "The Pandemic Has Exacerbated the Transformation of Grandparenthood." *The Washington Post*, 18 Oct. 2021, www.washingtonpost.com/outlook/2021/10/18/pandemic-has-exacerbated-transformation-grandparenthood. Accessed 21 Feb. 2023.

Sy, Stephanie, and Diane Lincoln Estes. "Raising Children for a Second Time, 'Grandfamilies' Struggle during the Pandemic." *PBSNewsHour*, 23 Feb. 2021, www.pbs.org/newshour/show/raising-children-for-a-second-time-grandfamilies-struggle-during-the-pandemic. Accessed 21 Feb. 2023.

Turner, Ashley. "Retirees Will Outnumber Children for the First Time in US History, Report Says." *U.S. News*, 14 Mar. 2018, www.cnbc.com/2018/03/14/retirees-will-outnumber-kids-for-the-first-time-in-us-history-report. Accessed 21 Feb. 2023.

Ward, Allison. "Grandparents' Advice amid Pandemic Isolation: Stay Present, Positive for Grandkids, Ohio State Study Says." *The Columbus Dispatch*, 6 Jan. 2021, www.dispatch.com/story/news/local/2021/01/06/grandparents-should-stay-present-positive-grandkids-osu-study-says/4025936001. Accessed 21 Feb. 2023.

Wildsmith, Elizabeth, Jennifer Manlove, and Elizabeth Cook. "Dramatic Increase in the Proportion of Births Outside of Marriage in the United States from 1990 to 2016. *Child Trends*, 8 August 2018. www.childtrends.org/publications/dramatic-increase-in-percentage-of-births-outside-marriage-among-whites-hispanics-and-women-with-higher-education-levels. Accessed 5 Mar. 2023.

Chapter 7.

Paperwork: Mental Health Is Not New; It Has Just Been Filed Away

Hillary Di Menna

We go to the hospital in matching leopard print coats. Landmarks of our lives on display, like a film reel being unravelled. We drive by our favourite ice cream spot and the Starbucks that we stop in to get our little black dog a puppaccino. My calm is unnervingly natural, yet at odds, with my usual overwhelmingly large feelings. Trips to the emergency room to plead for mental healthcare are not new to me, but they are for this scared child—the newly thirteen-year-old (no amount of using the term "Quaranteen" could cute away COVID-19 stress) sitting in the back of the car and rambling about how we will all die from COVID-19. Flashbacks of mental health assessment forms and tiny checkboxes rush to mind, 'acts as if driven by a motor?' check. It is March 4, 2021.

We get out of the car and send my partner home. He can't come in due to restrictions. Before he goes, I ask him to apologize to the neighbours. The events that led to this hospital visit were so loud that our fellow apartment dwellers had gathered in the hallway outside our door. I make a mental note to look into disability rights in case our property manager attempts to scare us off with a phony eviction notice again. A hospital bracelet wraps around their tiny wrist. My child (they/them) has become smaller since an hour ago. They are quieter now but still rambling, still bubbling over with emotions too big for a body so small to contain. These bursting feelings used to show themselves in dance and song ('loss of interest in activities once enjoyed?' check).

We wait in seats separated by plastic dividers, comfort hidden away like a baker's goods. I get the vigilance, as our family has been especially cautious throughout the pandemic. We wore masks right away, without question. They transferred to online school, and I made a career change to work from home. We kept to a schedule, showered regularly, and put on clean clothes as we would if we were still going out. We went on walks, so many walks, enough walks to push the dog into faking injury to avoid them. We were doing all the things we were told to do to be good citizens in the face of a plague as well as to preserve our own mental health. As someone aware of how disconnected the mental healthcare system is, as someone who has been around the winding block peppered with dead-end signs more than a few times, I thought I knew what I was doing. Was I not the person who made room for mental health days where we painted skateboards pink before plastering them with magazine clippings and stickers? I have forever fought against mainstream messaging around mental health, messaging deeply rooted in misogynistic ideas of hysterical women in a constant state of overreaction. Feelings of failing in the face of the seemingly inevitable and guilt over my genetics push against my temples, but this fear has to wait.

Our arms reach around the divider so that our hands can clasp. I haven't interrupted the rambles. My daughter looks up at me with a new panic in their blue-grey eyes: "Are they going to take me away?" "I go where you go;" I tell them. Hours pass. I wonder if we haven't demonstrated trauma accurately enough to get care, or if the delay is COVID-19 related. Getting mental healthcare is tricky. You need to be crazy enough—enough being defined by whoever is in charge of assessing at the time. The rules change per person, the same ways they do with case workers. You need to also not be so crazy that you get taken away from your family. The rules change on this as well, but I know how we look on paper—a young mom with a mental health history, the stigma that comes from escaping domestic violence. I got a university degree just so I could learn the language to articulate the barriers we face: the language nice middle-class folks with pretty scarves like to hear behind their Ontario Works or childcare subsidy desks, the language they like to hear in family court. Maybe I'm projecting. That's what people keep telling me. It's just teen angst. It's just COVID-19. It's just hormones. Don't worry. Be strong. Be better.

PAPERWORK: MENTAL HEALTH IS NOT NEW; IT HAS JUST BEEN FILED AWAY

A man cries out for help. He's already handcuffed, but multiple officers hold him down anyway. We watch him with hope that he can feel our compassion. The passing of time is marked by a kind man behind a desk. "We are just about to find you a bed," he says every forty-five minutes, or so.

Although my baby witchlet does not want to be held overnight, they don't know the system yet, so they answer the doctor's questions honestly, leading to an "on form" situation, which means a seventy-two hour hold. I am grateful for this, to be honest. A bed cannot be found. We are told the adult mental health unit would be too overwhelming. Where we are is so loud and busy; my teen's sensory overload is palpable. We are given one banana-flavoured popsicle each. We sit together on a gurney, across from the doctor, behind the curtain separating us from the noise. "I have to stay here," my daughter panics. I turn to them and promise I'm staying, as if my saying it first would override any hospital rules saying otherwise. There is no argument from the doctor. I could stay. The doctor rushes off, but lets us know we will be checked on. This does not happen, but even if it did, what would these check-ins achieve: "Hey just to remind you, you are on form and we don't know where to put you so stay behind this curtain, bye."

I have my partner bring over blankets, a change of clothes, snacks, pillows, colouring books, and markers. I can't fall asleep, but my little one finally does. I list comfort items as if they are building blocks so that I can shield them from the cold loneliness I felt when in their position. I rotate between cuddling them on the gurney and sitting in a gurney-side chair, watching the clock, willing the hospital Tim Horton's to open seven hours early. I tell myself that it will be okay, that no matter what happens, it will be different for them, and that they won't end up with a brain like mine because they won't be alone. I watch them sleep wrapped up in my coat. Almost thirteen years ago, to the day, we were back in Oshawa, and my newborn was wrapped up in those generic hospital blankets—the ones with pink and blue stripes, covered in pilling—and an oversized pink hat. That night, the hospital was a different kind of loud: The cries of stirring newborns were those of hope.

I crawl into the gurney and hold them close, as I did our first night together, in our bed in a shared maternity ward room. IVs aren't in the way this time, just fear. We hear shouting. It sounds like a patient is running away without any clothes on. The man from the waiting room is crying; from what I gather, the poor guy is coming off something. Two security guards start mocking him. "Help me, help me;" they laugh. My baby's eyes open wide: "I'm getting out of here and telling them to shut up." This little one still has some fight. "Alright," my mind whispers, "it's the same me and you. We are rekindling the fire that has gotten us this far, from the hospital room in Oshawa, to this hospital space in Toronto." There is still some fight. Let's go.

If you want to feel isolated but overwhelmed by human responsibility, all at once, I suggest an emotionally draining visit to the emergency room. While there, I miss a home delivery of a birthday present for the thirteen-year-old who started this new chapter of their life with a bang as well as several calls from someone who, the last time we spoke, spent an hour telling me how mental health issues are all made up. I also somehow make it through a phone call from a prospective employer, while at the hospital—a surprise interview. I chase this all down, after we get home, with dehumanizing psychiatry appointments followed by a new hunt for escalated mental health services. To think, other people like to get a jump start to the day with a morning jog.

It's a weird position to be in: to both acknowledge the privilege of finding a psychiatrist covered by OHIP while also being angry at them. It's like you're supposed to take whatever retraumatizing they throw your way with a smile because the system is so broken it's a miracle you found care in the first place. Yet here we are, my teen and I, home from the hospital, sitting in front of a laptop screen, staring at this doctor, completely miserable. Not too long ago, this doctor was praising me for being a fierce advocate for my little one. Now, I am the mother who couldn't help her family without medical intervention, and today's call radiates my failure. Deep down, I know I did the right thing with the tools I had, but at this moment, I'm forced to ask myself, what so many neurotypical minds have before: "Am I projecting?" Even the psychiatrist responds to a nervous ramble of mine by asking my daughter, "Was your mom being a bit much there?" Psychiatrists are not known for their bedside manner. I do not expect much more than a medical assessment from a psychiatrist, as counselling is a different department. Everything in the realm of mental health is a different department. I still expect some basic human decency. How I don't know better after decades in the game? I don't know. Perhaps, it is a mother's wishful thinking—a belief that I can bend the system for the sake of my baby. My own kind of stubborn magic manipulated life to work for me this far, after all, so why am I failing when it matters the most? We sit in silence. I am told by the doctor not to speak, and my child refuses to. I understand the need to give my child agency, but if there is nothing being vocalized, how can we receive help? When the appointment ends, I reach out to the doctor, asking if we can have a quick one on one, so that I can tell her what happened; surely it should be on record somewhere for future care. I am denied my request and told that if I cannot cope again, to bring my daughter to the emergency room. The phrase "cannot cope" sets fire to my mind, flames fuelled by frustration. A broken bone is given a cast because it needs support, but the bone is not lectured for having inadequate coping skills. To support mental health is to acknowledge the system is broken; blaming coping skills, a mother's coping skills, is much easier. I call an agency we are on a waiting list for and try a different department.

The way the youth mental health system works is that no one cares until it is almost too late. It does not get better the older you get. Once suicide is brought into the equation, you may get an upgrade from a school counsellor, who suggests private tutoring or a consultation with a counsellor at an outside agency, where your child may receive twelve counselling sessions. Twelve sessions seem to be the maximum in the nonprofit healthcare world. I had been begging for help for my child for years. Things become more complicated when there are multiple mental health concerns, and the stress of family court, where this child is repeatedly asked to repeat their own trauma in a tidy paperwork appropriate way. When there is a lot going on, you need a lot of help, but when there is a lot going on, there are more opportunities to be referred to a different department. Even now, folks scramble to explain away what my child is struggling with and what I struggle with with such explanations as "only hormones," "just teen angst," and "simply COVID-19." These are factors related to, not divorced from, the mental health challenges we are facing. These social constructions make for obstacles because to acknowledge the need to care for one another is to acknowledge the importance of community over profit. So everything gets divided into the individual. Departments are where paperwork can get lost in between. I know this all too well from my own experiences navigating the system. Although these experiences make navigating these same systems for my child a bit easier, they do not erase the barriers of waiting lists and specific program eligibility criteria.

Like most things to do with motherhood, it is difficult to talk about raising a neurodivergent child without sounding as if you are complaining. It is a challenge to get the point across that, again, with most things to do with motherhood, the complaints aren't to do with the child themselves. The problems are to do with barriers constructed by misogyny and capitalism. If mental healthcare was truly informed and accessible, there wouldn't be as many issues. If mental health was genuinely considered important, people, like my child and me, would not be considered troublemakers for being forced to exist on an uneven playing field. If community and nurturance were valued, we wouldn't be so tired. I recently ended a phone call with: "Soon there will be no mothers to make these appointments because we are all going to drop dead from exhaustion." When I shared this comment, thinly veiled as a humorous truth over social media, I received several responses from other mothers: "Count me in." We love our children, and the accusation, of otherwise, is said by those who want to deflect from the deeply rooted issues. It isn't the first time a mother has been blamed for the world's serpents.

Long before I discovered the truth about my family's mental health history, back when I thought it was simply a failing on my part (note: one's mental health is never a personal moral failing), we were sitting in a Tim Horton's in Oshawa. My then four-year-old was being loud and energetic, with a charm that allows a person to get away with pretty much anything. This is why it was hard, trying to articulate what was happening, the intricacies of the logistics of simply getting out the door each day. Even though I am often shushed with "Kids are difficult" or diagnosed as "a stupid and single young mother in Oshawa" disorder, I forever remind myself that I am a good mom, and I knew something was up long ago. A man gets up to leave the coffee shop and stops at our table to say bye to my child by name. "How did he know my name," my little one asks me, shocked and wide eyed, having no concept of the amount of times I need to tell them to "watch out/come back/wait" every time we are out. "Everyone here knows your name;" the man laughs, as the door's bell chimes before an Ontario winter wind loudly pulls the door shut.

My baby witchlet loves preschool. They attend two, and workers from each praise my little one's confidence and love of performance. The first preschool shares the same community health building as my counsellor, and the second preschool is recently built and located near where we are living. It is built on a tiny piece of land that used to have a small house, a house that, less than ten years prior, housed a series of rejected teens. That house was condemned and torn down. It was when I was living there that I met my child's father and where I fell in love with another angry girl who was no stranger to emergency room visits. She remains my best friend over twenty years later. I refer to this friend in the hospital waiting room on March 4, in some awkward attempt to let my teen know that they are in good company. I don't believe there are accidents, and I believe that the preschool, where my child spent so many sunny days, was meant to heal the dejection of the young souls who lived there before.

The transition to junior kindergarten is a shock. Folks aren't as charmed by the energetic child with a tattooed mom. The uncompromising structure that has created a culture where we make jokes at the expense of kids crushed by their day-to-day ("Haha, kids always want to get out of school; let us never ask why") moves swiftly in squashing my child's enthusiasm. I think maybe things will be better once we move to the city, and for a year, things are better. We find an amazing subsidized daycare, and senior kindergarten is an area where my child can take up space in their princess dresses while telling their classmates stories. I accompany them on field trips and brag about how happy my child is at school. Then, grade one happens; grade two follows, as does grade three—each school year experience worse than the one before. The "bad kid" label happens fast. My child can't sit still; my child is having a hard time focussing. Instead of acknowledging an obvious need for accommodations, school administration believes a transition from French immersion to the English program will be a cure all. The transition is not the quick fix it was thought to be. Instead, my "bad" child is "difficult" not only for not being able to focus but also for wandering out of their new class to go find their friends across the hall in their old class. My child is too loud, too energetic, too interested in making friends. Even their raspy voice is scrutinized. Their first-grade teacher cited some theory that raspy voices are linked to behaviour issues, before getting to the real point: "It is obvious that since you are a student yourself, you don't have enough time to properly discipline this child."

"I don't believe she said that," the second-grade teacher tells me a year later, during one of our first meetings over my child's too loudness, where I bring her up to speed after personally enduring way too many useless meetings where no solutions are suggested, only grievances. I will never apologize for my child being assertive, as I encourage advocacy for the self and others. When I get a complaint call that my child didn't follow the rules of quiet time because they got up to hug their friend who was crying at their desk, I feel my time is being wasted.

However, I do mind when my child is almost getting hit by cars because they cannot fight the impulse to run in the middle of the road to pick up a piece of string that had caught their eye, and I do care when my primary-school-aged child begs me to drop out. One day, as we get off the bus, my child looks at me. With tears in those regularly curious eyes, they say: "I couldn't do it, Mom. I try listening to all the conversations, but they get confusing, and it is too much for me."

A mom in the schoolyard comments, "My child has ADHD, too." We didn't have the diagnosis yet, but it was interesting to hear someone vocalize my suspicions when everyone else was calling my child a "bad kid."

The referral to the ADHD clinic involves a lot of paperwork, but it seems like we are on the right track. We have an official diagnosis. I cry from the validation, and for the information I need to learn more about how I can care for my child the way they need. My child skips beside me, touching everything, and I think to myself, "I think I get it, now." This joy is short lived, as the next step is to have the grade-three teacher fill out the paperwork, and the teacher keeps forgetting. Calls go unreturned. Letters are not read. It isn't until I get to school early one morning and meet her, as she is coming in, that she has no choice but to talk to me. She tells me she has been ignoring me because she doesn't believe in the diagnosis. The reason being my child has the ability to focus on the arts and their friends, so they must not be trying.

I become a nuisance, calling the school until the paperwork is complete. It works, as not only do I get the paperwork and the ball rolling for accommodations, but the principal also provides me with numbers to connect with doctors for a psychoeducational assessment. A psychoeducational assessment helps establish school accommodations, and it is an important tool in the school accommodations game. The catch is you can either wait on a list for years to see one at no cost, or you pay privately. I try talking to a pretty-scarf-wearing friend about it. They tell me in a condescending tone (the kind that confuses their privilege with something earned through merit and good morals) that I do not need a psychoeducational assessment and that I should simply call XYZ services. XYZ services are those that do not exist. Many people who don't need the system seem to truly believe quick and direct support services exist because it seems only fair that care is accessible (or to justify classist constructions of societal leeching). The naivety may be well intentioned, though usually patronizing. System navigation is exhausting enough without having one's experiences questioned at every turn. We get the psychoeducational assessment. We need information from the ADHD clinic, but they do not return our calls, so we get a referral to another ADHD specialist. The specialist is lovely and informed and retiring shortly after we meet—resulting in more waiting rooms, more answering machines, more departments.

My child is assigned to a school counsellor, two, actually. The first is wonderful and helps us out when the school questions why we are so often late. She understands ADHD and shows compassion when we are forced to go through another round of a traumatic family court process. Thankfully, she allows my child to speak about their complex feelings around all that is going on. The school counsellor shuffle happens. The next counsellor says there will be no talk of family court and asks, "have we tried lavender oil for the ADHD?" Unsurprisingly, the lack of support is not healthy. We try outside counselling services. One agency has a two-session cap. Another cancels its programs due to an insufficient number of registered participants.

A change in schools helps, although the school counsellor we are assigned is a let down. She refuses to speak to my child and, instead, refers me to a costly parenting course that takes place during work hours. She explains to me that there are accompanying books, but they may be "too academic" for me. She knows nothing of my child or me, including my recent master's degree, that involved me already reading these suggested titles. I dismiss her wisdom/classism as being another talking head in a pretty scarf. The new school is an upgrade, and I have mastered the art of attending meetings for all sorts of abbreviations—for example, IEP (individual education plan) and IPRC (identification, placement, and review committee)—in red lipstick and a (faux) leather jacket, notebook in hand, with binders of supporting documentation in my backpack. Though organizational systems and confidence boosting wardrobes cannot push back against what is bubbling, we soon find ourselves in a psychiatrist's hospital office to talk about this sixth grader's self-harm. We meet a fantastic team, and two sessions later, the department moves hospitals. No one calls us about the change. I find out when trying to follow up on our next appointment. Reception says the department has moved, and, no, they don't know where. We live on waiting lists; some my child eventually ages out of before even hearing back from the program. I know that waiting lists are where we need to be. When we need help, and are told, by whoever is in charge at the moment, to be on the XYZ list, I can say that part is done, check that off the to-do list, so now what?

A fellow student overhears my child telling their friend how suicide lets you be in charge of how you die, before sharing their own plan. News travels to a teacher who, in turn, calls me. I am used to calls home, but the tone of this call shakes me. I have survived so many of my friends, many lost to suicide, that I have survivor's guilt. I have attended two funerals in the past month alone. Immediately after the call, I leave my work office and call one of the lists we are on for psychiatry. We get bumped up as a priority and get an appointment next week. Shaken, I reach out to a loved one for support, and I am told not to cry because I need to be strong and not emotional. I feel selfish for even needing support. It is a feeling reminding me that this is how the world operates, which defines community care as a weakness and a selfish need.

A new counsellor is assigned, but with even more cuts to public school funding, the ensuing and valid teacher's strike, and the beginnings of COVID-19-induced online schooling, she disappears. On my own mental-health sick leave, I am able to help my child keep up with school. The same cannot be said for the next school year. Teachers come and go in fast rotation. The public school system was destroyed before COVID-19, and now routine is impossible. I can tell something is bubbling inside my child. I know something is wrong. The psychiatrist keeps pushing MentalHealthTO and other one-time services that won't help our situation because care is not a one-time shot. We need actual continued care past the generic one liners offered on a phone line—the one liners I already know, as a crisis line volunteer myself.

The first time I think about going to the emergency room, I let a friend talk me out of it. I immediately regret opening up to him. The hour of being told it is all in my head only adds to the years of gaslighting I have endured, as someone in need of mental healthcare. I'm the one who finds the plans written out in a sparkly pink diary. I'm the person who is threatened when the big feelings escape. I'm the one who knows her child so intimately and intensely that if something is off, I know. Yet all I hear is the Greek chorus: "It's just teen angst. It's just COVID-19. It's all in your head, that hysterical head."

What we call "the incident" happens the next day, the day we go to the emergency room in matching coats. My child gets released earlier than seventy-two hours; I am told it is because I seem to have a grip on the signals. This contradicts what the psychiatrist later says, when I am told that if I can't cope I should go to a different department. And it contradicts what the mindfulness martial arts teacher says when he won't believe that my child with ADHD isn't focussing in his class for kids with ADHD not because of ADHD but rather my failing as a mother for not promoting more mindfulness at home (as I am a mother whose mind is not full enough?) or for having a relative bring them to a class instead of my nondriving, several-contracts-working, and emotionally drained self. I know what our early discharge actually means: We are on our own.

March 2008, our first night together. I stare, dreamily determined, into my baby's eyes. I ignore our slumlord's phone calls with threats of eviction. I don't worry about the home we will go back to and quickly escape. I don't hear the wild wind from the storm happening outside. I was born during an earthquake, myself, after all. On this night in March 2008, I draw on the strength that had me survive this long, and I promise this power to my baby. I vow this strength will move us past simply surviving, and to the thriving mark. This determination is, again, conjured up in 2021 in the emergency room parking lot. COVID-19 has exposed the chaos behind the world's illusionary curtain. Ruby slippers, come save us. When departments with fancy titles move us around, my womb will forever be our home base. I love this wild haired child louder than any screams of shame and doubt. Mothering this kind of magic can't be taught, graded, or assessed.

I ignore all the negative outsider voices. The voices that say I am projecting, that I'm not a good mom, and that I should ignore the suffering because it is simply teen angst. I ignore these voices, as they are the same ones that failed me when I was a girl, when I was suffering with nowhere to go other than falling down cracks. These voices don't matter.

It has been said that a parent should make sure to (especially) receive therapy when their child becomes the age they were when their tower crashed. Putting the reality of therapy being inaccessible aside, I understand this sentiment. By the time I was my child's age, I did not have support. I was on my own until being adopted as an adult, legally speaking. (Whatever adult truly means remains a mystery to me. I certainly did not feel adult at eighteen.) I have no parenting experience to draw from. I did not have a "me." My daughter has me, though, with deep pockets full of experience and advocacy. I learn about nervous systems, school accommodations, and the different kinds of specialists. I fight feelings of hopelessness through a pathologized hypervigilance. I create plans A-Z, with subsections, and appendixes. My child won't fall through the cracks because I lay my body over the ruptures. If the people behind the voices won't help dust me off, then I will brush them off.

There are voices loud enough to reach me when my mind spirals too far into the future, far into the land of what ifs. What if my daughter never learns to live on their own? What if I run out of ideas? What if I die young like my mother? The neighbourhood pastor calls me on the phone. My chosen family visits me with soup. The voice of internet strangers from a mothering and motherhood group in my often neglected inbox and the voice of our old daycare worker remind me that dirtied pink pants don't mean I'm a bad mother, only that my child feels safe enough to get dirty. These voices are the hymns worth learning.

After the incident we get bumped again, to the top of the waitlist, for another agency. Some of its programming has been wonderful, some has not, but we finally have a counsellor who cares about us and advocates for youth mental health the way we all should. Bless them forever and always.

Youth mental health needed to be advocated for before the pandemic. We never had a real mental healthcare foundation to build upon, and now as the world falls apart, we see that we let the cracks get so big that they are all consuming. The problem won't be solved with positive notations on children's resiliency or trendy, once-a-year, capitalist constructed hashtags. Things are not okay, and until this is accepted, we cannot move on.

My five-year-old leaves their cat plushie on the streetcar. My eyes survey upwards to different signs and maps within the TTC station. Looking at the turning tracks, I know they make sense to those who built them but not to me. Strong legs from years of searching and vocal chords accustomed to making us heard, I chase the bus and retrieve the cat. For my witchlet, I will forever chase what I need to.

Our life is made up of appointments, some where I am told I am too involved, others where I am told I am not involved enough. I follow what works for my baby—that's the lead I take. The opinions of others have been muted because "blah blah blah hormones, teen angst, COVID-19" is not only ignorant and redundant but also boring. Life is too short for such nonsense.

Mental healthcare is constructed as a privilege and a lot of us will put up with a lot of hurt and retraumatization just to receive it. Even being able to talk about mental health, without fear of punishment, is a privilege. A disclosure of poor mental health can affect job security, housing security, and relationships. Such a disclosure affects one's standing in a courtroom setting and one's label as a fit parent. We aren't supposed to take sick days. Even after a well-documented need for mental health accommodations, in the eye of COVID-19's storm, we receive letters home about school attendance. We need to take action, beyond buzzwords, for the sake of our children and the communities raising them.

We still have routine, but it is not focussed on what the systems that got us into this mess deem important. Our routine focusses on compassion, community, and rollerskating. Youth mental health has been weaponized by the folks who continuously slash mental healthcare and endanger the most vulnerable in order to reopen an economy beneficial to a few. Some days, this insincere interest in mental health is offensive to me; other days, I remember the power of me and my witchlet: pink skateboards, bright coloured wigs, and chasing cats on buses.

I can't say if the kids will be alright, but I can say they will remember. They will remember the strength of their families through love, faith, and choice. They will remember those who failed to protect them. Secured within the armour of princess dresses, they will remember where the cracks are, and they won't let future generations fall because they will know the failings of a world that believes living life while one's body is shifting shape, one's heart is thundering loudly, and one's mind is surviving plague is simply just hormones, just teen angst, or just COVID-19.

March 2022, my three black cats fight for my attention as I laugh over the phone, speaking with our counsellor for my check in. Moments before, I hit send on the most recent draft of this chapter. It has been a year of different programs, counselling sessions, and visits to the psychiatrist. A year full of joyful moments, eating coco bread sandwiches from our favourite neighbourhood spot and planting gardens with the neighbours, but also difficult ones, including tearful visits to the ever-patient principal's office and vaccine lineups. Like a garden ourselves, we are growing, adapting, and making it work. Somehow, amidst it all, my daughter breaks their ankle, and not to be outdone, I break my wrist only a few months later. Like our bones, we heal with the right support. We know there are cracks, but we also know the power of our magic.

Chapter 8.

Coping with COVID-19: Child-Parent Reflections on Perceived Stressors

Lisa H. Rosen, Linda J. Rubin, and Meredith G. Higgins

Pandemic-Related Stressors

> "The world changed ... it's hard to wrap your head around it."
> —Student participant

The COVID-19 pandemic, profoundly and abruptly, changed children's lives and those of their parents, as reflected in the opening quote of a male adolescent, a study participant, speaking with his mother. For children, there were sudden changes to routine with schools closing. Fear of catching the virus surged, and many children contracted COVID-19 or had a loved one who had become ill (De Araújo et al.). Especially during the early waves of the pandemic, children's interactions with peers and friends were limited. Being physically isolated reduced children's access to their social infrastructure, which could serve an important protective role (Dalton; Vogel et al.).

Parents also faced tremendous stressors during the pandemic. As was the case for children, parents reported fear of contracting the virus. Many adults have contracted COVID-19, as did their friends and family. School closures affected parents who had to take on considerably more childcare work, and this was especially the case for mothers (Barroso and Horowitz; Igielnik). Balancing this additional parenting obligation with existing responsibilities often led to feelings of physical and emotional exhaustion (Cummins and Brannon). Working parents experienced stress due to pandemic-related changes in the nature of their job. Some experienced loss of employment or reduced hours, and those who maintained their job often reported stress due to pandemic-related changes, such as telework (Kapoor; Rožman and Tominc). The rise in telework offered flexibility but was also associated with loneliness due to decreased social interaction as well as challenges to maintaining work-life balance (Charalampous et al.).

Importantly, both child and parent pandemic-related stressors can spill over and affect the family system (Hussong et al.; Sun et al.). The pandemic directly affected children, but there were also indirect effects through their parents. The stress parents experienced during the pandemic affected family functioning. As parents are important models, children's ability to cope with the stress of the pandemic is influenced by their parents' coping style. Beth Russel and colleagues suggest that "the stresses and strains of parenting during disasters may amplify caregiver burden and mental health symptoms, potentially compromising parenting behavior sufficiently to impact the parent child relationship—a significant predictor of children's outcomes during times of prolonged stress" (672). Correspondingly, children's pandemic-related stress affected their parents, and "pandemic stressors for parents may also include how children cope with their own negative life events, such as changes in schools and isolation related to the pandemic" (Hussong et al. 361). Due to prolonged school closures, parents might have felt particularly responsible for their children's development and experienced guilt related to pandemic parenting (Staneva).

The current chapter centres on the lived experiences of early adolescents and their parents. We focussed our parent-child interviews on pandemic-related stressors during the early adolescent period (ten to fourteen years of age) because this is a time when peer contact is so strongly craved and risk-taking behaviour often increases (Andrews et al.). Thus, social distancing may have been especially difficult for early adolescents. This chapter also examines the pandemic-related stressors that were most salient for this age group and their parents.

Mental Health during the Pandemic

Identifying the most salient pandemic-related stressors for early adolescents and their parents may help guide intervention work, given the negative mental health outcomes associated with the pandemic for youth and adults. Despite children typically facing fewer physical health consequences from COVID-19, due to social distancing guidelines and the lack of traditional school routines during the early waves of the pandemic, there may be long-term effects on development and mental health, as children worried about loved ones contracting the virus. Paul Ramchandani suggests that "although the direct impact of COVID-19 on children seems to be less severe than on adults ... indirect and hidden consequences will have a lasting effect" (21). Ongoing longitudinal studies show a decrease in indices of psychological adjustment following the onset of the pandemic (Vogel), and the extent to which youth viewed COVID-19 as personally disruptive was associated with increased internalizing (e.g., anxiety, depression) and externalizing (e.g., anger) symptoms (Skinner et al.). School disruptions may be particularly impactful for children, with the potential to affect learning as well as academic motivation (Agostinelli et al.). Effects of the pandemic may also be noted in adolescents' emotional development, as they had to cope with negative emotion over a prolonged period of time. In terms of social development, youth had fewer opportunities to interact with peers, exert autonomy, and explore their identity (Hussong, Benner et al.).

Parental support likely acts as a buffer against the stress of the pandemic; however, as adolescents are spending more time with family, they are also in the midst of a developmental period when they are striving towards independence. During this time window, when children may have needed their parents most, many parents are facing great stress that may strain their resources and negatively influence their parenting (O'Reilly and Green; Westrupp et al.).

Like their children, parents reported greater mental health concerns during the pandemic. Parents reported higher levels of depression and anxiety since the onset of the pandemic (O'Reilly and Green). The pandemic might also have been associated with greater parenting irritability and consumption of alcohol (Westrupp et al.). For parents and their children, "the pandemic is both a shared historical event and an individual varying one" (Hussong, Benner et al. 821). Although families shared many stressors, some may have experienced stressors of greater intensity and duration. The stress of the pandemic and subsequent mental health outcomes might have been especially pronounced for BIPOC families (Black, Indigenous, and people of colour), working-class families, and single mothers, in part, due to the potential economic hardships of the pandemic (Gur et al.; Mehta; Yoshikawa et al.).

Current Study

Our research team consisted of six interviewers, who conducted a total of ten child-parent interviews from June 2021 through October 2021. Child participants reported their gender as boy (n = 7), girl (n = 2), and non-binary (n = 1). Seven mothers and three fathers participated and reported their race/ethnicity as white (n = 4), Black (n = 3), and Hispanic (n = 3). Due to the pandemic, we conducted all interviews online and recorded them for later transcription.

Prior to the interview, both children and parents completed a brief survey. Children responded to two open-ended questions as part of the survey: "Many problems or difficulties have happened because of the coronavirus pandemic and social distancing guidelines. Some examples are changes in school and after-school activities. Think of a problem that you have had and write a short description of the situation," and "What is a problem or conflict you have had with a peer during COVID-19? Please share about it." Correspondingly, parents reported on a problem they had due to COVID-19, a problem their child had experienced because of COVID-19, and a peer problem their child had experienced during the pandemic.

Following completion of the survey, the research assistant introduced the interview. Child-parent dyads were asked to participate in three observational tasks. Each task was presented individually, and dyads discussed each task for five minutes, bringing the total discussion time to fifteen minutes for all three tasks. The research assistants turned their cameras off during discussion to allow children and parents to talk but turned their camera back on when introducing the next prompt.

For the first observational task, the researcher reminded participants that they each came up with a problem related to COVID-19, and each person was asked to talk about anything related to the problems. This task was designed to elicit discussion on problems most salient to children and parents during the pandemic. The second and third observational tasks were designed to examine the social impact of the pandemic. For the second observational task, child-parent dyads were asked to discuss a problem the child had experienced with a peer during the pandemic. The third and final task focussed on social distancing, and both children and parents were asked to reflect on changes that have happened due to social distancing guidelines, also known as the six-foot-apart rule.

We hoped to examine how general pandemic stressors, as well as how the profound social changes brought about by the pandemic, affected children and their parents. Under social-distancing guidelines, there were significant decreases in face-to-face peer interactions and a corresponding increase in peer communication thorough electronic channels (Goldschmidt). As such, the importance of examining the effects of social distancing has been highlighted (Andrews et al.; Hussong et al.). Positive interactions with peers have the potential to serve as a powerful protective factor, which can buffer against the effects of different forms of adversity, whereas negative peer experiences, including victimization, confer risk for the development of myriad forms of health and adjustment problems for children (Bukowski et al.). With increased peer communication via electronic media, experts suggested there could be a rise in cyberbullying during the COVID-19 crisis (Imran et al.), as a great deal of research on children's electronic communication has focussed on antisocial behaviour. Conversely, children's electronic communication can take positive and prosocial forms (Erreygers et al.; Underwood et al.), which could serve a powerful protective role during this pandemic. Our interviews sought to address both negative and positive influences of peers during this unprecedented time.

Lived Experiences of Children and Parents during the Pandemic

Thematic analysis following the process outlined by Virginia Braun and Victoria Clarke was applied to the transcribed interviews. Five interview themes are presented to illustrate the lived experiences of early adolescents and their parents during the pandemic. We provide a representative example of each theme and, in so doing, identify each child participant by an assigned set of initials.

Fears for Physical Health of Loved Ones

One pressing concern was the physical health of family members. In particular, multiple dyads focussed on grandparents and fear for their health, as noted in the exchange of one son and his mother:

> Mother of RB: I think that was, that was harder for me because I don't think you all worried about it [getting grandparents sick], like if you went over there. I don't know. I worried a lot, like if we went over there, I would try not to stand too close to them, or I would try not to breathe anywhere near them because I was really worried about giving them COVID.
>
> RB: We were kind of dumb about COVID like that. Or I didn't know much about it.
>
> Mother of RB: So you weren't too worried?
>
> RB: Yeah
>
> Mother of RB: I worried a lot though...

This theme of concern for health of family members recurred in other interviews; this stress was more pronounced for parents in the dyads interviewed.

Irritation with Masks

Although many noted that masks were protective, several of the children were irritated about wearing them. This was especially evident in one mother-daughter interaction:

> Mother of AB: Yeah. I wrote that you had—that was your problem, too, that you had to wear masks at school.... And you hate the masks, right? Huh?
>
> AB: I want to burn them.
>
> Mother of AB: You want to burn them?
>
> AB: Yes.

Other children mentioned their annoyance with masks but under circumstances that were more specific. For instance, some talked about how it was challenging to wear a mask during athletics or in hot weather, suggesting it was the mask itself that was problematic, rather than what the mask represents about the contagious nature of COVID-19.

Loss of Experiences and Opportunities

Another recurring theme was perceived loss. Child-parent dyads reported on loss and missed opportunities in many domains. Children reported missing events and fun experiences, such as holidays, including Halloween. Missing celebrations, trips, and time with family were highlighted by numerous child-parent dyads. In the exchange below, a mother and son reflect on the loss of opportunities for travel and time with family.

> AM: So, you know about one time we were supposed to go to California? And do all that fun stuff? I was really excited about that.
>
> Mother of AM: Me, too. I know. And I was excited because you guys have never ridden on a plane before.
>
> AM: Yeah, and that was one of the things I wanted to do. I've never ridden on a plane. It would be cool.
>
> Mother of AM: And that would have been like one of the first real family vacations we'd ever had, too, right? It was kind of a bummer. We didn't get to go to Disney World or Disneyland, and we didn't get to ride on a plane.
>
> AM: I just feel like California would have been really fun. We would have been able to see family members.
>
> Mother of AM: Yeah, we would have been able to see some of our family.

This exchange illustrates the salience of loss as experienced by missed opportunities for travel and time with family.

Changes in Friendships and Peer Dynamics

The theme of loss was also evident in missing friends, with some dyads reflecting on the loneliness they experienced from pandemic restrictions. Parents pointed out the social toll the pandemic took on their children, as seen in the following sentiments conveyed from father to son: "I saw that affected you, not being able to see your classmates, and interact with your classmates and the ones who are your friends. Because you did all the virtual [school] so not able to, you know, just sit in a classroom. I did notice that you, not being able to interact with your classmates, was pretty challenging for you."

A similar sentiment was echoed in a mother-son discussion: "I saw it affecting your peer relationships during COVID. So, yeah, I think that you missed your friends because I feel like you're definitely a very social person, you like to be with people."

During a developmental period in which early adolescents crave peer contact, they were unable to interact with their friends, face to face, and parents recognized the stress this created for their children.

Some dyads noted that some families were more limited in the time they engaged with others outside the home during the pandemic, which changed how children interacted with their closest friends. Some parents opted to delay the return to school for virtual instruction, which affected social dynamics at school. The effect of this delayed return to school is evident in one parent's response: "When we had the lockdown part, you couldn't see anybody for a long time.... And then when you got to go to school, you got to see a limited number of people. Because your real close friends either weren't in your class and you didn't get to interact with them, or ... they were homeschooled because of COVID." Beyond the effects of virtual school, some parents limited children's interactions that kept friends physically apart, as seen in the following mother-child exchange:

> Mom of AC: Okay, and your best friend, you can't see her anymore, right? Sam?
>
> AC: Yeah, I can't.
>
> Mom of AC: Because her mom doesn't want anyone... her mom really, really fears COVID. So, we try to be respectful, and we don't go over. But she won't, you won't be able to see her until she is vaccinated, which will probably be in September this month.
>
> AC: Yeah, yes, at the end of the month. We would just have to wait after that.
>
> Mom of AC: But that has really affected you because you used to spend the night over there.
>
> AC: Like all the time.

In almost every dyad, the effect of the pandemic in limiting or, in some way, changing peer contact, was noted.

Interestingly, several dyads, specifically, discussed missing physical contact with their peers. Some children mentioned missing fist bumping and giving high fives as evident in this mother-son discussion:

> LR: It was more one of things [sic], like throughout the whole grade, that the social distancing. I know that was a problem at school because like it's almost like you just want to go in the hallway, like give your friend a fist bump or something.
>
> Mom of LR: But I get what you were saying, before, as an athlete. You love to be able to, you know ... give your friends a high five or a fist bump. How does that make you feel?
>
> LR: Just mind blowing, that the whole world changed.

In addition to fist bumping, some dyads discussed how social distancing had affected the ability to give a friend a hug.

Children and parents noted the effect of missed interactions with peers on feelings as well as on development. Missed interactions led to feelings of sadness and loss, as is evident in what participants shared. Interestingly, an early adolescent male insightfully reflected on how the pandemic affected his social development:

> AM: I feel like the pandemic has stalled everyone's maturity.
>
> Mother of AM: That's a valid point. Do you feel like you have more friends now or less friends now?
>
> AM: I feel like I have a little bit more because I've tried socializing a lot to get my socializing skills back.
>
> Mom of AM: Yeah. I think, like you said, when the pandemic hit, you didn't get to interact with other kids as often as you used to. And so, when we finally started getting kids back into our home again ... you struggled with certain things like the time P. was at our house. You were upsetting him by dunking him in the pool, and he was clearly really upset with you, but you couldn't tell that he was upset with you, and so, like those types of things you've had to slowly learn again. That's the only time I've ever really noticed a problem you've had with a peer because of the pandemic.

Limited opportunities for peer interactions during early adolescence were challenging, and once children were able to resume face-to-face interactions, some reported a process of readjusting.

Although children missed the opportunity to interact with one another face to face, many of the families we interviewed discussed creative ways of coming together with peers in safe ways during the pandemic. Sometimes these opportunities to connect safely were orchestrated by their school, such as a socially distanced field day. Other times, children moved their face-to-face interactions to the virtual world. Many dyads noted an increase in multiplayer video games, such as in this mother-son interaction:

> AM: I, mostly, was just hanging out with the boys on games.
>
> Mom of AM: On video games?
>
> AM: For seven months straight, we played this one game; I don't think you remember it; it was like a fighting game ... it helped me to socialize with my friends online.

Although face-to-face opportunities were limited, many children were able to connect in ways that allowed for social distancing, including online gaming.

Mental Health Concerns

The stress of the pandemic affected the mental health of early adolescents and their parents. During the interviews, some parents were incredibly honest about the ways the pandemic influenced their wellbeing, such as the following exchange between a mother and son.

> Mom of AM: Well for the first time in my life, I started experiencing depression a little bit, too, during the pandemic. And that's something I had never really dealt with before, and so that was kind of new to me.... I went to a counsellor, and it helped a lot to talk to somebody. And luckily, a lot of counsellors started doing like, counselling sessions on the computer. That was really helpful for me.
>
> AM: I can understand that because a lack of social interaction would really hurt so much emotional stability.

Mom of AM: Yeah. Did you ever pick up on the fact that I was depressed during the pandemic?

AM: No!

Mom of AM: Really?

AM: I thought you were normal. I thought you were just tired. I thought either you were just very tired or very stressed out.

Mom of AM: Yeah, there was probably a little bit of both those two, right?

AM: I know whenever you're tired or stressed out, it's just hard for me to pick which one it is because [being] tired and being stressed always kinda look alike.

Mom of AM: Well, a lot of the times, they go hand in hand.

AM: Yeah.... I didn't know what some signs of depression was... before. I didn't know how to identify it, or anything like that.

Even though not all dyads had as open discussion as outlined above, many children reported being aware of the stress their parents were under, and parents could identify stressors affecting their children.

Although some dyads highlighted how COVID-19 had influenced their wellbeing and the wellbeing of their loved ones, others reported forgetting about or minimizing the stress of COVID-19. One mother-son dyad suggested that the negative effects of COVID could be quickly forgotten:

Mom of RB: It's surprising like how quickly I feel like we forget the more unpleasant parts [of COVID-19].

RB: Probably because we're humans.

Mom of RB: You think so? You think humans forget the unpleasant parts?

RB: Yeah.

Mom of RB: I think sometimes that's true.

RB: It's helpful, until your mom reminds you about it after you finally forgot!

In dyads such as this, it seemed protective to focus beyond COVID-19 and think of the future.

Sometimes, one member of the dyad minimized the effects of COVID. In these dyads, the child, more frequently than the parent, minimized the impact of COVID-19. One mother reported experiencing long-term effects of having contracted COVID-19, but as seen in the exchange below, her daughter reported that she did not experience her mother's illness and lingering symptoms as stressful.

> Mom of AB: And then I had a lot of issues, health issues, leftover from having COVID.... How has that affected you with Mommy having some of the problems that I've had?
>
> AB: No, it hasn't really affected me.
>
> Mom of AB: Like, the falling asleep and the things, like that hasn't affected you? Except that it's taken some time away from you, I felt ... like I'd fall asleep when I got home because I was so tired, and I couldn't stay awake ... when I would have time with you, but yet I didn't have time with you because I fell asleep.
>
> AB: Yeah, that was a problem, but nothing really affected me.

As seen in this exchange, some downplayed the effects of COVID-19, and this was more common among child participants.

Parents, sometimes, indicated disagreement with a child's interpretation that minimized the stress of COVID-19, as seen in the following interaction between a father and son:

> Father of CM: Okay. You didn't have an opportunity to do that [play with friends] on a daily basis like you do when you go to school every day, when you were in remote work. So your inability to see people and interact and have friends I think was difficult.
>
> CM: No, I was cool with it
>
> Father of CM... it was different and not normal and you...
>
> CM: I didn't understand it.
>
> Father of CM: Sure. But I think the fact that you weren't able to do that [play with friends]... I think that is tough for a kid.

CM: No

Father of CM: Even though it may not, you may not think so, but that's what I was thinking.

CM: It wasn't tough.

Although some children might have minimized the effects of the pandemic, parents frequently attempted to discuss the stress they thought their children had experienced.

Discussion

This study focussed on early adolescence, which is a time when children crave peer contact (Andrews et al.). Throughout the interviews, it was clear that many children desperately missed face-to-face peer interactions, including parties/celebrations, sports, extracurricular activities, and school events. At this age, children might have been uncertain as to how to connect in meaningful ways with their peers during social distancing. Some of the youth interviewed were creative in using technology to connect with peers in safe ways, but they missed face-to-face interactions and physical forms of contact. The children interviewed did not mention increased experiences of cyberbullying, as some experts feared (Imran et al.); rather, they were able to socialize with peers online.

Although the social costs of being isolated were quite evident in many dyads, some families discussed the fear of spreading the illness to loved ones, such as grandparents. The perceived need to connect with peers was at odds with the desire to keep the family safe during the early stages of the pandemic, which resulted in significant stress for children and their parents. Social support can serve a protective role and help to foster resilience in times of adversity (Hussong, Benner et al.). However, with social distancing, both children and their parents were unable to associate with others, as was routinely done prior to the pandemic. As COVID-19 cases went down in number, it was challenging for some to adjust to the return of face-to-face interactions, as they had grown accustomed to interacting online and in socially distanced ways.

Families discussed a range of stressors, but lack of social interaction and masking requirements were repeated topics brought up by many children. It is possible that these were the most visible and obvious changes for youth. Although masking has been a politicized issue (Lyons and Fowler), youth in these interviews did not focus on the politics of wearing masks but rather the discomfort.

Throughout these interviews, many dyads had open and honest discussions of how the pandemic had affected their development and mental health. Researchers have suggested that the pandemic will adversely affect adolescents' social development (Hussong, Benner et al.), and this fear was also discussed by one astute child participant, who speculated that the pandemic affected his and his peers' social maturity. Consistent with quantitative studies (e.g., Westrupp et al.), some of the interviewed parents indicated that the pandemic had been associated with negative mental health outcomes. Other parents and children noted forgetting about the pandemic or seemed to minimize its effects. The families interviewed seemed to employ different styles of coping with the pandemic, as was identified in larger, quantitative studies (e.g., Fluharty and Fancourt).

These parent-child discussions about pressing challenges related to COVID-19 were of particular importance. When the recording was stopped, some dyads thanked us for the opportunity and expressed appreciation because they had not talked about the problems caused by the pandemic in a significant way prior to the interview. Janette Herbers and colleagues noted that there is "surprisingly limited research on the processes through which parents support and protect their children's development, particularly during acute periods of adversity" (420). Although the pandemic was an extremely stressful period, having open communication about challenges appeared protective, suggesting the critical importance of parent-child discussion in times of adversity.

Acknowledgments

This research was supported by a grant from the Research Enhancement Program at Texas Woman's University. We also wish to acknowledge the parents and children who contributed to this research.

Works Cited

Agostinelli, Francesco, et al. "When the Great Equalizer Shuts Down: Schools, Peers, and Parents in Pandemic Times." *Journal of Public Economics*, vol. 206, 2022, pp. 1-10.

Andrews, Jack L., et al. "Peer Influence in Adolescence: Public-Health Implications for COVID-19." *Trends in Cognitive Sciences*, vol. 24, no. 8, 2020, pp. 585-87.

Barroso, Amanda, and Juliana Menasce Horowitz. "The Pandemic has Highlighted Many Challenges for Mothers, But They Aren't Necessarily New." *Pew Research Center*, 17 March 2021, https://www.pewresearch.org/fact-tank/2021/03/17/the-pandemic-has-highlighted-many-challenges-for-mothers-but-they-arent-necessarily-new/. Accessed 23 Feb. 2023.

Braun, Virginia, and Victoria Clarke. "Using Thematic Analysis in Psychology." *Qualitative Research in Psychology*, vol. 3, no. 2, 2006, pp. 77-101.

Bukowski, William, et al. "Peer Relations as a Developmental Context". *Social Development: Relationships in Infancy, Child, and Adolescence*, edited by Marion Underwood and Lisa Rosen, Guilford Press, 2011, pp. 153-79.

Charalampous, Maria, et al. "'It Needs to Be the Right Blend': a Qualitative Exploration of Remote e-Workers' Experience and Well-Being at Work." *Employee Relations*, vol. 44, no. 2, 2022, pp. 335-55.

Cummins, Molly Wiant, and Grace Ellen Brannon. "The Balancing Act Is Magnified: U.S. Mothers' Struggles amidst a Pandemic." *Mothers, Mothering, and COVID-19: Dispatches from the Pandemic*, edited by Andrea O'Reilly and Fiona Joy Green, Demeter Press, 2021, pp. 211–220.

Dalton, Louise, et al. "Protecting the Psychological Health of Children through Effective Communication about COVID-19." *The Lancet*, vol. 4, no. 5, 2020, pp. 346-47.

De Araújo, Liubiana Arantes, et al. "The Potential Impact of the COVID-19 Pandemic on Child Growth and Development: A Systematic Review." *Jornal de pediatria*, vol. 97, no. 4, 2021, pp. 369-77.

Erreygers, Sara, et al. "Feel Good, Do Good Online? Spillover and Crossover Effects of Happiness on Adolescents' Online Prosocial Behavior." *Journal of Happiness Studies*, vol. 20, no. 4, 2018, pp. 1241-58.

Fluharty, Meg, and Daisy Fancourt. "How Have People Been Coping during the COVID-19 Pandemic? Patterns and Predictors of Coping Strategies amongst 26,016 UK Adults." *BMC Psychology*, vol. 9, no. 1, 2021, pp. 1-12.

Friedman, May, and Emily Satterthwaite. "Same Storm, Different Boats: Some Thoughts on Gender, Race, and Class in the Time of COVID-19." *Mothers, Mothering, and COVID-19: Dispatches from the Pandemic*, edited by Andrea O'Reilly and Fiona Joy Green, Demeter Press, 2021, pp. 53-64.

Goldschmidt, Karen. "The COVID-19 Pandemic: Technology use to Support the Wellbeing of Children." *Journal of Pediatric Nursing*, vol. 53, 2020, pp. 88-90.

Gur, Raquel, et al. "The Disproportionate Burden of the COVID-19 Pandemic Among Pregnant Black Women." *Psychiatry Research*, vol. 293, 2020, pp. 1-8.

Herbers, Janette E, et al. "Parenting and Coregulation: Adaptive Systems for Competence in Children Experiencing Homelessness." *American Journal of Orthopsychiatry*, vol. 84, no. 4, 2014, pp. 420-30.

Hussong, Andrea, April Benner et al. "Adolescence amid a Pandemic: Short-Term and Long-Term Implications." *Journal of Research on Adolescence*, vol. 31, no. 3, pp. 820-35.

Hussong, Andrea, et al. "COVID-19 Life Events Spill-Over on Family Functioning and Adolescent Adjustment." *The Journal of Early Adolescence*, vol. 42, no. 3, 2022, pp. 359-88.

Igielnik, Ruth. *A Rising Share of Parents in the U.S. Say It's Been Difficult to Handle Child Care During the Pandemic*. Pew Research Center, 26 Jan. 2021, www.pewresearch.org/fact-tank/2021/01/26/a-rising-share-of-working-parents-in-the-u-s-say-its-been-difficult-to-handle-child-care-during-the-pandemic/#:~:text=Overall%2C%20about%20half%20of%20employed,said%20this%20in%20March%202020. Accessed 23 Feb. 2023.

Imran, Nazish, et al. "Mental Health Considerations for Children and Adolescents in COVID-19 Pandemic." *Pakistan Journal of Medical Sciences*, vol. 36, no. S4, 2020, pp. S67-72.

Kapoor, Vartika, et al. "Perceived Stress and Psychological Well-Being of Working Mothers during COVID-19: a Mediated Moderated Roles of Teleworking and Resilience." *Employee Relations*, vol. 43, no. 6, 2021, pp. 1290-1309.

Lyons, Jeffrey, and Luke Fowler. "Is It Still a Mandate If We Don't Enforce It? The Politics of COVID-Related Mask Mandates in Conservative States." *State & Local Government Review*, vol. 53, no. 2, 2021, pp. 106-121.

Mehta, Punam. "Are We Not the Heroes?: Racialized Single Mothers during the COVID-19 Lockdown." *Mothers, Mothering, and COVID-19: Dispatches from the Pandemic*, edited by Andrea O'Reilly and Fiona Joy Green, Demeter Press, 2021, pp. 459-66.

O'Reilly, Andrea, and Fiona Joy Green, editors. *Mothers, Mothering, and COVID-19: Dispatches from the Pandemic*. Demeter Press, 2021.

Ramchandani, Paul. "Children and COVID-19." *New Scientist*, vol. 246, 2020, p. 21.

Rožman, Maja, and Polona Tominc. "The Physical, Emotional and Behavioral Symptoms of Health Problems among Employees before and during the COVID-19 Epidemic." *Employee Relations*, vol. 44, no. 7, 2021, pp. 19-45.

Russell, Beth, et al. "Initial Challenges of Caregiving During COVID-19: Caregiver Burden, Mental Health, and the Parent-Child Relationship". *Child Psychiatry & Human Development*, vol. 51, 2020, pp. 671-682.

Skinner, Ann T., et al. "Parent–Adolescent Relationship Quality as a Moderator of Links between COVID-19 Disruption and Reported Changes in Mothers' and Young Adults' Adjustment in Five Countries." *Developmental Psychology*, vol. 57, no. 10, 2021, pp. 1648-66.

Staneva, Aleksandra. "Mothering during a Pandemic and the Internalization of Blame and Responsibility." *Mothers, Mothering, and COVID-19: Dispatches from the Pandemic*, edited by Andrea O'Reilly and Fiona Joy Green, Demeter Press, 2021, pp. 411-22.

Sun, Jing, et al. "Child Behavior Problems during COVID-19: Associations with Parent Distress and Child Social-Emotional Skills." *Journal of Applied Developmental Psychology*, vol. 78, 2022, pp. 1-9.

Underwood, Marion K., et al. "The BlackBerry Project: The Hidden World of Adolescents' Text Messaging and Relations with Internalizing Symptoms." *Journal of Research on Adolescence*, vol. 25, no. 1,

2015, pp. 101-17.

Vogel, Mandy, et al. "Well-being and COVID-19-Related Worries of German Children and Adolescents: A Longitudinal Study from Pre-COVID to the End of Lockdown in Spring 2020." *JCPP Advances,* vol. 1, 2021, pp. 1-9.

Westrupp, E. M., et al. "Child, Parent, and Family Mental Health and Functioning in Australia during COVID-19: Comparison to Pre-Pandemic Data." *European Child & Adolescent Psychiatry*, vol. 22, 2021, pp. 1-14.

Yoshikawa, Hirokazu, et al. "Effects of the Global Coronavirus Disease-2019 Pandemic on Early Childhood Development: Short- and Long-Term Risks and Mitigating Program and Policy Actions." *The Journal of Pediatrics*, vol. 223, 2020, pp. 188-93.

Chapter 9.

Between the Screens: Pandemic Life and Therapy with Children and Adolescents

Kiley Gottschalk, Tracey L. Hurd, Angela R. Jones, and Laura Matlack

It is the first session during the pandemic and nine-year-old Mary has just found out that school will not be meeting in person. Mary has customized her Zoom backdrop to have two tigers. The session went, as follows:

Mary: See these two tigers?

Therapist: Yes. One is so black; it's like the eyes pop out, and that other one looks like almost fire on the coat.

Mary: I made them! One is the good one, and the other is more fiery.

Therapist: Hmmm. Both sound so powerful.

Mary: They are, like good and bad, like one on each shoulder.

Therapist: But I can't really tell, which is the good and the bad.

Mary: Right, because there's always some mixture of good and bad. I mean nothing is going to be 100 per cent good—that's not how it is.

Therapist: Some mixture. And then looking at the tigers, I almost feel that mixture... like I don't know which one feels safe.

Mary: That's because you can't tell. Because they're mixed up.

Therapist: It's all so hard to tell.

Were the kids alright during the pandemic? In this chapter, we will explore the way the pandemic shaped the experiences of children and youth. As psychologists, we write from the vantage points of parent and clinician, considering the lived tensions, possibilities, losses, and joys of children's lives during pandemic constraints. The child in the opening vignette from a telehealth clinical session gives a glimpse of the conflicted experiences that children and youth expressed during the pandemic. Their interior emotional experiences were made known directly through metaphor, talk, actions, and play. Children and teens told us about their feelings. What might be good or bad, scary or safe, was not always clear. Children's pandemic lives paralleled family, cultural, and community dynamics. Children felt, at once, centrally present and invisible in their family lives. Zoom forums for school and therapy created new tensions between autonomy and belongingness.

Donald Winnicott said, "It's a joy to be hidden and a disaster not to be found" ("Communicating" 186). For most families, pandemic crisis conditions created more time together. The lack of privacy was often felt by all family members, but its significance for children and youth was often overlooked.

Small, regular acts of independence, such as being a member of a school classroom, help children develop a sense of who they are outside their families. In these acts, children learn about themselves and realize that they will be the only ones that know everything about themselves. This realization is radical. They experience a sense of not being fully known by others, which nurtures their growing sense of internal experience and of who they are in the world. Many incidentals of life, at school or with peers, traditionally go unseen by parents and families. Children experience the joys of being hidden—to feel safely not fully known to their parents—through such experiences, but pandemic conditions made the joys of being hidden in these meaningful ways more difficult.

Although children and youth struggled with the lack of opportunity to be hidden, they often, paradoxically, struggled with the pain of not being found. Parallelism was part of many families' pandemic life. Both directly and indirectly, children experienced being hidden in plain sight.

Thomas Ogden notes the following:

> The need to be recognized, but not exposed is universal, but perhaps most painfully evident in latency age children and adolescents, when in health, it is a joy to hide from one's parents (while personal identity is being formed, and along with it, a readiness to be recognized) and at the same time they have an intense need to be looked for, to be sought out, not to be neglected, not to be allowed to disappear. (43)

One high school-aged patient described being "right there but not seen" at home: "The first thing I would do, if the pandemic ended, would be to just tell all the extroverts in my family—which is everyone—to just leave me in the house alone." "That would be honest," he added.

Tensions of being hidden and unseen became part of therapy with children and youth since the beginning of the pandemic. With their therapists, they could be both intimate and rejecting. Some demanded to be made the host (the technical controller) of Zoom therapy sessions. Others muted the microphone of their therapists, enforced rules never spoken, or simply refused to speak, talking only through Zoom's typing-only chat feature. Some engaged in direct talk therapy instead of playing, choosing to be face to face with urgency. Others played deeply, creating fantasy worlds that seemed to exist just beyond the Zoom frame, which awakened in the therapist the uneasy feeling that she could not see or grasp the whole picture. In all of it, the pain of not being seen enough, or perhaps in the right way by others, was evident. Children and youth struggled deeply with the presence of absence in their lives. The essential human struggle to be known but not exposed was frequently highlighted. Due to less interaction with peers and less autonomy, children's and youth's needs for this attuned level of being known often went unmet. At its best, treatment with children provided a critical, nonfamily place for these needs.

In this chapter, reflections on family life and clinical work with young, school-aged patients will illustrate how children struggled to get their needs met and make sense of their place in pandemic life. We offer four voices. Our identities, as white cisgender women working with largely privileged, white, middle-class children, shape our work. Laura Matlack writes from her perspective as a psychologist-parent about her own family during the pandemic. Kiley Gottschalk, Tracey Hurd, and

Angela Jones write as psychologist-clinicians about their clinical work with children and youth. Though written from four perspectives, each echoes the pandemic struggles of being hidden and found for children and youth. Shared emotional connection to each other and to pandemic experiences emerged though our collaborative writing.

Robert Stolorow uses the term "emotional dwelling" to describe a process that involves more than empathic engagement, but attunement to and companionship with the other's emotional pain. Emotional dwelling provides "participatory comportment that is especially important in the therapeutic approach to emotional trauma" (Stolorow 81). The experience of being joined in bearing what seems unbearable can be deeply healing. The pandemic created the context of shared trauma for us all. We offer these four segments as both testimony to and part of our collective emotional dwelling.

A Parent's Perspective

Parenting during the Pandemic (Laura Matlack)

The saying goes, "It takes a village to raise a child." During the pandemic, for many parents and children, that village suddenly and astonishingly vanished. This rupture of the normal fabric of community was intensified by persistent uncertainty about how long and, to what degree, the separation from our various forms of support and connection would last. As a therapist and a parent, I wondered what this tear in the fabric, and ongoing lack of clarity, would mean for the relationships in my life.

Sometimes in the initial days of the pandemic, I found myself thinking about early settlers on the frontier and what it must have been like to go for long stretches working and parenting in isolation, seeing no other humans besides one's own immediate family. Maybe, this was a way of comforting myself that things could be worse. At least, we had the newly vital sharing of comradeship with neighbours and connections with loved ones via Zoom. Watching the recently formed evening rituals of banging pots and pans, I was moved by the ingenious, inexorable expression of gratitude, ongoing existence, and the wish to band together in one of the few ways possible to feel the unity of the tribe.

At the outset of the pandemic, the abrupt loss of many, or all, forms of nonparental childcare quite literally took my breath away. For our six-year-old son, the normal developmental trajectory of ventures into the world was balanced with the safe haven of home, collapsed into a cocoon, where our son was constantly with or looked after by one of his parents. For us as parents, there was an impossible equation with the shortage of time; the math simply did not add up. The crisis itself, and this unworkable time arrangement, demanded that we come up with a new set of priorities and regimen, but doing so was made all the harder by not knowing for what duration we were constructing a plan. This led to multiple stages where the coping model no longer worked, was set aside, sometimes thrown away, and something new had to be invented.

It is interesting to think about how I, as a parent, and my son, as a child, thought and felt about safety and danger during the various phases of the pandemic. Although the playgrounds were closed, and we saw men walking in hazmat suits near our home, the danger itself was unseeable. After a hike, north of Boston, on one of the first weekends of the pandemic, I wrote in an email to friends: "When we were on top of a hill at the Fells today and looking down on I93 and Boston in the distance, one of the strangest things I realized is that, mostly, everything looks completely normal and the same. There was the same load of traffic that I might have expected on a Sunday afternoon, and in fact, the park was oversubscribed." It was so confusing to have the world utterly transformed yet visually unchanged—and not to be able to pinpoint the danger.

Additionally, although the primary danger was disease, there was an ongoing compulsion to try and predict as well as to prioritize the secondary dangers for us and our son. What will we look back on and wish we had done? What enables our son to feel safe and calm in this transformed environment? How do we nurture the space to play and explore amid all this? How much structure, freedom, and indulgence is good? How much rigidity and requirement do we put in the daily schedule? What does supporting his social and emotional needs mean in this situation? How do my husband and I figure out what sacrifices are all right to make and what is sacred, especially around taking care of ourselves? How do we keep alive a sense of joy, gratitude, awe, optimism, and connection to the larger natural and human world?

My son did not express fear. He seemed to use the knowledge that children rarely were getting dangerously sick as a shield to, at least consciously, ward off danger and worry. Thus, it was notable when he became preoccupied about the danger of nuclear power plants after he read a story about the Fukushima Daiichi nuclear disaster. Although the narrative included florid descriptions of the tsunami, and we were living within sight of the ocean, it was the nuclear meltdown that was the focus of his distress. The location of nuclear power plants was the core of his worried inquiries, and I wondered if there was a certain appeal of a danger, that could be corralled and quarantined, if you will, even as it was connected to the deep unseeable danger of the earth's crust shifting and generating dangerous undulations on the sea's surface.

As the quarantine we all are experiencing has lessened, for many individuals and families, there is the opposite process—the rejoining of the village. After the disruption, the construction of new normals, the silver linings, the loss and grieving, and the bending of time, the re-entry into the larger world comes with many reactions and facets. As a now third grader, my son has demonstrated much vigour as, in his case, he navigates returning to the Boston area after a year absence. Just as he had to quickly adjust to much more time with us, he is now being asked to step into multiple forms of independence and autonomy. This is clearly enjoyable and gratifying to him. All the same, he has made it clear that he wants to reserve a weekend morning for "getting in my sleeper and reading books together in bed." I understand this as a wish to cocoon, once again, and a bridge between what was and what is becoming.

Three Clinician Perspectives

In March of 2020, as families were figuring out the previously unimaginable equations of childcare, education, and work, therapists were figuring out how to use online platforms, such as Zoom, to host secure psychotherapy sessions with patients. Many of us, who had previously felt certain that we would never make video sessions a regular part of our clinical work, found ourselves looking for a professional enough background in a private enough space for a schedule full of appointments. While some child patients felt that Zoom wasn't working for them and stopped their remote therapy, many children found ways to play and have done and are doing important emotional work in a difficult time. The following pages share clinical vignettes from three child treatments.

Clinical Vignette with Six-Year-Old "Jon"[1] (Angela Jones)

It is the summer of 2020. Six-year-old Jon's father signs onto our Zoom meeting. I began meeting with Jon in the spring of 2020, and Zoom is the only way we have done therapy together. I see more of some parents and less of others these days because it is so easy for children to sign on by themselves. Jon's father has some questions about how to talk to his children about their nanny having visa troubles. He apologizes for not telling me, ahead of time, that he wanted to talk and then thanks me for thinking through his questions with him. He says he will go and get Jon. I'm glad to have had a moment to check in. I wait for a long time, wondering if I hear a small sound or if I see the desk chair move slightly. Sometimes Jon begins our sessions by hiding from me, out of the range of the camera. In person, in the office, I know when the child is there and hiding. I know the child is in the room, and I can pretend to look in the wrong places for the right amount of time. I can always find the child. Now, on Zoom, children hide outside the frame and the microphone often doesn't pick up the noise, or Zoom filters it out. I think Jon is here now, but I am not sure. I begin the remote-session process of finding him as follows:

> Therapist: Is anyone there? [pause] Jon? I think I saw the chair move.

I wonder if I am speaking to an empty room. Jon is sometimes slow to arrive and may still be downstairs finishing his dinner.

> Therapist: Are you there? Is there a ghost?

Just as I decide there is no one there, the chair does move, just slightly, but enough that I am sure Jon is moving it.

> Therapist: Hello ghost, how nice to see you! Or not see you, I guess.

The chair moves again, then spins all the way around.

> Therapist: Oh, there is definitely a ghost here.

Jon jumps into the frame suddenly, laughing, then sits and spins in the chair, demanding that I read to him, delightfully in charge of our session.

I am working much harder than I would, in person, to find Jon but perhaps he has had just as much joy in hiding as he would have had in the office, and perhaps he has felt just as found. After several repetitions of this ghost theme with Jon and another child patient, I wonder about the ghosts. A ghost evokes for me the many COVID-19 losses, the deaths and illnesses and changes in children's lives. It also allows for being both seen and unseen, and it gives the children a way to be completely in control, more completely than they could have been in the office. Perhaps this play creates an opportunity to gain some mastery over the absences in their lives—the time away from school, the lack of playdates indoors, and the missed camps and family gatherings. The children choose for themselves when to be there and when to be hidden. Additionally, there is a negative space in a ghost that is the presence of an absence. There is an absence of my own physical presence for Jon, who has not ever met me in person, and the absence of his beloved nanny who had been there and was now far away.

Jon's father brings a great deal of creativity to making our Zoom sessions possible. He finds the right quiet, or when appropriate, not so quiet space for our meetings, adjusting the details if something isn't working well. He makes sure to have dinner or a snack ready and sometimes has games and toys available. He keeps an eye on the technology and helps us get reconnected if the meeting is interrupted. The need to set limits on behaviours at home is sometimes in conflict with the need to leave space in the therapy session, and he is a good collaborator with me to find this balance.

In the fall of 2021, Jon's father asks if he can bring Jon in person for a meeting outside. Everyone in the family is astonished by how tall I am, and although I knew Jon was small, he seems so much smaller in person than he looked in our Zoom sessions. Everything feels more real in person. Jon and I go on a walk in the woods near my office, and he explores the strange bridge there and then finds some geese. We talk about whether the geese are scary or not, and he runs after them, becoming the scarer himself. He runs fast enough and boldly enough that some of the last, lazy birds, who haven't fled to the pond yet take flight. He is delighted at this but then sorry there are no more geese to run after. Here is a new, more embodied way to find mastery over the potential dangers in life, and the insubstantial ghost is no longer needed.

In a recent session, in winter of 2021, we are back on Zoom to accommodate possible COVID-19 exposure. When Jon's father comes into the Zoom meeting, I can see Jon lying on the floor in a place where he would have been hidden previously, but now he is in full view. Jon's father says, "Oh, I moved the camera, sorry about that Jon." It is wonderful for me to see the curtain pulled back on this routine from our earlier sessions. Jon seems unfazed and pops up and into the chair for our meeting. COVID-19 accommodations have become ordinary for him; Jon's father has found a way for the nanny to return, and Jon and I have a well-developed routine that leaves space both for closeness and for distance.

I have great faith in the ability of children to find ways to play, unless there is something really in the way. Play allows children to make sense of what is happening in their world and to weather the inevitable storms. Jon's ghost play created a space for him to gain mastery and make meaning of the themes of absence in his pandemic life. I sometimes wonder if it was as useful to meet for therapy on Zoom as it would have been in person, but Jon and many other children were able to get enough of what they needed from remote therapy with good enough support from their parents in making this work. Winnicott describes "good enough mothering" as attuned adaptation by a parent to a child's needs that accounts for their capacity to tolerate frustration (Winnicott, "Transitional" 94). Many parents found this balance with their children during the COVID-19 crisis, attending to some needs and frustrating others, which allowed opportunities for healthy development in a difficult time.

Clinical Vignette with Eleven-Year-Old "Joan" (Tracey Hurd)

We connect via the telehealth platform. She says, "Nothing is really new today; I'm shopping for a new laptop," as if we had already said hello. We are on Zoom for our biweekly session. It is a routine that has been going on for almost two years. Joan was in my office on that last day, the day before the pandemic lockdown. She took a couple of weeks off but then came back on Zoom; she was nine years old at the start and is now eleven.

Joan asks me if I know anything about dreams. Again, I experience Joan's demeanour as feeling mid-sentence, although her question and topic are new. She trusts that I will follow her lead and remember her past, at once. Her face is still, and through the computer, it feels so close to mine. We can see each other's pores, although we are miles apart. A psychoanalyst friend likens meeting on Zoom to being as close as one would be if going to kiss. I wonder if we are too close. On Zoom, I can't exactly tell if she is looking at me; our relationship is technology mediated and not quite live. We rely on the pinprick camera to translate our images and then project them. Everything is once removed. We are constantly reminded that we are apart, yet we are so close. We return to the dream:

Therapist: I find dreams so interesting. I'm interested in yours.

Joan: They're crazy though. Like in this dream, it's all regular, but then there's the end.

Therapist: Regular and then something at the end?

Joan: It was confusing. The part where I eat my older sister was unexpected.

Therapist: How did that all work?

Joan: Like I just started to eat her—not gross, but that's what was happening.

Therapist: Did you want to eat her?

Joan: Not really. It was just what I did.

Therapist: What do you make of that?

Joan: Like an analysis? You mean, is it some wish to not have her here anymore, always bugging me? [laughs]

Therapist: Well, wanting to end annoying bugging does feel reasonable. Eating her up would end that for sure. Your family is together more now—less school, and hangouts with friends for sure...being around each other so much could definitely feel like bugging

There is a pause, but it is shorter than it would be in person. Space is harder to judge when we are not together—I tighten up time and move things along more than I do in person.

Therapist: Do you think that sounds right?

Joan: Not really

My conjecturing is off, and I said too much of it. I filled the conversation somehow thinking that was the same as connecting.

Therapist: Hmm, then what?

Joan: Not much happened in the dream.

Therapist: You were with your sister; it seemed kind of regular.

Joan: Like at home.

Therapist: At home... your room?

Joan: It was here, but I am not sure where. I keep thinking about how I started to eat her.

Therapist: Eating her... Dreams can have—

Joan: I just started eating her

[Pause]

Therapist: Eating her... of course that would stay with you... memorable.

Joan: Why would I do that?

Therapist: I wonder if the opposite of what I said before might be at work.

Joan: Like how?

Therapist: Maybe eating her was not about getting rid of her or getting rid of the bugging. Maybe you eat her up in the dream so that she is right there with you, really with you, eaten up, but in you? Really with you...

Joan: [kind of laughs] That's some crazy stuff... but maybe.

Therapist: People seem to get both too much of their families and not enough attention at the same time during this pandemic.

Joan: We're together all the time, so we don't notice each other.

I think about the pain of being hidden in plain sight. The yearnings of latency and early teens are so heightened by pandemic conditions, which take away small nuggets of independence. Less time with peers has been challenging for Joan. Independence, the recognition of her own mind, and her need to belong and matter outside of her family are healthy impulses that can feel so acute during this stage of life. Joan misses her peers more than she knows.

The session pivots. Joan shares a new screen, and we play chess online. I am too slow and deliberate. Joan decides that watching her play might be "useful" to me, and I agree. I surrender to this paradigm where Joan becomes all aspects of this game. She is both herself and her opponent. My presence has been consumed, and now I am on the sidelines, marvelling at her moves. Joan is at the centre of it all. She is not constrained by the unknown disappointments of an opponent that has failed her before. We exist together in this metaphor of an aspect of her internal pandemic life. We are not face to face but looking together at the screen. I feel such a connection with and from her. My mind drifts, and I notice anew how perfectly comfortable I am in the sweater I am wearing—the temperature feels just right in so many ways.

When Joan switched from talking about the dream to chess, I had thought she was moderating our closeness, perhaps even our too closeness. I realized, however, that she was adjusting our way of connecting so that we were more together. I was misled by her words, exploring the meaning of her dream, when she was really asking me to just join with her in the experience of pondering. She had invited me to join her in the emotional dwelling (Stolorow 81), the essential human experience of love and hate for her family. Joan needed to know that I was able to bear and feel the weight of her experience. The dream was the container she offered, but talking about it, didn't meet her needs. She needed to be intentionally together with me, found as she is, and known and not known at once. I marvel about how Joan shaped our time together so that her needs could be met. Our Zoom consulting room experience affirms that Joan's healthy pulse towards her own needs and growth has prevailed.

Clinical Vignette with Ten-Year-Old "Katie" (Kiley Gottschalk)

All our play in the months leading up to the pandemic had revolved around a single imaginary plot. A troop of orphaned monster figurines had been marooned on an island, represented by the area rug on the floor of my office. In the first few weeks, the monsters had worked together to survive the ever-present threat of Mother Nature in the form of imaginary windstorms and gigantic waves as well as monster-hungry creatures that inhabited the island woods. Over time, the island had grown lush with our handmade creature comforts for the monsters, including sleeping bags made of strips of cloth, small picnic lunches drawn and cut out of construction paper, and beach toys made from repurposed dollhouse accessories. Each session began with our carefully unboxing and thoughtfully placing each creation from a toy bin that stored the treasures safely between sessions. The island had become a place to relax and play. It seemed to hold limitless possibilities.

In March, as COVID-19 began to spread through our Boston suburbs, Katie and I abruptly began meeting virtually on Zoom for our appointments to comply with the public health guidelines of a pandemic that would keep us physically distant for the foreseeable future.

Katie and I have been meeting virtually for nearly two years. The toy bin of monster island supplies sits on the same shelf it always has, but it has not been opened in months. Our weekly session should have started several minutes ago. I begin to type out an email to her mother, wondering if she might have forgotten about our appointment when a second frame enters the Zoom application.

I assume that Katie must have been running late, although as more time passes, I become less certain. Her video feed remains technically connected but appears to be intentionally disabled by Katie. Save for occasional technical difficulties, Katie is in control of when her video is on or off, when and if I see her face. I sit quietly for a moment, wondering out loud about what might be happening when a third frame enters the application. An image of a sinister-looking, wide-eyed doll appears in the frame seated at a familiar desk that I know resides in Katie's bedroom. There is no verbal exchange between us, but with countless remote play therapy sessions now in our history together, I can understand the presence of the doll as Katie's attempt to engage me in something. I decide to type to Katie using the chat feature to get more information without breaking the early, emerging rules of play that Katie has set for us with her cameras and her silence. A typed conversation develops:

Therapist: Hello?

Doll: Hello.

Therapist: Who are you?

Doll: I am a haunted doll.

> Therapist: A haunted doll? Where is Katie? What are you doing in her bedroom?
>
> Doll: Wouldn't you like to know, hahaha [evil laugh]

This beginning exchange feels like confirmation that we are playing, but without Katie physically in my office or even showing her own face on Zoom, I am left without the clues I might have had access to in person about how she might want or need our play to develop. I decide to invite more information, but I am careful to protect the possibility in whatever dynamic may be taking shape.

> Therapist: Katie, are you there? Katie, if you can read this, try to type me something so that I know you're safe from the haunted doll!

Katie's chat remains silent for several minutes. Katie is not going to type back right away. She is not going to turn on her video feed. In our telehealth framework, she can be in the play but not in the play at the same moment. The suspense builds.

Without any visual cues, I am anxiously aware of my own uneasiness with this game and the powerful effect it is having on me. It has become a familiar feeling in the Zoom-era of child therapy. I have not yet seen Katie, my patient, on Zoom. I have only seen her doll. I do not yet know how Katie looks or feels this afternoon. I feel waves of disorientation and near paranoia. Who is this doll and where is Katie, actually? Am I foolish for trusting that she is safe? Is this really just play? Should I expect answers to these questions or simply trust that the power of play will prevail over the uneasiness it evokes with so much physical distance between us?

The pandemic poses an ever-present, evolving disruption to Katie's childhood, and I am aware of how hard the past two years have been for her. I work so hard to be present in the play through this challenging medium—to tolerate disruption and change with her while still inhabiting the role of her therapist. This vignette exemplifies the complexities of remote play therapy, where boundaries are blurrier and critical and where the nonverbal material that we once relied on can feel fleeting if not completely out of reach. Had this play taken place in person, Katie might have held the scary, haunted doll up to me and spoken for the doll in an altered tone of voice. Inhabiting the same physical space, Katie and

I would know, with certainty, that the voice of the doll still belongs to Katie. Katie and I would be aware that although the doll may look scary, she is still a toy. I would understand more about Katie's affect. We could delight together in the most rewarding and restorative parts of play, hopping back and forth between the real world and fantasy. Together, we could imagine a scary, imaginary world in which an evil doll threatens to take over, but when it becomes too real for either one of us, we could quickly and carefully, re-enter the realm of my office, marking the transition with a giggle or joke or stage whisper. In remote play, or in a chat box, it can feel hard to know if that transition is needed or where to find the bridge back to reality.

I often imagine that Katie is sharing through her play how it feels to navigate one's childhood in a pandemic. Themes of ambiguity about who is in charge, what is safe and secure, and how or if this will all end resonate through our hours spent online. Katie shows me the extraordinarily fine line between fun and fearful, free and rule bound. Just when we think we have found a way to make things safe and routine, the reliable and impactful unpredictability of the virus threatens to upend everything.

Conclusion

When the pandemic took hold, many families suddenly found themselves needing to vastly increase the scope of their childcare responsibilities and to create entire worlds for their children within the four walls of their home. Therapists, supporting these families, contended with the additional challenge of adapting to a new medium, marking an unprecedented adjustment to long-established practise. As children, and the systems that support them, scrambled to adapt to a new way of life, the once considered short-term pandemic stretched on for weeks, then months, then years. Many child-therapist dyads found ways to bridge the physical space between them and inhabit worlds that neither had before known could exist.

The pandemic posed and continues to pose complex challenges and threats to the safe and predictable conditions that psychotherapists once relied upon to provide child patients with containment and space to explore their internal worlds. The emotional traumas of life during the pandemic have created conditions for the emotional dwelling required to endure it. The long-term effects of this layered strain on systems and child development remain unknown, but as illustrated by the narratives discussed in this chapter, children, families, and their therapeutic supports possess remarkable adaptivity.

Endnotes

[1] All names are pseudonyms.

Works Cited

Benjamin, Jessica. "Beyond Doer and Done To: An Intersubjective View of Thirdness." *Psychoanalytic Quarterly*, vol. 73, no. 1, 2004, pp. 5-46.

Ogden, Thomas. *Coming to Life in the Consulting Room: Toward a New Analytic Sensibility*. Routledge, 2022.

Stolorow, Robert. "Undergoing the Situation: Emotional Dwelling is More Than Empathic Understanding." *International Journal of Psychoanalytic Self Psychology*, vol. 9, no. 1, 2014, pp. 80-83.

Winnicott, Donald. "Communicating and Not Communicating Leading to a Certain Study of Opposites." *Maturational Processes and the Facilitating Environment*, International Universities Press, 1965, pp. 179-92.

Winnicott, Donald. "Transitional Objects and Transitional Phenomena —A Study of the First Not-Me Possession." *The International Journal of Psychoanalysis*, vol. 34, 1953, pp. 89-97.

Part III.
How We Helped Children Cope

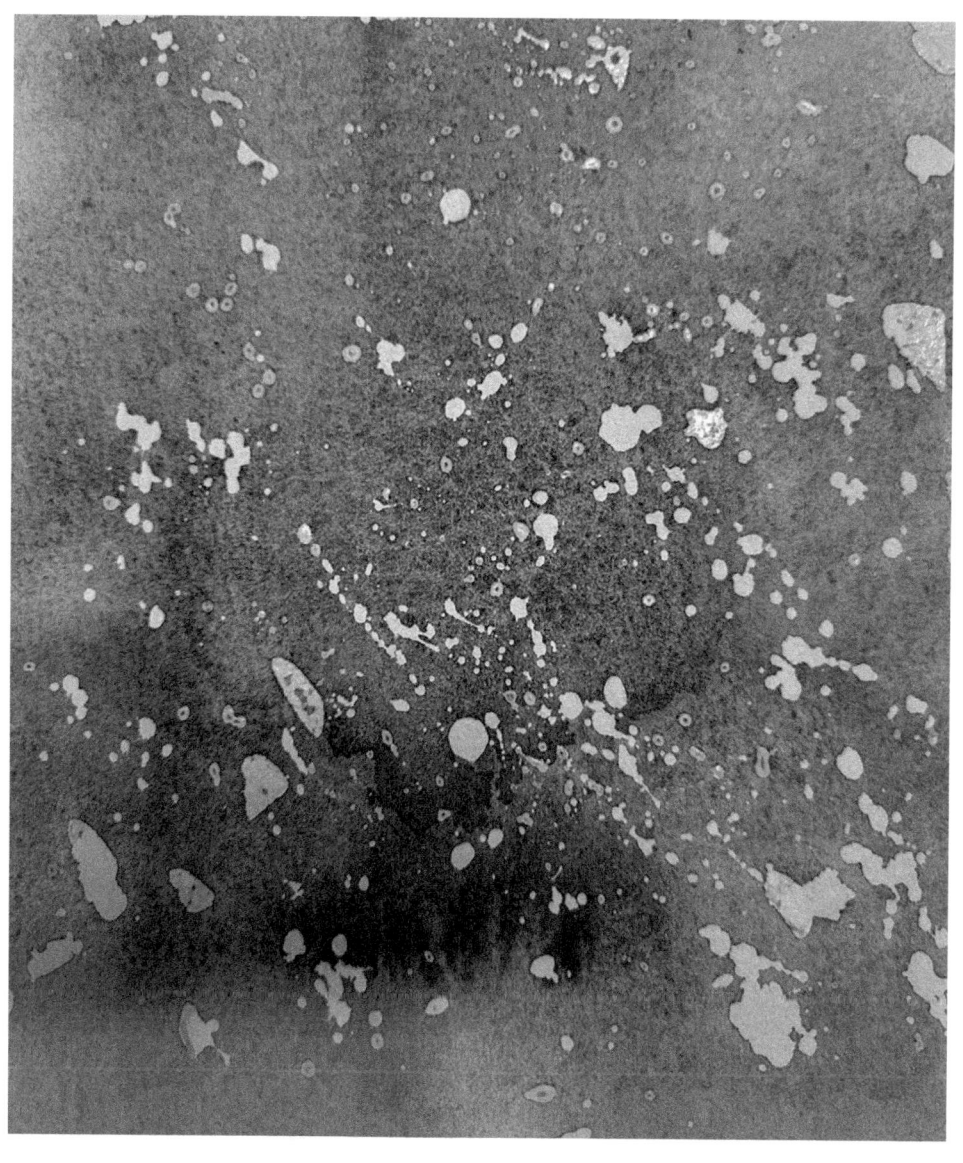

Chapter 10.

Gchi-Apptendaagoziwag akina Niizhigwag Idaanisag: The Lives of My Two Daughters Are Precious

Renée E. Mazinegiizhigoo-kwe Bédard

Among the Anishinaabeg,[1] we teach our children about the Nigaanaajimowin dibaajimowinan (prophecy teachings), which tell us that there will be moments in our history that will cause human beings to suffer hardships like we are now living through. The teachings guide us to rely on our cultural knowledge, ceremonies, and communities to survive. We are told to protect our children, retreat from others, and seek refuge with our families, medicines, and the land. Throughout the pandemic, my husband and I have told our children that those traditional Anishinaabeg practises will see our family through the crisis. We honour their feelings, opinions, and stories about their journey through the pandemic as children. Protecting the mental health of our children ensures that they continue to live well as Anishinaabeg people: Anishinaabe mino-bimaadiziwin. The goal is to make sure they learn how to navigate being a good human being by living through the COVID-19 pandemic as an Anishinaabeg.

In this chapter, I share those traditional teachings that I use to guard and guide my children's wellbeing and mental health through the COVID-19 pandemic. As an Anishinaabeg mother, I use the teachings of the Niizhwaaso-ishkoden Ningaanaajimowin (Seven Fires Prophecy) as the foundation of the information, methods, and knowledge required to navigate these tumultuous times as a parent. Within the prophecy are teachings called the niizhwaaswi-gichitwaa-miigiwewinan (Seven Sacred Gifts) or Seven Grandmother or Grandfather Teachings that I use to guide my children's ability to holistically cope with the challenges and traumas that arise from living through a pandemic. Not only do these teachings aid children in understanding their emotions, but they also give practical strategies for dealing with emotions in a culturally based model for balanced mental health, along with maintaining a healthy body and spirit. For parents, they provide key pedagogical instructions on how to guide, nurture, and foster our children's wellbeing. Furthermore, I explore how the Seven Grandmother's Teachings are used to ensure that my daughters continue to live through the pandemic using Anishinaabeg-centric ancestral traditional knowledge, learn to articulate their mental health needs, and follow the miikana (pathway) for living in a good way as Anishinaabeg children. Lastly, I offer some concluding thoughts.

Anishinaabeg Narratives as Parental Bundles

Anishinaabeg have sacred bundles that carry our ceremonial items and sacred objects, which represent our cultural traditions, knowledge, and customs. There are also those things that are unseen or nonphysical objects inside the bundle but are present, nonetheless. These things include stories associated with objects, personal narratives that an individual has about an object, and teachings that have been given by Elders, community, or family. An Anishinaabeg individual will carry these unseen bundles in our minds, hearts, and emotions. We share them with our family, our children, our community, and those in need.

Traditional Anishinaabeg narratives or stories are like sacred bundles filled with information we can take out to map out and navigate our miikana-bimaadizi (road of life), but they also contain the instructions of how to do it in the most ethical way. There are two types of narratives: the aakizookaanag (sacred narratives; stories; prophecies; legends) and the dibaajimowinan (personal narratives; stories; histories). Those good ways of living and moving through life embody the accumulated wisdom of generations upon generations of people who researched and practised how to live well as an Anishinaabeg. Passing down narratives from generation to generation enables each successive learner to garner lessons from the experiences and work of those who have come before. As Anishinaabeg writer Basil Johnston-*ban*[2] explains:

> Our ancestors had no books from which to draw knowledge.... Ages ago our ancestors learned that children and even grown ups were endowed with a measure of timidity and self doubt.... The purpose of stories is to instruct and entertain.... For our ancestors the lessons that they wanted to pass on to their descendants was meant to bring about growth of heart, spirit, mind and the senses to provide youth with the means to meet the challenges of life. (Johnston, *The Gift of the Stars* 6-11)

What I leave behind for my children are the many narratives shared with me by my family, Elders, and cultural teachers but also what I have experienced. Stories are the offerings parents leave behind for their children, grandchildren, and great-grandchildren. Anishinaabeg scholar Niigonwedom James Sinclair explains that Anishinaabeg narrative expressions are "bagijiganan," meaning offerings "embodying an intellectual praxis called minobimaadiziwin ("the good life") from the past to the present" (Sinclair ii). For me, Anishinaabeg narratives are the bundles I pick up from our ancestors, use today, and safeguard for my children and children's children. The interactions between parents and children through sharing narratives demonstrate and affirm relationality from generation to generation, continuing an inclusive sense of cultural identity and nationhood. In terms of using the offerings of wisdom and knowledge embedded in the narratives, contemporary Anishinaabeg parents can utilize them in all areas of life to guide each of our children's mino-miikana-bimaadizi (good path in life) and ensure that their mental, physical, and emotional health needs are met and that their spiritual wellbeing is maintained.

When COVID-19 came to Turtle Island (North America), I began to unpack my bundles to find the resources I required to teach my children to not only cope but also thrive in uncertain and sometimes traumatic circumstances, such as repeated vaccinations, the continuous fear of catching COVID-19, or their schools closing again for at-home online learning. I am reminded of the warning calls of the echo-maker, maang, the northern loon, to prepare.

When the Loon Calls

My memories of childhood are filled with the songs of the maangwag (loons) at sunset echoing across the channels of the French River on my traditional territory of Okikendawt or Dokis First Nation. I would sit on the rocks at sunset and into the early evening listening to their calls to one another. The call of the loon is haunting and soulful. They sing at sunset to connect with their mates or other loons in order to group up for safety. In Anishinaabeg traditions, the loon has the unique gift of being able to travel between our Earthly realm and the underworld of the Nibi-Manidoowag (Water Spirits) or Aadizokanaa-Giigoonyag (Sacred Fish Beings). These beings travel through matter, space, and time in a different manner than human beings. They see holistically, in what Anishinaabeg Elder Jim Dumont describes as, "a whole and comprehensive vision that entails not only vision before but also vision behind (a three-hundred-and-sixty-degree-vision). This [is] a circular vision ... the all-around-vision" (Dumont 31-32). The loon teaches us that our past is connected to our present and our future. Because it sees in an all-encompassing manner through time and space, its job is to warn the human beings. The loon is a metaphor or sign for escaping danger, offering warnings, foretelling challenges ahead, and reminding us to look back to the teachings of our ancestors for answers of how to handle the path ahead, but it also sings warnings to go home, find home, and seek refuge (Johnston, *Ojibway Heritage*, 54, 61-63; Johnston, *Honor Earth Mother*, 83-88; Bourdeau-Waboose 1-24).

Today, I find myself thinking about the calls of the loon in a context related to the COVID-19 pandemic and those prophecies we hold as Anishinaabeg regarding the Niizhwaaso-ishkoden Ningaanaajimowin (Seven Fires Prophecy) or simply Niizhwaaswi Ishkoden (The Seven Fires). When the COVID-19 virus spread across the world, resulting in a global pandemic, all human beings across the earth retreated to the safety of their homes. Homes became places of refuge where we could control and maintain both the health and wellbeing of our families, partners, and ourselves. For me as an Anishinaabeg woman, wife, and mother, I listened to the echo-maker's call to "go home" and "stay home" as reminders of our traditional Anishinaabeg prophecies, particularly the Seven Fires Prophecy. The calls to go home that echoed over and over on radio, television and the internet, reminded me of the echo-maker's calls. They were sounding around the world as a warning and a reminder to Anishinaabeg of our prophecies that foretold of hardships during the time of the Seventh Fire—a challenging time for us Anishinaabeg to live through but also a time to wake up and do better, be better, and live better as human beings.

The prophecy teaches us that during the time of the Seventh Fire, human beings will suffer great hardships that cause us to retreat, stay home, and guard our family's health and overall wellbeing: inendamowin, wiiyaw, jichaag, and ode' (mind, body, soul-spirit, and heart). We will have some difficult choices to make during these times. The prophecy is contained in the collection of stories concerning the Miigis, which are aadizokaanag (sacred stories), often called the "Great Anishinaabeg Migration" (Sinclair 175). The Anishinaabeg scholar Niigonwedom James Sinclair explains that the "story of Niizhwaaso-ishkoden Ningaanaajimowin begins sometime between 600-700 AD, when ancestors of Anishinaabeg resided on the shores of what is now the Atlantic Ocean, in a political and social alliance often called the Waabinaakii ('Day Break People') Confederacy" (176). Seven prophets, whom we refer to as grandmothers or grandfathers, came to the Anishinaabeg and foretold a time that has come to pass. Sinclair describes the arrival of the seventh prophecy as follows:

> The seventh prophet, who had glowing eyes, declared that Niizhwaaso Ishkode would be a time both of destruction and possibility. While many would perish during this time, the final stopping place would be found. By this time, the Earth would be poisoned. The vision of the Miigis would be almost gone, and all life would be in peril. Then, a people called the Oshki Anishinaabeg (the "New Anishinaabeg") would emerge, Anishinaabeg who would desire to know who they are, where they have come from, and what they have inherited. Many would try to heal the earth and re-learn stories, histories, and traditional ways, re-creating themselves through the Midéwiwin and other venues. The Light-skinned people, at this time, would be given another choice: to revisit the possibilities of the Fourth Fire and fully extend the hand of niikonisiwin, or not. If so, the Eighth Fire and a "powerful and united nation" would begin. If not, the light-skinned people, and those who they had convinced to join them, would destroy themselves and perhaps everyone else too.

> Elders and storytellers claim that this is the time of today....
> These Anishinaabeg ... face many choices. (180).

The prophecy teachings are rooted in the concept of choices and the importance of making decisions that are good for ourselves, our families, and community.

In the next section of this chapter, I share a matricentric retelling of the Seven Fires Prophecy story and the Grandmother's Teachings. I share this story so that readers can enter into the Anishinaabeg worldview and the maternal perspectives I use to navigate the dangerous times imposed by living during the pandemic. The prophecy teachings enable parents to keep our children's wellbeing prioritized and provide direct guidance on how to uphold their overall wellbeing. The story is shared from the perspectives of a Kwe (woman), doodoom (mother), and nindaanisag (my daughters), who will listen to these words and want to see themselves reflected. We are taught as Anishinaabeg to personalize and make the old stories applicable to our lives today. I refer to the teachings as the Seven Grandmother's Teachings because I write from a matricentric feminist perspective that prioritizes the inclusion of the feminine; however, others can and do refer to these teachings exclusively as the Grandfather's Teachings. However, in my opinion, these teachings are not gender exclusive and different communities refer to them as either Grandmother or Grandfather Teachings. In this way, I share the following story from a female gendered perspective that is also inclusive of all those who identify as female, male, or LGBTTIQQ2SA+. I have been taught to both tell or read a story as I would want to see myself presented but also to remember the original as I was told it, which prioritized the Grandfather and male perspective in order to preserve the legacy of the original storyteller.

The inspiration for this retelling lies in the versions of the story presented by Anishinaabeg Elder Edward Benton Banai-*ban*, Niigonwedom James Sinclair, and Anishinaabeg scholar Basil Johnston-*ban* (Benton-Banai, 89-93; Sinclair 175; Johnston, *Honour Earth Mother* 84-85). The Niizhwaaso-ishkoden Ningaanaajimowin is also embedded in narratives like the loon's role in the story of the Seven Prophets, in *Honour Earth Mother: Mino-Audjaudauh Mizzu-kummik Quae* by Johnston, in *Where Only the Elders Go* by Bourdeau-Waboose, and in *Nanabush and the Dancing Ducks* told by Daphne Odjig. This is a narrative that is repeated, over and over, in similar embodiments (Johnston, *Honour*

Earth Mother 84-85; Bourdeau-Waboose; Odjig). All these versions and variations, encoded with teachings to set human beings on, or back on if the case arise, the good path. They act as reminders of the gchi-inaa-konigewinan (Good Laws of Creation; Great Laws; Binding Laws; Sacred Laws), which are the intellectual praxis I use as a mother to guide my cultural role as the teacher to my children. With this said, I share with readers the story and teachings of the Seven Fires Prophecy, with its Seven Gifts from the Grandmother Prophets, which I save for my children and grandchildren.

Niizhwaaswi-Gichitwaa-Miigiwewinan (Seven Sacred Gifts)

Long, long ago, when Anishinaabeg peoples were new to the world, they struggled to survive and learn how to live well on the land in relation to the Gchi-inaakonigewinan (Great Laws). The animals, fish, insects, and plant nations of Aki (the Earth) did as much as they could, but the human beings continued to become weaker and began dying in large numbers to starvation and disease.

Gizhew-Manidoo (Creator; Great Mystery; Great Spirit) sent seven manidoowag (spirit beings) called the niizhwaaswi-nookomisag (Seven Grandmothers) with their niizhwaaswi-gichitwaa-miigiwewinan (seven sacred gifts) to visit with the human beings and instruct them how to live in a balanced way. These beings were sent out from the Spirit world as guardians, teachers, and guides. These guardian spirits sent an Oshkaabewis (helper), ahead of them, to find a baby to instruct in the ways of living a good life as a human being.

Oshkaabewis looked and looked but could not find a baby who would be best to teach and carry knowledge back to the Anishinaabeg. Oshkaabewis grew very sad and worried they[3] would never find a person worthy enough to bring back to the niizhwaaswi-nookomisag. On the helper's final search, they found the baby named Abinoojiinh (child). Oshkaabewis heard Abinoojiinh's parents describe the child as smart, quick to learn, and adventurous. All babies are fresh from being in the Spirit World and come directly from the side of Gizhew-Manidoo, so Oshkaabewiskwe knew that Abinoojiinh was the one they were meant to bring back to the Seven Grandmothers.

Oshkaabewis sought out the parents of Abinoojiinh and told them of their mission. They gave the parents a beautiful hide pouch of semaa (sacred tobacco) as a formal gift before requesting permission to take their child to the Spirit World to meet the niizhwaaswi-nookomisag and receive their niizhwaaswi-gichitwaa-miigiwewinan for the wellbeing of all Anishinaabeg. Oshkaabewis explained that the child would be given gifts to bring back the Anishinaabeg so that they might survive and thrive. The parents did not want to let their child go but agreed knowing this was a great blessing for their child and people.

Oshkaabewis travelled to the wiigiwaam (lodge) of the Seven Grandmothers. It was a long trip to the Sky World, past the stars, moon, and planets. Upon arrival, the grandmothers flocked around cooing and pinching the cheeks of the sweet baby. They hugged, fed, and sang to Abinoojiinh until the baby fell asleep. Oshkaabewis was instructed to put the child to bed and in the morning, they would begin the lessons.

The next morning, at dawn, the Oshkaabewis was instructed to show Abinoojiinh all the four quadrants of the Star World. By the time they returned, Abinoojiinh was seven years old. Abinoojiinh was brought to the Seven Grandmothers' lodge for further study. The grandmothers welcomed Abinoojiinh to the lodge and sat the child down with these Seven Grandmothers. One of the grandmothers took out a bundle blanket and inside lay a miskwaabik-akik (copper vessel). Their Oshkaabewis came forward and laid out the blanket in front of Abinoojiinh and poured some water into the miskwaabik-akik. The bundle blanket was decorated in four colours, which the grandmothers said represented each of the four quadrants of Creation. First, there was waabanong (eastern direction), the colour being ozaawaa. Second was zhaawanong (southern direction), which is represented by the colour miskwaa (red). Third was ningaabii'anong (western direction), and it was embodied by makadewaa (black). Lastly, there was giiwedinong (northern direction), which is represented by the colour waabishkaa (white). The grandmothers asked Abinoojiinh to look inside the miskwaabik-akik and tell them what she saw. Abinoojiinh stared into the miskwaabik-akik and saw the universe unfold before her, her life, and the future for her people. When she was done, the grandmothers each took a turn holding the miskwaabik-akik and sharing with Abinoojiinh a lesson.

The first lesson began with the eastern direction and the teachings of that time of year, which was springtime. Each of the grandmothers shared warnings and knowledge of the challenges the Anishinaabeg would come to endure over the coming generations. They called them the Seven Fires and, each fire, contained knowledge of how the people should live. The first, second and third grandmothers gave Abinoojiinh many spiritual teachings and spoke of the great migration of their people from the east coast of Turtle Island (North America) to the Nayanno-nibiimaang Gichigamiin (the Great Lakes; Fresh Water Seas).

Next, the fourth and fifth grandmothers warned of the coming of Europeans, struggles, and the false promises that would be made to the Anishinaabeg. The sixth grandmother told of the time of boarding schools and residential schools where the children would be stolen away. Much would be lost, forgotten, and hidden away during this time. The seventh grandmother shared that the Anishinaabeg would do the work of regaining their cultural ways. This grandmother spoke of two roads. If they stayed to the mino-miikana (good road) and continued learning their cultural ways they would ultimately light the sacred eighth fire, the final fire, an eternal fire of peace, love, brotherhood, and sisterhood. The second road was the path of ruin initiated by the coming of Europeans and their descendants. If Anishinaabeg continued to walk that second road with the settler-colonial peoples, they would all see ruin, suffering, and death of all Earth's people. She also said that it was the time of the oshkibimaadiziig (the New People), who will retrace their steps to find their way back to what is left of the mino-miikana. They will seek out the Elders, the medicines, the knowledge, and they will speak out for the land. Their path will not be easy but is necessary.

Each grandmother gave Seven Gifts to Abinoojiinh to take back with her to help the Anishinaabeg return to the good road. The first grandmother gifted Abinoojiinh the lesson of dabasendiziwin (humility). The second grandmother taught a lesson of the summertime and the southern direction relating to Gwayakwaadiziwin (honesty). Next, the teachings travelled westward and to the teachings of the fall. The third grandmother provided Abinoojiinh the teachings on minaadendamowin (respect). The fourth grandmother's teachings began the final teachings: the lessons of the north and the wintertime. She shared knowledge about Zoongide'ewin (bravery or courage). The fifth grandmother gave Abinoojiinh the lesson concerning the responsibilities and duties of nibwaakaawin (wisdom). The sixth grandmother provided guidance on the lesson of debwewin (truth). Lastly, the seventh grandmother shared one of the most important teachings, which is zaagi'idiwin (love). The grandmothers explained and taught gikendaasowin (knowledge; intelligence) for each gift. When they were done, the Oshkaabewis emptied the vessel and wrapped it in the blanket as a bundle for Abinoojiinh to carry home. They instructed Abinoojiinh to take it home and share all the teachings they had given her. The grandmothers told her to transmit the knowledge in the right way, explained how to use it, when to use it, and how to preserve it for future generations.

At the end of their lessons, Abinoojiinh had matured into a woman, and they called her Kwe. They instructed the Oshkaabewis to return Kwe to her people. It took a long time to arrive and when Kwe did arrive, she was an old mindimooyenh (old woman). Oshkaabewis told her that she was not longer just a woman, but an Elder now, so her new name was going to be Mindimooyenh, so that she might teach the children the good way.

When they did find Mindimooyenh's village and people, they had travelled westward and were resettled on Lake Nipissing. She knew that her parents were no longer alive, but she was happy to see her relatives. With all of these relatives gathered around her, the mindimooyenh was led to sit down. There was a small kwezens (girl) standing behind her mother's skirts and she called her over to sit with her. Mindimooyenh told the kwezens that she was going to give her a great many gifts to share with their people. She opened the bundle, took out a copper pail, filled it with water, and began teaching the young kwezens all that she had learned from the Seven Grandmothers. Mindimooyenh shared the Seven Grandmothers' gifts to the Anishinaabeg and all their wisdom of the Gchi-inaakonigewinan (Great Laws). Next, she instructed her how to use it, when to use it, and how to take care of it for future generations. Mindimooyenh told the kwezens that this knowledge would help the people to follow the Anishinaabeg-mino-miikana-bimaadiziwin (good path of life teachings for human beings). Mindimooyenh spent many moons teaching the young girl. Through Mindimooyenh's wisdom, the girl taught the people how to live on the Earth as good human beings and walk through life in a peaceful, respectful, and loving way. They learned about the four directions and the delicate balance of life and living in harmony with all of creation.

A year into the young girl's apprenticeship, the girl became sick. Mindimooyenh prayed to the Seven Grandmothers on what to do. The community members cried, and on the lake, the zhiishiibag (ducks) trumpeted, and the maangwag (loons) wailed. A dream was sent to Mindimooyenh, teaching her how to make a water drum, the songs to sing, the medicines, and the teachings of healing that would be needed.

The grandmothers and Elders of the community built the water drum for that little girl. They sang the songs and beat the drum so that it echoed across the lake. Maang (loon), the echo-maker, sang back and with the Anishinaabeg people in their pain for their little girl. To this day, the loon still cries for the pains of the Anishinaabeg and the well-being of all children. When Anishinaabeg hear the echo-maker's call, we remember the Seven Prophets and their Seven Gifts brought for the children to lead us out of hard times and into the future.

Prophecy as Anishinaabeg Maternal Pedagogy

The story of Abinoojiinh, turned Kwe, and lastly, turned Mindimooyenh, is the story of survival and teachings that echo through time to remind Anishinaabeg families, especially parents, of how to raise our children well during times of challenge but also in the good times. The Seven Gifts are the tools of parenting through the pandemic in real ways and with real guidance of how to ensure the health of children: mentally, emotionally, physically, and spiritually. The story is pedagogy that we put into practise with each successive generation as tools to survive, thrive, and seek wellness in all aspects of life, but it has become especially useful during the pandemic.

The Anishinaabeg prophecy story of the Seven Gifts from the Grandmother Prophets provides a valuable ceremonial bundle filled with resources, including knowledge, teaching practices, and methods to maintain the wellbeing and overall health of our children. Our children are going through a lot of mental and emotional trauma, along with physical and spiritual trauma, as they live through the COVID-19 pandemic. I think of my youngest daughter who was so afraid of the COVID-19 vaccines that she hid under the bed and after getting the vaccine threw up in her mask due to the stress of the ordeal. I turn to the Seven Gifts of prophecy for the teachings embedded in them to guide me as I parent through the toughest time in my life and potentially my children's lives. My Anishinaabeg ancestral grandmothers also used this prophecy bundle to survive a host of traumatic events, such as displacement from territory due to signing the Robinson-Huron Treaty (1850), the Indian Act, loss of resources, loss of language and culture, diseases, the residential school systems, and so much more.

Prophecy is like a backpack full of information and methods of teaching and learning that parents can use to help our children thrive mentally, emotionally, physically, and spiritually. Inside the Seven Fire Prophecy, Anishinaabeg parents have been gifted the Seven Grandmother Teachings or Seven Grandmothers' Gifts. These teachings show us "the specific and interconnected ways circles of Anishinaabeg relationality operate," which are "formed through three concepts, enawendiwin (strands connecting all parts of creation together), waawiyeyaag (interwoven systems of circularity) and waawiyekamig (cosmic uterus; universe)":

> The teachings of enawendiwin tell us that everything in the universe is interconnected through the energies that hold the universe together. Women explain to their daughters the teaching of endawendiwin by sharing the stories and lessons of Nookomis-Asabikeshiinh (Grandmother Spider) and her grandchildren's spider webs that interweave so many strands of thread. We share with our daughters that there is a cosmic web that holds together the universe, like the tissues of our body. The body of the universe is a sacred home for human beings. This is why Anishinaabeg call it waawiyekamig or the cosmic uterus. Through all these interconnected teachings, Anishinaabeg come to understand that we share the universe with other life and things that fill that space. We are related to and connected to everything else in a cycle of life, living, death, and rebirth. Everything in our universe is born out of the essential chemical elements that make up our universe, everything is sustained by those elements. When we die, our physical bodies return to being those raw elements, and then, new life is reborn from our elements. Thus, we are interwoven into the cosmic systems of circularity through time, space and reality. (Sinclair ii)

From these teachings, from the Anishinaabeg concept of nindinawemaganidog (all of my relations), comes a law that we share with our children to show them that they were thought of seven generations back by their ancestors and grandmothers of long ago. Down through the generations it was passed, like a favourite handmade quilt.

As Elder Benton-Banai points out, Anishinaabeg parents are the first teachers of their children, and it is their role to instruct children in these teachings:

> Children are born with fully-developed senses and are aware of what is happening around them. They can even communicate with the Spirit World. Most of us, as human beings, are so far removed from the Spirit World that we cannot tell what an infant is saying. Let us learn from the Seven Grandfathers the importance of giving our young children the teachings they will need to guide them in their later lives. (61)

Anishinaabeg parents are taught before our children even arrive to not only begin to speak these teachings but to model them so that a child's world is positioned within prophecy as lived experience before they even take a breath. Anishinaabeg believe we are born into the teachings as gifts from our parents, Elders, and community. I began teaching my children from the moment they were lowered to my breast on how to act in a good way as a human being based on the Seven Grandmothers' teachings. Both my daughters learned how to act towards my body in relation to the needs of their bodies, how to communicate their needs, how to learn the ethics of relationality between their needs and my needs as a mother, nourisher, woman, and teacher. When our children learn in this way, we nurture their wellbeing of inendamowin, wiiyaw, jichaag and ode' (mind, body, soul-spirit, and heart). Upholding the balance of those four quadrants of wellbeing is the duty and responsibility of parents. Whole health, balance, and wellbeing is the foundation of the Seven Gifts of the Grandmother Prophets.

As a mother, I think about those roles and what I want to embody for my children on how to be a good human being during these challenging times. Again, I look to the prophecy story and find the teachings of the Seven Gifts, which are my inheritance and the inheritance of my in-daanisag (daughters). In relation to COVID-19 and the pandemic, I teach my children by not only modelling the behaviour of these Grandmother Teachings but also by guiding them to embody these teachings and to experience these teachings firsthand, so that they can relate specific instances within their lives where these teachings manifest.

Dabasendiziwin (humility) is the first Grandmother Teaching of the prophecy. During the COVID-19 restrictions, human beings learned that we all must humble ourselves regarding the greater needs of our communities and nations to survive. For instance, "look to Wolf—ma'iingan—for humility. Observe how ma'iingan does not live for himself but for the pack. Watch him bow his head in the presence of others. He does this out of deference, not fright. Ma'iingan understands what a small part of the whole he plays. his ultimate punishment is to be cast away from his community" (Bouchard and Martin 6). To make ourselves part of the pack, thinking regarding our actions in relation to the holistic needs of our human relations, is a personal sacrifice, but it has the reward of sustaining and protecting our loved ones—particularly, the grandmothers, grandfathers, and Elders, who are most vulnerable to the dangers to COVID-19. Yet my daughters mentally struggled to contextualize why they had to be separated from others. When my children ask why we stay at home during lockdown, why we stay away from loved ones, why we wear our masks, and why we get our vaccinations, I use the concept of the pack and nature as our community. The wolfpack acts in a specific way; it upholds the bagwaji-inaakonigewinan (natural laws) of the ecosystem as well as the wellbeing of the greater community. In coming to understand this, my children find their purpose, a path forward, and ways to mentally justify and culturally situate the new tasks they are being asked to perform.

The second teaching is gwayakwaadiziwin (honesty). My daughters are taught to be honest about their feelings and emotions regarding life under the restrictions and dangers of COVID-19. Both my husband and I always allow our children to express the complex wave of emotions regarding how they are trying to live through the pandemic. Emotional communication always allows them to release those feelings, energies, and articulate what feelings are valid, flawed, or can be problem solved. Bapakwanagemagoog (red pines) stand tall in the forests along the French River on the traditional territory of my daughters and myself. A bapakwanagemag stands out among the other trees because it has rough bark, long pointy needles, and is not as fluffy as other trees. It looks different, but it stands true to itself, and it has a purpose. Its roots and needles provide materials for baskets; its bark, branches, and trunk provide homes for both insects and birds, and, lastly, the pine sap provides medicine. The red pine reminds us it is okay to be ourselves and not hide our feelings from others. An honest person is one who stands tall like bapakwanagemag. In this way, my daughters can find the truth in how they, as individuals, choose to see the pandemic, how they think about it, and how they feel they want to make choices about it. All their thoughts, ideas and opinions are their personal truths.

Next, is the teaching of minaadendamowin (respect). Children are always learning and negotiating the dynamics of how to demonstrate respect, how to earn respect, or how to ask for respect from the people around them. As parents, we are also learning how to respect our children who are individuals on their own life paths and not to interfere with their miikana (path) but also guide them how to live ethically as an Anishinaabeg in relation to the cosmic order laid out in the gichi-inaakonigewinan (Great Laws). In Anishinaabemowin, this is defined as aanjigone, which Michi Saagiig Nishnaabeg scholar Leanne Betasamosake Simpson translates to the "ethics of non-interference," which she explores by introducing the teaching of Elder Gdigaa Migizi, Doug Williams of Curve Lake First Nation (Simpson 54). Elder Gdigaa Migizi explains the following:

> In exploring this "ethic of non-interference"...the Nishnaabe concept of Aanjigone ... is the idea that one needs to be very, very careful with making judgments and with the act of criticism. Aanjigone is a concept that promotes the framing of Nishnaabeg values and ethics in the positive. It means that if we criticize something, our spiritual being may take on the very things we are criticizing...Our responsibility is to live our lives according to the teachings and values that were given to us with great love by Gzhwe Mnidoo (qtd. in Simpson 54)

In this way, the ethic of non-interference does not mean we let children run wild. It means that we respect and foster their mental capacity to make choices. Simple things are helpful tools like allowing my daughters to pick face masks that make them feel confident or asking them to explain all the ways in which they are protecting themselves at school from COVID-19 and what new things they have learned that they can teach their parents about living through this time. Even if we know the information, we let them understand that their research, their knowledge gathering, and their experiences will inform how we all live as a family.

Aanjigone is fundamental to ensuring that my children know I respect their mental capacity to navigate choices while still ensuring that I am there to catch them, guide them, and support their life path decisions. Despite the changes to their young lives, the ethical codes we promote in our family household continue throughout the pandemic. The outside world may change and vary, but our teachings, their responsibilities, and our relationality to one another remain constant. Furthermore, their training in learning how to become good children, and later adults, continues on course.

The fourth prophecy gift is knowledge of zoongide'ewin (bravery or courage). Through the pandemic, I have been amazed at the courage, bravery, and resulting resilience exhibited by my daughters. We teach them that change is the only constant human beings face. Like a wave, ebbing and flowing, we must learn to face changes in our lives. Our ancestors survived a great deal. Their grandmother and great aunties went to a residential school and survived, so they come from brave women who were once little girls like themselves. Every choice they make builds confidence and assuredness. Bravery to live through new challenges comes easier if we know that we are supported, so having a strong familial foundation is essential. When geese travel, they travel together with family and community in the shape of a "v." Each member supports the other, and they take turns sharing the load of being at the front of the "v" shape so that others at the back have an easier path forward. As parents, we each share the burden of leadership, and our job is to ease the way for our children but not completely shield them from leadership decision making. Each member needs training and the feeling of control that rises from it. For instance, throughout the pandemic, when my daughters have been at home learning online, I have allowed them to determine when online learning was too much of a burden to guard their mental health. We would take breaks for a walk, do an art project, or just watch some television. They help each other out with schoolwork or navigating technology, so that it becomes less scary, but also helps each of them feel like they are leaders. Being able to make decisions, share the burden, aid others, and make choices for the family allow children to feel they are contributing to familial life rather than just being passive participants. Bravery comes when action and experiences are allowed to happen.

The fifth teaching represents nibwaakaawin (wisdom), the art of wisdom. According to Anishinaabeg Elder Shirley Ida Williams:

It means "the art of kindness in knowledge" ... Nbwaakawin means to put others before one's own self. In other words, you can think about yourself after you have thought about others, so that even though you might have knowledge or know about a particular concept, you cannot always show what you know. In a sense, Nbwaakawin keeps the ego in check (which is the third level of consciousness in Nishnaabeg thought). This concept refers to the highest form of wisdom and it cautions people to be careful with that wisdom and use it in an appropriate way. If one follows Nbwaakawin, one will know how to handle this kind of wisdom and also remain in a humble state. (qtd. in Simpson 126)

Nibwaakaawin also reminds us that it is through our relations in nature and all the wisdom they must share, we can learn valuable teachings to use to direct our life journey (Bouchard and Martin 12). The wolf does not live its life wishing it is a fish, and the bird does not wish it is the bear, so we can find wisdom here to not live our lives based on desires or wishes for how we could be rather than enjoying the unique gifts we were given. David Bouchard and Joseph Martin write:

Look to the beaver—Amik—for wisdom. Amik has formidable teeth. Do you know what will become of Amik if he does not use his gift? His teeth will grow until they are no longer of any use to him. They will hinder him. Amik uses his gift wisely to thrive and so must you. Now is the time to ponder over life, death and rebirth. And be grateful for the gift you have been given in this life. (12)

COVID-19 forced a lot of people to remain at home, to observe their lives, and to take in all that they were and did in their lives. During the first year of the pandemic, we literally saw our children day in and day out, and it became apparent to me that my eldest daughter loved to lead and problem solve, whereas my youngest daughter loved nature, animals, and learning about her culture. The prophecy teaches us to nurture our children's interests and gifts so that they can find emotional and mental fulfillment in knowing they are performing what comes natural to them.

The sixth teaching is about debwewin (truth). For teachings of truth, we look to the constancy of Aki, the Earth. Everything comes from the

Earth, and everything returns to it. The seasons come year after year. Truth lies in constancy, reliability, and steadfastness. Our children rely on us to be the models of good human beings and citizens. Fundamentally, "truth is to know all these teachings. Debwewining onji-gikendan gagiikwewinan" (Bouchard and Martin 12). Parents must live the truth we want our children to reflect upon the world. Debwewin, the art of truth, is rooted in the teachings of the heart. Elder Gdigaa Migizi teaches that debwewin is embodied in "the sound of the heart [and] speaking from the heart" (qtd. in Simpson 125). He stresses that "his understanding of Debwewin was not physical but involved the idea that "being a good person was being a person whose word you could trust" (qtd. in Simpson 125). Every child should feel that they can follow and trust their heart and that their parents cherish their emotions. I want my daughters to trust their heart. So when I place my hand over their hearts and tell them they have good hearts and to use their heart, they are receiving the healing medicine from the teaching of debwewin.

The last gift holds the teaching of zaagi'idiwin (love). On the French River, there are many tourists with big boats that fly around without regard for much other than their own fun times. The mother maangwag (loons) carrying their babies on their backs across the deep waters of the river are vulnerable to those boats running them over. I always hold my breath when I watch a mother loon lift her body high, stretch her wings, and drop her babies into the water so that they dive to safety. She makes herself big and echoes a call of warning so that the boat will both see and hear her and hopefully drive around. Her love for her babies is so big and brave. I learned to be a parent by watching the devotion of the maangwag mothers who work hard for their children. As Bouchard and Martin note: "There is no shortcut to achieving the state of love and you cannot know love unless you are courageous. You cannot know love unless you are honest. Love is based on the wisdom to understand one's self and the humility to accept weaknesses as well as being proud of one's strengths. Love has, at its very core, the other teachings" (15). To ensure the overall wellbeing and mental health of my children, I work to embody all the teachings in myself, but try to manifest it also in my children, so that they can come to know zaagi'idiwin as Anishinaabeg know its scope and complexity. Only through knowing all these teachings, within each of us, can we become a true-hearted human being or Anishinaabeg.

These Grandmother Teachings provide Anishinaabeg parents the values and ethics we need to pass on to our children to teach them to respect all of life, including their own. These seven values of conduct can be seen as an "internalized set of beliefs or principles of behaviour held by individuals or groups. They are expressed in the ways people think and act" (Danard 12). As Anishinaabeg, we can come to connect cultural values of conduct that "continue to be considered a strong basis for the initial development and lifelong growth of a human being into an active, purposeful and honorable member of her or his community" (Danard 2). Furthermore, through the Seven Grandmother Teachings we can learn how to teach our own children the good ways to contextualize these ancient teachings within their own assembly of personal memories and firsthand experiences. This can then be used to enable and empower them to form their own choices to be active participants in developing a family plan of action with their parents.

The COVID-19 pandemic has certainly been a time of trauma and will likely continue for several years. The trauma will mark our young children's lives and mould who they will become as adults, but each generation carries these challenges. I have my own baggage from childhood that I carry, but what helped me to carry forwards is learning about my culture from what my mother held and her mother before her. Like seeds, her knowledge and experience shaped my identity. Passing on, teaching, educating and immersing Anishinaabeg children in cultural ways of knowing, being and living, is critically essential to their ability to move through and past the mental and emotional traumas of living through time periods like the COVID-19 pandemic and to continue to build their Anishinaabeg identities as good human beings. Anishinaabeg maternal pedagogy is grounded in following the knowledge, teachings, practices, and ceremonies of our mothers, grandmothers, their grandmothers, and all those grandmothers that came before.

Concluding Thoughts

When we look at that prophecy story, as parents who facilitate, teach, and mentor the growth or education of our children into their identities as Anishinaabeg, we can see valuable pedagogical directions to follow in guiding the wellbeing of children. As a mother, I look to the lessons I need to get out of the prophecy teachings to parent my children, during this tumultuous time, in a way that embodies the Anishinaabeg worldview of how to be good human beings on this Earth. So when I read the Seven Grandmother Teachings, I see within them parental teachings that aid me in guiding the mental and emotional balance, physical health, and spiritual path. Through these teachings, I can ensure that my children will continue to grow in a good way if I follow them as procedures of parenting while living through the darker times of prophecy. Prophecy echoes through time and living through it spins us down the path of life in often challenging ways. I watch my children spinning down their miikanan (paths), and I set before them the guideposts and maps of their ancestral grandmothers: knowledge, teachings, language, customs, ceremony, and stories. Prophecy is unfolding, but my daughters will survive and thrive. I share this poem written for my daughters.

Gchi-Apptendaagoziwag akina Niizhigwag Idaanisag

Prophecy unfolds.
Spin, Spin, Spin.

Pick up the stories, my daughters.
You can only survive by picking up your mother's teachings.
You can only find a path forward holding the stories I leave you.
My words form deep roots that bind you in enawendiwin[4], like strands of grandmother spider's eyebigwasab connecting you to the cosmos.
Deep roots grow down into Aki, your mother the Earth, and are not reached by the disease and fire of winter's frost.
It will not reach you my little ones.

Spin, Spin, Spin.
Arise from the ashes, new, clean, and fresh again.
You are the light in the shadows.
You will spring us forward into the bounty of summer.

Prophecy unfolds.
Spin, Spin, Spin... my little Fancy Shawl dancers.
Dance us through this time like memengwaag[5] carried on a summer breeze.
Around and around you spin.

Prophecy unfolds.
Spin, Spin, Spin.

Endnotes

1. Anishinaabeg are Indigenous peoples from the lands around Nayaano-wiishkbiwii-nibiimaang Gichigamiin (The Five Freshwater Seas: Great Lakes). Our traditional territory crosses the borders of Canada and the United States of America. We have lived on the lands of Turtle Island (North American continent) since time immemorial.
2. In Anishinaabemowin, *-ban* or *-ba* is a preterit suffix that is added to a noun stem to indicate a past state or absence. For instance, -ban is added to a noun to indicate that the person is now deceased. To honour that they have passed to the Spirit Realm, I have chosen to write it as -ban at the end of their name. To not bother or draw the attention of the Spirit of the deceased who is busy with their existence in that Spirit realm, Anishinaabeg are encouraged to alter or add to the name *-ban* or *-ba*. I have chosen not to attach it directly to the name of each deceased person repeatedly. Furthermore, I have chosen to italicize *-ban* to make it visually resonate as different and alter the name in the traditional manner.
3. I have chosen here to use a gender-neutral pronoun so that the reader can envision the gender of their choosing.
4. Enawendiwin refers to the concept of "relating." It speaks to our relationship(s) with all of Creation or everything in the universe.
5. Memengwaag translates to butterflies.

Works Cited

Benton-Banai, Edward. *The Mishomis Book: The Voice of the Ojibway*. University of Minnesota Press, 1988.

Bouchard, David, and Joseph Martin. *Seven Sacred Teachings Niizhwaaswi Gagiikwewin*. MTW Publishers, 2009.

Bourdeau-Waboose, Jan. *Where Only the Elders Go—Moon Lake Loon Lake*. Penumbra Press, 2003.

Danard, Deborah. *Medicine Wheel Surviving Suicide—Strengthening Life Bundle*. PhD dissertation, University of Toronto, 2016.

Dumont, James. "Journey to Daylight-Land: Through Ojibwa Eyes." *Laurentian University Review*, vol. 8, no. 2, 1976, pp. 31-43.

Johnston, Basil. *Honour Earth Mother: Mino-Audjaudauh Mizzu-Kummik-Quae*. Kegedonce Press, 2003.

Johnston, Basil. *The Gift of the Stars: Anangoog Meegwiwaewinan*. Kegedonce Press, 2010.

Johnston, Basil. *Ojibway Heritage*. McClelland & Steward, 1976.

Simpson, Leanne. *Dancing On Our Turtle's Back: Stories of Nishnaabeg Re-Creation, Resurgence, and New Emergence*. ARP Books, 2011.

Sinclair, Niigonwedom James. *Nindoodemag Bagijiganan: A History of Anishinaabeg Narrative*. The University of British Columbia, PhD dissertation, 2013.

Chapter 11.

Noticing: A Story of a Mother's and Son's Arts-Based Discussions about the Pandemic

Lauren E. Burrow and Ethan S. Burrow

As a MotherScholar (Burrow, et al.), I continue to grow in my understanding and acceptance of my chosen identity—an identity that both inescapably intersects and overtly overlaps between my mother and scholar selves. This past year,[1] during an ongoing global COVID-19 pandemic and unresolved civil rights unrest, I have taken care to specifically consider and appreciate the role my young children (currently ten to thirteen years old) inherently and intentionally play in my currently co-mingled personal and professional space. Upon receipt of my COVID-19 vaccine and my state's push to return to normal, I have taken time to critically self-reflect on the reality of MotherScholaring during a global pandemic, chronicling the successes and frustrations resulting from my personal-professional blended identity being confined to full-time work and childcare at home. My children are frequently the subject of and/or inspiration for my research and have co-taught and copresented with me on a variety of teacher education-related topics, but in this chapter, I push myself to explicitly invite my youngest child, Ethan, to coauthor a narrative examination of his shared existence with me, his MotherScholar.

To construct a mini story that captures many big moments, I used multiple qualitative methods to both self-reflect and then, later, interview Ethan in a discussion-based format. Primary data collection included photo elicitation, in which I used family photo books to ask him about how he perceived our shared experiences of 2020. Next, we labeled our feelings through an arts-based association activity featuring Katsushika Hokusai's (葛飾北斎) *Thirty-six Views of Mount Fuji*. And, finally, we returned to reflect on our family photo books and wrote response poems guided by a prompt from Naomi Shihab Nye. My intention with this chapter is to honour my youngest child with his own space to make sense of and comment on a most significant time in our lives while also modelling potential asking-and-answering methods by which other mothers could inquire into the perceptions of their children during times of extreme stress so that they can better understand the interconnectedness of their shared experiences.

Introduction to Me, a MotherScholar

I am a white, cisgender female (a person whose gender identity is aligned with her sex assigned at birth) and married mother of three young adolescent children, who have been forced into completing their elementary school and middle-grade level studies through a free, public online school to maintain health and safety in a largely unvaccinated community. As a cisgender white mother with middle-class financial status, I acknowledge the privileges and accompanying power that I hold based purely on my identities. Additionally, I take seriously my responsibility to educate my own white children about the urgency to disrupt our white privilege and the system of white supremacy by respecting spaces that prioritize and amplify diverse voices to inform us of critical cultural and racialized issues. Throughout these tumultuous times, I have been privileged enough to retain employment as an associate professor of education studies at a public state university and can mostly complete my work responsibilities from the safety of a remote location. However, as a MotherScholar, I have been obligated to maintain a prepandemic level of faculty workload in teaching, service, and scholarship while also managing household chores and the supervision of my children's schooling—all in the same house space.

I claim an identity of a MotherScholar—an identity that reminds me and signals to others that I am both forced to and willingly embrace a reality in which my two identities manifest as a blended coexistence, which is always flowing throughout both my personal and professional times and spaces (Burrow et al). Coined by Cheryl Matias and further explored by Yvette Lapayese: "Mother-scholars drive the feminist impulse to dismantle patriarchal binaries—namely, the sharp divide between the intellect and the maternal, the public and the private" ("Mother-Scholars Intellectualize"17) while also "[finding] creative ways to insert [the] maternal identity, specifically in academic spaces and [into] scholarship" ("Mother-Scholars Maternalize" 23).

The Journey to a Mother-Child Coauthoring

My version of MotherScholarhood has led me to include my children, actively and intentionally, in my scholarship. For example, my children have accompanied me, sometimes welcomed and sometimes shunned, to conferences around the United States, and as a result, I have proudly watched all three of my children present at various state and national conferences on their own. Individually, and in collaboration with other MotherScholars, I have frequently presented and published the lessons I have learned about finding and accepting my identity as a Mother-Scholar—an identity I can only hold because of my children—and about protecting and celebrating my MotherScholarhood during COVID-19 (Spradley et al.; Olson et al.).

This chapter is my opportunity to shift from writing about my children to making space for my youngest to write with me. As we enter another year of at-home school and work due to COVID-19 it seems only logical and natural to include him as a coauthor so that he can share, in his own words, his feelings about being a son of a MotherScholar during a global pandemic.

After all, our stories have always been intertwined—from being the one whom I nursed while finishing my dissertation to the one who quieted down while bouncing on a friendly attendee's knee while I presented at my first international conference. Nowadays, he is the one who listens in and plays along as I teach my preservice teachers on Zoom during a global pandemic, the one who asked to accompany me when I received my teaching excellence award from my college, because he was just "so proud of me," and the one who has rarely strayed from my mother's orbit throughout this pandemic.

Methods for Our Discussions
Photo and Art Elicitation
Photovoice is a visual research method associated with action research that seeks to empower the voices of consistently marginalized and/or vulnerable groups through photography and functions as a form of social action (Wang). For this chapter, a similar method, photo elicitation, was used to facilitate interactive interviewing between me and Ethan using preselected photographs. Similar to Julie Rust's use of personal photography in her autoethnography of being a Mother-Scholar, my discussions with Ethan were prompted by looking at family photo books and selected screenshots from my Instagram. Finally, we engaged in what I am terming "art elicitation" in which we discussed famous artworks to identify personal connections between them and our feelings about our COVID-19 realities.

Poetry
This collaborative self-study is a continuation of my conscious choice to draw on a natural tendency towards poetic verse to continue my quest to find some logic in these illogical times and to continue my rejection of traditional research practice (Percer), which is not powerful enough to handle the beautiful complexity of my nontraditional experiences of MotherScholaring during a pandemic. Ethan and I agree with Monica Prendergast that thinking poetically helped us identify the most relevant themes and phrases out of the storm of emotions swirling within and around us during the pandemic.

Storytelling
In my work, I join fellow MotherScholars in acknowledging my motherly "propensity for storytelling at bedtimes, around dinner tables, on social media, during carpoolings, and over glasses of wine" (Burrow et al., 4246), my professional pedagogical practice of "storytelling in front of peers at conferences, on the pages of [my] publications, as an instructional delivery method in [my] classrooms" (4246), and my feminist commitment to share my scholarship in a way that "honors [my] individual MotherScholar voice, in what is typically a patriarchal space, a preferred and valued research methodology and dissemination in

traditional quantitative formats" (4246). Having grown up listening to me tell my stories in class, at bedtimes, at conferences, and during car rides, Ethan joins me in wanting to share his own story in this chapter.

My "Noticings" about My Children during the Pandemic

In the early months of the pandemic, I began noticing the goodbyes that my children never got to say to friends, family, and teachers as their schools and our town collectively shut down to quarantine from COVID-19. Then, as the pandemic dragged on, and most of our local community moved on from or gave up on COVID-19 safety practices and returned to normal life, I noticed all the social interactions—such as sleepovers, sports play, school events, and other previously typical hallmarks of childhood—that my COVID-19-conscientious family was missing out on. I noticed what COVID-19 was taking away from my children, and I did what I could for each of them to show that I saw what they were going through and that I really cared. To that end, I created collective coping experiences that we could share together to try to compensate for the tragedy, unfairness, and confusion my children endured because of the pandemic.

Music—To Make the Mood or Match the Mood?

My eldest child and only daughter, Nicole, is a second-semester seventh grader. Her pronouns are she/hers. She is a talented and self-taught artist, who tries to use her art to share her social justice beliefs and values with others. She has presented at a national English teacher conference and has had a poem published. In March 2020, she said goodbye to her friends for spring break and has not seen any of them since, save for an extra special birthday visit, which still required quarantining to prepare for the get together. She has had to graduate elementary school and transition to middle school, all on a screen from her bedroom. Early in the pandemic, when we felt most cooped up and isolated, when nothing made sense and everything was frustrating, there were days when our emotions ran so high and our patience and resilience ran so low that we just had to get out of the house. We would get into the car and just drive. We got lost together, took a turn here, a turn there, and eventually turned the GPS back on to direct us home. Before we would set out on these drives, I would always ask her: "Do you want the music to match our mood or make our mood?" This meant did we need Taylor Swift's pop albums to lift us out of our COVID-19-induced funks or did we need Taylor's *Folklore* and *Evermore* albums to meet us where our hearts were at and just let us cry? We would sometimes talk about the unique issues of her becoming a teenager during a pandemic; at other times, she would just narrate funny TikToks to me, but the soundtrack of our pandemic got us through the bad times and the good.

Marvel to the Rescue

Triston is my middle child and eldest son. He is a sixth grader who loves reading manga (comics or graphic novels originating from Japan) and watching anime (Japanese animation). He wants to learn the basics of coding so he can someday build his own video game. He has frequently cotaught comic book writing lessons in my preservice teacher writing methods courses, and he hopes to teach a new lesson about the creative writing skills that can be authentically practiced during *Dungeons and Dragons* play. Triston has always loved movies, and going to the movie theater is one of his favorite pastimes. In fact, prior to 2020, he had frequently celebrated his springtime birthday at the local movie theater, timed to the release of the latest Marvel movie. So when his 2020 *Black Widow*-themed birthday party plans had to be cancelled, it hit us that COVID-19 was truly going to alter our lives. As a true middle child, he handled it in stride and delighted at the opportunity to turn family movie nights into rewatching the entire Marvel Cinematic Universe (MCU) from the beginning.

Then, Disney+ came along. Having access to all the previous Marvel movies, at-home new releases, and brand-new series became a way to pass the boredom and provided us all much to talk about. Throughout the pandemic, we tested each other with Marvel trivia, debated fandom (community of fans around a shared enjoyment of an aspect of popular culture, such as books, movies, TV shows, bands, or sports teams) theories, and analyzed the social justice messages of comic books. These conversations even became part of our night-time routine; the conversations sometimes lasted so long that they had to be paused and picked up again in the morning. By early 2022, we have been able to cautiously and occasionally return to the movie theatre for a new release, but only after it has been out long enough for everyone else to see it first. Enjoying weekday movie outings with theaters all to ourselves is one of the perks we love most about an at-home lifestyle while others return to their prepandemic work and school schedules.

Noticing Them Noticing, Too

Just as I have taken notice of my children throughout the pandemic, I have also noticed them paying attention, too—observing current events; noticing responses, or lack thereof, from local, national, and international leaders; and reflecting on what it means to be part of a global society. Most importantly, during a time when they are noticing so many people, who are taking no notice of others, they are noticing what it looks like to care. As months have turned into years, I have noticed how all my children have made a significant shift into becoming humans who genuinely care about others, starting with me, their mother. I have noticed how this pandemic has given my daughter lots of practice checking in with me just as I check in with her. Often, while I am chained to a computer late at night trying to finish one more publication proposal, grade one more paper, or reach out to one more struggling student—she stops by my home-desk to ask, "How are you doing? What can I bring you?" And I have noticed how this pandemic has transformed my once stoic middle son into a walk-by hugger, who senses when I might be feeling overwhelmed, a little blue, or frustrated. He models awareness of and respect for consent as he first asks if he can give me a hug "because, you know, not everybody wants a hug sometimes."

Like so many other mothers, I have worried about what COVID-19 has taken away from my children, but maybe not all of it should be mourned. With only a tinge of selfishness, I will admit to being relieved that my eldest has missed out on the bullying and drama that can accompany the pubescent years. I am grateful that missing out on in-person school has taken away the societal push for them to skip over childhood and rush into adolescence. Overall, I am noticing that while unexpected, unpredictable, and certainly unwanted, the pandemic has created extraordinary opportunities for my children to grow into the caring human beings that our world will always need. While I keep taking time to pause and take notice of how my children are surviving and, in some ways, even thriving in a pandemic, I am also now taking time to share in this chapter what Ethan has noticed about himself during the pandemic.

Ethan, my youngest son, is a fourth grader. He loves science and writing stories in the style of Dav Pilkey's *Dog Man* series. He is so pleased that at-home school lets him write and draw along with his current favorite author, Jarrett Lerner's virtual classes. He is a phenomenal video game player and enjoys playing with his dog, Lightning. He is also ready for COVID-19 to go away! When I first asked Ethan if he wanted to cowrite this chapter with me, I explained that the premise of the collection was to see if "the kids are alright" during this pandemic, to which he immediately responded: "Ooooh! Can I tell you this TikTok joke I saw? ... Two guys are in heaven, and they are looking back at 2020, and the one says, 'Yeah, that was the worst year of my life.' Then, two dogs are in heaven, and they are looking back at 2020, and the one says, 'Yeah, that was the best year of my life.'" That was when I knew that I had picked the best coauthor for this particular chapter.

For this portion of the chapter, I utilized arts-based data collection methods, which I have previously used in my own scholarship and self-care, to invite Ethan to reflect on, take notice of, and articulate his feelings during the pandemic. As his mother, I determined that the best way to include him in this chapter was to make space for him to tell his pandemic story. To create a space that was age appropriate, I made sure our data collection centered on simple chats about familiar family photographs and famous artworks. In this chapter, the story collection process is presented in the order that it occurred, from the most familiar to the most abstract, but his reflections have been rearranged to create story flow. Ultimately, although I used scholarly methods, these are just some conversations between a MotherScholar and her son.

To start our reflective conversations, I paired photo elicitation with a poetic prompt. Our discussion began with a prompt that Youth Poet Laureate Naomi Shihab Nye had shared during a 2020 online session of *Barrio Writers*, a summer creative writing camp I co-taught for under-represented and marginalized youth: "What did it take? What did it give?" I asked him to consider what COVID-19 had taken away from us and what it might have given us. I started our photo-guided chat with my own example: "it gave us masks and took away handshakes." Together, we looked at two books featuring family photos taken throughout 2020. As I turned each page, I asked him to scan the memories and then talk about what COVID-19 took from and gave to us, as evidenced in the photos. On some pages, he did not have much to say; on others, he would assert: "I don't know how to say it like a poem, but I'll just talk about the photo and figure that out later." As we progressed through the poetic photo talk, he even decided that "take" did not, necessarily, have to be a bad thing, like when COVID-19 "took away early bedtimes." Ethan's final poem is shared in the next section.

I next completed another photo elicitation activity with him. We looked at images I had previously selected from my private social media accounts when I was working on my own pandemic self-reflective publications. I showed each photo to him on my computer screen and asked him what he remembered about the experience, captured in the photo, and how he felt when looking at the memory. This form of guided reflection took on more of an interview-style discussion as I encouraged him with open-ended prompts, such as "You felt that way because?" Selections from Ethan's most vivid memories are shared in the next section.

For our final discussion, I prompted him to visually identify his feelings, through an arts-based association activity featuring artworks from the *Thirty-Six Views of Mount Fuji* series by Hokusai, a Japanese artist, ukiyo-e painter, and printmaker of the Edo period. This short activity is a version of the self-care exercise I completed during the "Summer Institute for Educators," a professional development hosted by the Smithsonian National Gallery of Art, Washington DC. In this contemplative activity, guided by "art looking," I showed Ethan a grid of the thirty-six woodblock prints (ink and color on paper) by Hokusai and explained that Mt. Fuji was depicted in every single one of the series' prints. To encourage a deeper look at each artwork, I challenged him to "find Mt. Fuji" in each one. Next, I guided him to reconsider the connection of the artworks to his COVID experiences:

> What if COVID was like Mt. Fuji? Just like Mt. Fuji is in all of these prints, sometimes big and taking up the whole space and sometimes small and almost forgotten, but still there. COVID is always in our lives; it just hasn't gone away yet. Look in some of the artworks people are at work and play, and Mt. Fuji/COVID is just there in the background. In others, it is totally in the way of their everyday lives.

Finally, I asked him to look at all the prints, again, and tell me which one(s) looked like the way he felt about COVID-19 in the beginning as compared to now. I am terming this new iteration of photo elicitation as art elicitation. Ethan's final answers are shared in the next section.

Ethan's Turn to Notice What I Remember and How It Made Me Feel: A Photo-Elicited Conversation

[Ethan discussing Figure 1]

>Ethan: I remember that day. I wanted to do a fashion show, like the one you and I had at home, but you were in your art conference [online] so you suggested we have an art fashion show instead.

>Lauren: I remember that too. I had forgotten that was why we did that activity. Thanks for reminding me. Thanks for letting me suggest an alternative to your original idea of a fashion show. And remember, Maw Maw and Papa Tuesday.(Ethan's name for his grandparents) were there, too. How did you feel that day?

>Ethan: HAPPY! I was happy to do what I wanted to do and see what others created. I like what I made, but I was even more excited to see what others did.

>Lauren: Can I tell you something? I love this picture. I loved that day. You are so creative and so fun. I loved that I could get my work done and play with you at the same time.

>Ethan: Yeah, it's like I got to be your work buddy that day. (See Figure 1 in the Appendix)

[Ethan and I discussing Figure 2 in the Appendix.]

>Lauren: Can I ask you, why do you make me these and leave them on my desk?

>Ethan: Because I knew it'd make you happy a friend while you're on Zoom.

Lauren: You're right. It did help to have some friends while I was in Zoom meetings. Thanks, buddy. (See Figure 2 in the Appendix)

That's What COVID-19 Feels Like: An Arts-based Association Activity

During our art looking and talking, Ethan chose four of Hokusai's prints that best represented his feelings about COVID-19 over time. *The Great Wave Off Kanagawa* is one of Hokusai's most famous prints. He used fluid lines and blue, white, and cream colours to depict large, rising, white-capped waves that had not yet crashed back into the sea water. In the middle of the print, far in the distance, is a snow-capped Mt. Fuji—small and almost blending in among the ominous, great waves. *Fine Wind, Clear Weather* or *Red Fuji* features the volcanic Mt. Fuji as the large, central focus of the print. Mt. Fuji is depicted, mostly in reddish tones, with thick, deep, greenery dotting its base and bunches of stratocumulus clouds set in the sky behind it. *Thunderstorm Beneath the Summit* or *Black Fuji* is similar to the *Red Fuji* print but with darker red, almost blackish tones, for the mountain and a line of cumulus clouds depicted behind it. Finally, *Umezawa in Sagami Province* is a scenic view of the mountain featuring bluish, greenish, cream, and white tones throughout the tranquil setting; it also features five red-crowned cranes (Japan's most sacred bird and a sign of happiness and good luck) drinking at a watering hole and two flying off into a sky full of cumulonimbus clouds. Mt. Fuji almost blends in among a natural setting of rolling, green hills.

> Ethan: At first, COVID was scary and far away like the first print, *The Great Wave Off Kanagawa*, and then, it got closer and closer and closer, like the second print, *Fine Wind, Clear Weather*, until we could think of nothing except COVID like in the last two prints. Sure, COVID still sucks, but it's not as bad now. It used to be like print number three, *Thunderstorm Beneath the Summit*.... We used to not know what to do and that was scary, but it's not as bad now. It's more like that print, *Umezawa in Sagami Province*.
>
> Lauren: Hey, Buddy, if we zoom in on that print, *Umezawa in Sagami Province*, the one you chose for what COVID is like now,

do you notice the birds? Do you see that detail? There's five of them, just like the five of us in our family.

Ethan looked up at me with a knowing, kind smile.

What It Took Away and What It Gave: A Poem Created from Photo Elicitation

I Remember…
By Ethan S. Burrow

It took away in-person school and going to bed really early.

It gave us time to hang out and stay up late to have movie nights.

It took away my mom going into the office.

It gave us an office for mom in the middle of our home.

It took away Halloween for a year or two.

It gave us new holiday traditions like hunting for candy in the backyard at night.

It took away my big sister's in-person graduation.

It gave us time to stay up late reading and playing.

It gave me time with grandparents—painting, walking, and building box forts.

It gave me and my mom and sister and brother Zoom birthdays.

It took away my brown hair …

and gave me blue hair for a day and blonde hair for a year.

It gave me time to build Lego scenes for my mom during her Zoom meetings.

It gave me the chance to attend online class in my Iron Man helmet.

So What's a Mother to Do? How to Check on Your Kids during Traumatic Times

It has been bad. There is no doubt about that. In fact, it has been traumatic: "The COVID-19 crisis can be defined as a collective trauma, which contributes to an upheaval of community connection and functioning" (Duane et al., abstract). In my previous work, I used poetry to make a space for me to self-cope, to take care of myself, and to check in on my own mixed-up feelings (Burrow and Jeffrey); now poetry has given me space to turn my attention to the feelings of my children. I have also used art and photography to analyze, label, document, and share a claimed MotherScholar identity (Burrow et al.), and now, I use it to let my child share his COVID-19-affected identity, too.

I again acknowledge that my multiple identities afford me the space, time, and means to routinely check in on myself and my family. Since these practices may not be feasible and accessible for all mothers, it is my intention to push future scholarship to include and advocate for those mothers that have been more severely impacted and harmed during this time, including Black and single mothers. For mothers experiencing the trauma of the pandemic alongside their children, perhaps a way to check in with yourself and your children is to allow familiar photographs to prompt discussions. Being intentional about a natural mother-child experience, like looking through old photographs, can lead to asking, listening, and responding. Starting prompts, for example, can include "Tell me what you remember about this photo" or "Tell me how you feel when you look at this photo." The conversations do not have to be forced, and memory associations need not be demanded—just take some time to remember together and listen to one another.

When words are hard to come by and the feelings just cannot be adequately explained, using famous artwork can help identify abstract emotions in visually aesthetic ways. The chosen artwork can be familiar ones but showing your children new ones can give a reason for them to explore, notice, and make new connections. In addition, sharing a series of artwork, can encourage comparisons and critical reflection. Sharing background about the artists and how/why they created the artwork can spark an initial understanding of and connection to the artwork and guide "art looking." Starting prompts can focus on the concrete and include such questions as "What do you notice in this artwork? What colors do you see? What shapes do you see? Who do you see? What are they doing? Can you figure out the setting?" Next, you can encourage more abstract connections with other prompts: "How do the colors make you feel? How do you think the people in the painting feel? How does this painting make you feel"? After completing a concrete and abstract analysis of the artwork, you can prompt your child to try to identify if any of the artwork represents the way they feel about COVID-19, current life situations, or recent experiences, for example, "If your feelings about COVID-19 were one of these paintings, which one would it be and why?" This art-association activity can be done while discussing public artwork, such as sculptures and murals, while out on a walk, or it could be a prepared reflection that takes the place of normal bedtime story readings.

Finally, poetry has a way of capturing, honouring, and sharing our most complex, innermost thoughts and feelings in a beautifully satisfying way. If you are unfamiliar with poetry, it can seem daunting and unapproachable, but many poems follow a template that children can easily be guided to complete. For example, the prompt I used with Ethan was the questions "What it took?" and "What it gave?" The "it" can be anything going on in your child's life. Ethan, then, paired the two lists in a purposeful way to finish his poem. A final easy-to-follow template is the popular *Where I'm From* poem by Renée Watson and George Ella Lyon, which involves interviewing and then adding Mad Lib-style responses to craft a reflective poem that takes notice of who you are, what you care about, and who matters most, even during a pandemic.

Whether through intentional questioning and listening, art analysis, or poetry writing, mothers can create moments to hear their children's thoughts about their everyday lives, their feelings about important moments, and their perspectives on the pandemic. This mother-child reflection time can hopefully reassure both mother and child that they are doing alright and that in retrospect, just like the TikTok dogs in heaven, these may even be the best years ever for our children.

Endnotes

1. This chapter captures a specific timespan of family experiences during the COVID-19 pandemic: spring 2020–early 2022; therefore, all references to my children's ages/grade levels and COVID-19 safety

protocols reflects our realities at the time of coauthorship. Our work and school realities have changed since the writing of this chapter, but this remains a snapshot of our truth—at that time.

Works Cited

Burrow, Lauren. "Let's Talk: Tips from a Preschool Teacher-Turned-Parent on How to Improve Teacher-Parent Communication." *Early Years*, vol. 33, no. 2, 2012, pp. 22-23.

Burrow, Lauren E., et al. "The Skits, Sketches, and Stories of Mother-Scholars." *The Qualitative Report*, vol. 25, no. 12, 2020, pp. 4245-73.

Burrow, Lauren E., and Tonya Jeffery. "The Poetry of the Pandemic." *Journal of Motherhood Initiative for Research and Community Involvement*, vol. 11, no. 2 / vol. 12, no. 1, 2020, pp. 47-73.

Duane, Addison M., et al. "Collective Trauma and Community Support: Lessons from Detroit." *Psychological Trauma: Theory, Research, Practice, and Policy*, vol. 12, no. 5, 2020, pp. 452-54.

Hokusai, Katsushika. *Fine Wind, Clear Weather* or *Red Fuji*. 1830-31. *Museum of Fine Arts Boston*, www.mfa.org/exhibitions/hokusai. Accessed 26 Feb. 2023.

Lapayese, Yvette V. "Mother-Scholars Intellectualize the Private Sphere. *Mother-Scholar: (Re)imagining K-12 Education*, edited by Shirley R. Steinberg, Sense Publishers, 2012, pp. 17-22.

Lapayese Yvette V. "Mother-Scholars Maternalize the 'Public' Sphere." *Mother-Scholar: (Re)imagining K-12 Education*, edited by Shirley R. Steinberg, Sense Publishers, 2012, pp. 23-28.

Matias, Cheryl. "Cheryl Matias, PhD and Mother of Twins: Counter Storytelling to Critically Analyze How I Navigated the Academic Application, Negotiation, and Relocation Process." American Educational Research Association (AERA), April 2011, New Orleans, LA.

Olson, Beal, et al. "Everything Is Topsy-Turvy": Academic Mothers Scramble to Keep Their Careers and Families Afloat during COVID -19." *AJE Forum*, 20 Aug. 2021, www.ajeforum.com/everything-is-topsy-turvy-academic-mothers-scramble-to-keep-their-careers-and-families-afloat-during-covid-19/. Accessed 26 Feb. 2023.

Percer, Liza Hayes. "Going Beyond the Demonstrable Range in Educational Scholarship: Exploring the Intersections of Poetry and Research." *The Qualitative Report*, vol. 7, no. 2, 2002, pp. 1-13.

Prendergast, Monica. "Poetic Inquiry Is... 29 Ways of Looking at Poetry as Qualitative Research." *Educational Insights*, vol. 13, no. 3, 2009, pp. 1-3.

Rust, Julie. "Mother-Scholar Tangles: Always Both This and That." *Ubiquity: The Journal of Literature, Literacy, and the Arts*, vol. 3, no. 2, 2016, pp. 87-120.

Spradley, E,. et al. "Crystalizing Layered Approaches to MotherScholar Expressions in COVID-19: A Photovoice and Autoethnographic Study." *Peabody Journal of Education*, vol. 97, no. 2, 2022, pp. 228-45.

Wang, Caroline C. "Photovoice: A Participatory Action Research Strategy Applied to Women's Health." *Journal of Women's Health*, vol. 8, no. 2, 1999, pp. 185-92.

Appendix

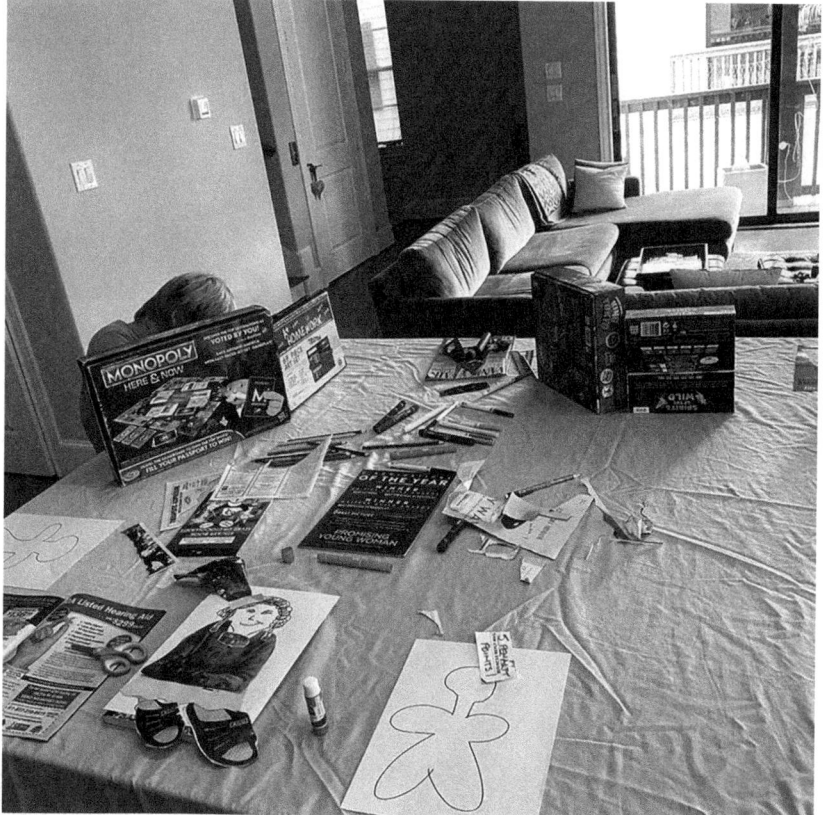

Figure 1. Ethan and other family members (not pictured) prepare their paper collage supermodels behind propped up game boards and art kits (i.e., their dressing rooms) for the runaway event.

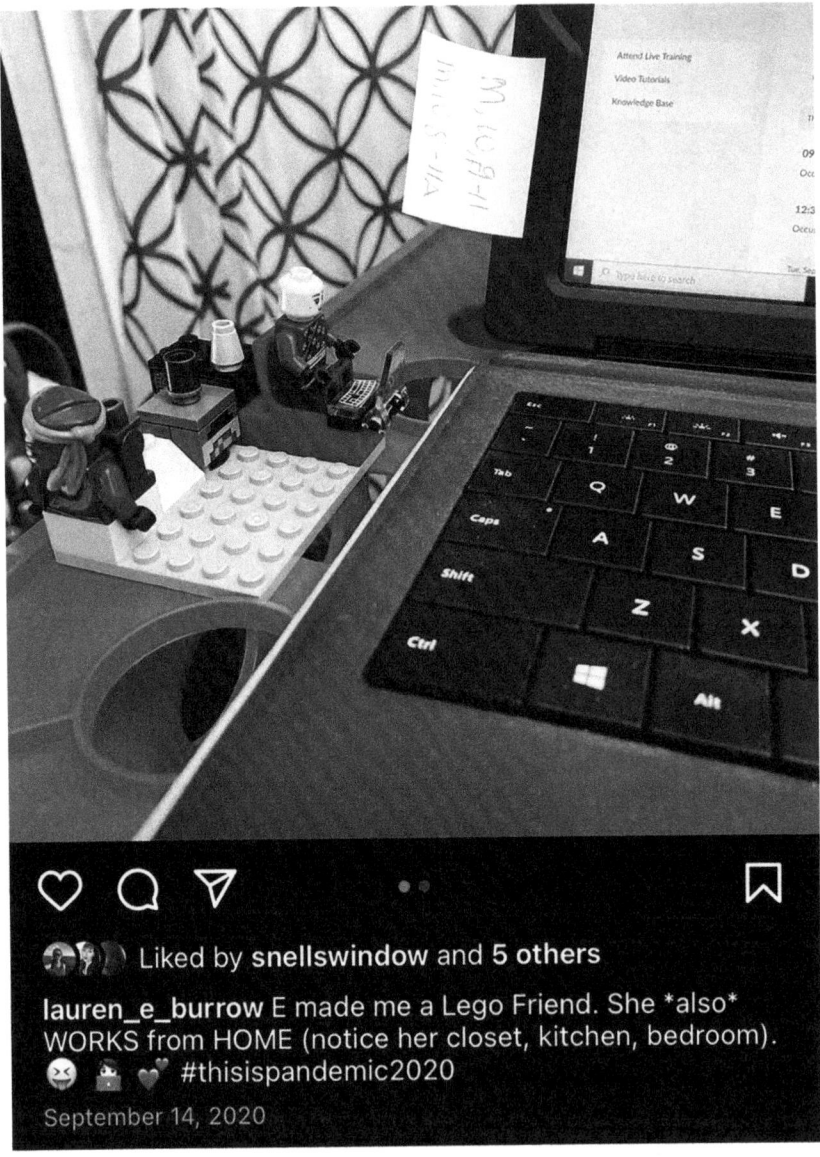

Figure 2. A screenshot from my Instagram account sharing one in a series of posts of the Lego scenes Ethan frequently built at night to leave as a "good morning" surprise for me at my home-office desk.

Chapter 12.

A Moment of Beauty: Verses of Hope for Children in a Pandemic

Mirelly da Silva Barros, Maria Wanderleya de Lavor Coriolano-Marinus, Bianca Rocha Gouveia, Adélia Karla Falcão Soares, Maria Ilk Nunes de Albuquerque, Weslla Karla Albuquerque, Talita Mendes Bomfim, Vitória Andrade Farias de Oliveira, and Brenda Elize Nunes da Hora

The present study aims to describe and reflect upon the construction of an e-book for children in the context of the COVID-19 pandemic and the dialogues achieved between sensitive care and aesthetics in nursing. Care through a transdisciplinary dialogue is one of the possible ways to better develop sensitive strategies and expand the horizons of care when understanding the aesthetic field as a space that allows for the alignment of nursing with sensitive care. In this way, this transdisciplinary dialogue, which is a communication between different types of knowledge, will allow an integral look at problems and situations, making care more attentive to human needs (Teixeira 90).

This type of sensitive care is part of the context of art because it has an aesthetic perspective that dialogues with care. Care, therefore, is art and science. While not dissociating itself from technique and scientific knowledge, sensitive care promotes the establishment of concrete inter personal relationships, connecting subjectivities with ways to enable the transformation of contexts and the improvement of actions (Teixeira 92; Morin 77). In this way, nursing goes through paths of complexity to develop and build sensitive care. Human beings are understood to have physical, psychological, emotional, and spiritual needs, and these, in turn, are related to contexts, which emerge as determinants for the state of health. (Assis et al. 337; Morin 84). Therefore, environmental, social, and economic conditions and issues—such as in cases of natural disasters, wars, and economic crises—have a direct impact on health and wellbeing, contributing to the development of diseases and reducing the quality of life.

The different impacts generated by the COVID-19 pandemic have had direct repercussions on childhood regarding the development of cognitive, emotional, and motor aspects, increased situations of vulnerability, the deprivation of affective needs, as well as worsening social relationships and living conditions resulting from increased parental unemployment and increased family stress (Araújo et al. 7; Linhares and Enumo 8; Cabral et al. 8). These challenges created the need for the construction of a poetic e-book for children and caregivers, intended to offer them a moment of beauty and a short tale of hope for the present times.

The pandemic has negatively affected the mental health status of children, as they have experienced fear, pessimism, and panic, leading to feelings of depression. Environments that did not encourage the expression of feelings or recognize the absence of established routines might have increased children's high levels of stress and further restricted their development (Cluver et al. 1).

It was with this context in mind that we decided to prepare the e-book *Cordelzinho para Sabiá Dormir* (translated as *A Folk Tale to Lull the Thrush to Sleep*). The book aimed to develop and apply strategies that combine science and playfulness for the subjective expression of children's feelings. To achieve this, we used storytelling, mediated by poetry and illustrated art, as tools to express aesthetic knowledge, combining transdisciplinary knowledge for the production of human care in the form of hope. Transdisciplinary knowledge allows the integration of different areas, which allows for a comprehensive look at the complex realities and contexts that occur in life.

Methodological Path

This is a descriptive study that emphasizes experience. The stages of the report followed Oscar Holliday's systematization, which divides the organization of the experience into the following stages: a) the starting point (introduction): b) the initial questions (last paragraph of the methodology); c) recovery of the lived process (axis I); d) deep reflections (axis II); and e) the points of arrival (final considerations) (72).

The experience to be examined was made by two nurses and a designer. One of the nurses is a teacher in the Postgraduate Program in Child and Adolescent Health (PPGSCA) at the Federal University of Pernambuco (UFPE), the other nurse is a master's student of the same Postgraduate Program, and the designer is an art and media graduate student at the Federal University from Campina Grande (UFCG). They came together to combine storytelling, poetry, and drawing as coping strategies for children during the COVID-19 pandemic.

Based on scientific knowledge about COVID-19 and the life context in which children and families lived these new experiences, the e-book *A Folk Tale to Lull the Thrush to Sleep* was created by the nurses through poetic sensitivity and illustrated art.

How could we use storytelling, the research method of the researchers, as a social technology that combines knowledge of scientific studies and experiences in dealing with the COVID-19 pandemic? Poetry was used to generate an approach that emphasized the playful universe of children, who were facing the pandemic's challenges and changes, through simple and poetic language.

In view of the current pandemic context, we also explored additional questions supported by the cocreation process. Can poetry be used as a strategy to strengthen hope for better days? How can we transform art and poetry into sensitive care strategies for children? Based on these questions, we will go over the process, of creating *A Folk Tale to Lull the Thrush to Sleep* and seek to provide reflections on the following themes: dialogues between science and art; the importance of storytelling and poetry in facing the COVID-19 pandemic; and sensitive care practices for children.

Results and Discussion

For a better understanding of our report, we divided it into two reflective axes. In the first axis, we describe the constructive process of *A Folk Tale to Lull the Thrush to Sleep*. We go over our steps and the cocreative process. In the second axis, we seek to highlight our inferences, regarding the transdisciplinary dialogue between poetry and aesthetics in nursing as a mediator for changing paths as proposed by Edgar Morin in his book *It's Time to Change Paths: The Lessons of the Coronavirus*.

Axis I: A Folk Tale to Lull the Thrush to Sleep: Building a Path for Sensitive Care

We could start by saying that the initial sketch of the e-book originated from an inner dream, the result of a garden that germinated within our souls. Walking during the COVID-10 pandemic had become limited, and the beauty that once seemed to only exist in distant places started to be noticed everywhere. Searching for places of beauty and hope is an incentive for the future; it makes the present possible. Seeing different faces of the pandemic awakened dormant feelings and desires, which guided us in the direction of new meanings.

These meanings, which were once poetically described and narrated, evoked a regenerated humanism that connects human beings through different aspects—such as affective, mental, and cultural—and awakened us to the sublimity of art, aesthetics, care, and poetry (Morin). Morin invites us to regard the need to learn the imperatives of personal reform to practise a regenerated humanism. He emphasizes that it is necessary to "live according to the poetic need for love, communion and aesthetic enchantment" (Morin 86).

In this way, we sought out possibilities to care for children, and from this desire emerged a poem written for children that addresses the events that marked the period of the COVID-19 pandemic between March 2020 and June 2021. The short e-book aims to lull children to sleep with a short tale of hope; it emphasizes that despite adversities, it is necessary to keep dreaming. The e-book was developed for children four to eight years old.

The choice of the e-book's title was inspired by the poetry of Manoel de Barros, when he said: "I have a candor for nonsense, when I grow up, I'll be a child. Those who decorate the blue of the morning are the thrushes" (389). Thus, from a desire for new dawns for children and for mornings of hope, the title was born: *A Folk Tale to Lull the Thrush to Sleep.* The thrush is a bird that lives naturally in several states of Brazil, including in the northeast region. It has a sweet and soft birdsong that is much admired, and for this reason, it is constantly present in poetic texts in which it has the ability, through its melody, to make the dawn and dusk more beautiful. Furthermore, children, as subjects, have the potential to transform and change the future as distributors of hope and, at the same time, to fulfill their destinies; thus, the thrush is the child who needs to hear this short tale of hope.

The e-book (Appendix 1, Figure 1) has only one illustration so far—the cover, which is permeated with meanings and represents Northeast Brazil, evidenced by the woodcut of the cordel, a folk, and the surrounding typical plants of the wild Northeast hinterland. The child, on the cover, is Black with a gentle face and wears a cangaceiro hat. He is held by the ribbons of Senhor do Bonfim, an amulet, that symbolize faith, spirituality, and hope. It is an artifact used by people living in the northeast of Brazil, who carries him along to live in that moment of beauty with a view to a future of hope and dreams. The choice of the representation of the woodcut on the cover of the e-book refers to the traditional aesthetics of cordel folk literature, in addition to valuing Northeast culture and Brazilian folklore using visual elements characteristic of the region, such as the typical vegetation and the simplicity of the country houses present in the scenario as well as the clothes worn by the character. In general, the elements represented in the illustration—such as the cangaceiro hat, leather sandals, cactus, starry sky, and Senhor do Bonfim ribbons—work to contextualize the story and represent valued aspects of Northeast culture. The presence of woodcuts in cordel literature is a striking feature. These forms of printing illustrate the pamphlets and dialogue with the text of the poetry. Not only do they increase the aesthetic value, but they also help condense the verses through the images, allowing for the freedom to interpret them.

Based on the relationship between the cordel tale and the woodcut, the purpose of the illustrated cover was to approach this aesthetic, seeking to use more blocky and less defined shapes, with little proportion, given that woodcuts have these characteristics. This also reinforces the playfulness of the scenario and character by not only allowing the children to feel represented but also permitting them to expand their imagination, travel in the story verses, and believe in the unpredictable.

The woodcut has only one background colour and the outline of the drawing is mostly black. In this way, we used an orange tone for the background and black as the outline. Our intention in colouring the Senhor do Bonfim ribbons was to demonstrate the characteristics that they have, due to the diversity of the colours and the meaning each one has. For the cangaceiro hat, a shade of brown was chosen due to the colour of the leather, which is a raw material commonly used in the northeast region.

In general, a picture can be used in many ways and carries a lot of importance when it comes to representing stories. Therefore, our intention in using this illustration technique on the cover of the e-book was to place the viewer in the story that will be told, value the elements of a specific culture, and propose playfulness within the verses.

For the textual and versed construction of the e-book (Appendix 1, Figures 2, 3, and 4), we used themes from two poems by Northeast poets. The first is entitled "Sabiá" ("Thrush") by Luiz Gonzaga, a singer and poet from Pernambuco, and the second theme is the poem, "A esperança" ("Hope") by Augusto dos Anjos, a poet from Paraíba (Côrtes, 197; Silva Filho and Melo 92). In this way, our starting point for the elaboration of the e-book verses was the already existing small excerpts/verses of the aforementioned poems, which are known in Brazil (Sautchuk 171). The versed text recalls early events of the pandemic and emphasises how social distancing interfered with the routine of children throughout the world; the text also shows ways of coping through remaining hopeful, represented by the experiences of Italian children and their phrase "andra tutto bene" ("everything will be fine").

The e-book tries to encourage hope and resilience among children and caregivers worldwide, establishing through verse, a community network with the perspective of restoring positive feelings by reestablishing the incentive to play and imagine through the use of supports that promote spirituality and beauty, which can help everyone face the current crisis. By highlighting the experiences of other children in the world and showing painting and drawing strategies, the e-book promotes creativity and healthy entertainment.

The verses of the e-book also bring children closer to the different realities of suffering; they encourage them to experience and remember feelings related to loss and longing and emphasise the need to ensure that love and hope are perennial guests in the dwellings of their hearts.

Therefore, the e-book, which looks to provide sensitive care to children during difficult times, in the end helps us to have "hope not in the best of worlds, but in a better world" (Morin 30).

Axis II: A Glimmer of Hope from the Perspective of Edgar Morin: Dialogue between Poetry and Aesthetics in Nursing for the Construction of Sensitive Care

The domains of beauty and sensitivity are presented by Morin in his book *It's Time to Change Paths: The Lessons of The Coronavirus* as a proposal for a new politics of civilization. The book is described as a means of making people feel happy, regenerating humanism, and increasing the quality of life. In the book, these themes are divided into three chapters: 15 Lessons from the Coronavirus, Post-Corona Challenges, and The Need to Change Paths (Morin 9).

The third chapter indicates that one way to recover life and strengthen "human resilience is the recognition of the need to reestablish poetic living, inspired by love, communion and aesthetic enchantment" (Morin 86). Furthermore, Morin invites us to practise sensitive and complex reasoning in relation to everything that affects human beings so that love directs our rationality and favours a collaborative destiny between human beings in different dimensions.

In the context of nursing, the search for new paths of humanity is to expand the possibilities of actions to provide support so that sensitive care can integrate these initiatives from its perception. Being aware of socioenvironmental relationships influences the aesthetic field and aligns with the subjectivity of each person (Teixeira 93). Sensitive care draws on delicate and complex motivations that affect professional actions, and through these efforts, it becomes possible to access elements of human wellness that are difficult to perceive in the context of care. It is not limited to physical illness; it also covers the subjectivity of emotions in their contexts, being, above all, diligently attentive to human needs (Pereira et al 363; Morin 87). Morin reminds us of the need to develop the ability to be altruistic (44). Altruism refers to human actions that help others. In the professional scenario, altruism places the nurse in an interconnected network with others to promote solidarity, benevolence, and understanding. This human consciousness can awaken us to the restoration of humanism in professional action based on the assumption that it is a way to build a better future that begins with actions taken today. Altruism, with a transdisciplinary dialogue, must be an integral part of nursing to meet the complex needs of human beings.

Sensitive care is informed by a sensitive reason, which leads to creativity in the context of nursing (Pereira et al., 361). We consider *A Folk Tale to Lull the Thrush to Sleep* as a tool to make children more hopeful during difficult times, including the COVID-19 pandemic.

The verses of the e-book were constructed from a dialogue between science, art, and poetry, and they aim to expand the possibilities of facing the COVID-19 pandemic for children. Thus, poetry becomes a powerful mediator for strengthening bonds between children and caregivers as well as allowing for the sharing of hopeful verses.

In this way, nursing care is based on three pillars: art (creativity, aesthetics), ethics (respect, understanding), and science (knowledge, research). Consequently, care is promoted, which improves the quality of life and contributes to human dignity (Santos et al. 24). These pillars were considered when we thought about writing the e-book because they unite drawing, poetry, beauty, and playfulness in understanding that the child is a subject of rights and dignity disseminating important information. Moreover, this e-book corroborates the indispensable mission of sensitive care, which is to find meanings in context and in people to enable creative communication between nurses and children. In addition, the e-book also contributes to children's right to beauty, as presented by the Brazilian National Plan for Early Childhood, which highlights the urgent need to offer children aesthetical and emotional experiences through contact with reading, art, and poetry (Rnpi 206). Sensitive reason enables nurses to fully observe the other in their context. Therefore, sensitive care, under the aegis of sensitive reason, allows us as professionals to have the ability to establish a connection with the reality around us, without neglecting emotion and appearance, since these are constituent elements of human beings (Erdtmann and Erdmann 525). Thus, we can see that the e-book works as a sensitive care tool for children, as living through the COVID-19 pandemic has had direct repercussions on children's growth and development, and these needs should be observed in the professional practice of nurses. Morin, from his perspective, argues that nurses can contribute to the establishment of a new path and a new way to care—offering a true glimmer of hope.

This hope can communicate to children the arrival of a new time: a time to play and a time to believe that dreams can come flying on the wings of hope, despite everything. Certainly, this short e-book also represents a new place to reflect on other ways to provide nursing care to children.

Final Considerations

Through verse, we connect children with their realities. The events described in the story will allow hope to appear in different environments and contexts. We announce the arrival of better days that need to be shared between children and their caregivers during moments of adversity, including the COVID-19 pandemic. The e-book will make it possible to visualize better days for humanity, especially for children.

Offering accessible information about the COVID-19 pandemic, without ignoring what children think and feel, is an appropriate way to reduce feelings of anxiety, fear, sadness, and anger. Storytelling allows us to discuss these issues with children in a playful and sensitive way. Therefore, it is necessary to direct and create methods of sensitive care for children, especially in this context of adversity, so that they can share their thoughts about the pandemic and feel understood.

In their book *The Path of Hope*, Hessel and Morin describe that "The world is both wonderful and horrible. Aesthetics help us to marvel and allows us to face the horror" (53). In this way, aesthetics awaken us to the beauty present in each moment but recognize the existence of beautiful days. Every day, whether difficult or easy, it is necessary to live. Certainly, the writings of Morin and Hessel show us the essential role of literature as an aesthetic vehicle that promotes poetic living; it allows for the discovery and understanding of everyday processes, as literature can create meanings that will lead us through life.

While aiming for a moment of beauty, we have combined art and poetry and used them for childcare strategies. We believe that drawings and storytelling are powerful tools to introduce aesthetics in the context of nursing care. However, it is important to emphasize that the pandemic demanded an expansion of our care perspectives while constructing the e-book. We had to bring it close to the children's reality and instigate their imagination and hope that a better world would be possible with vaccination.

There is hope distributed through our thoughts, echoed through us and the children, in the form of a song, that of a thrush, which allows us to believe in the potential of small details and in the sublime strength of the sensitive in the context of care.

Works Cited

Araújo, Liubiana Arantes de, et al. "The Potential Impact of the COVID-19 Pandemic on Child Growth and Development: A Systematic Review." *Jornal de Pediatria*, vol. 97, no. 4, 2021, pp. 369-77.

Assis, Marluce Maria Araújo, et al. "Cuidado integral em saúde: dilemas e desafios da Enfermagem." *Rev Bras Enferm.*, vol. 68, no. 2, 2015, pp. 333-38.

Barros, Manoel de. *Tratado Geral das Grandezas do* ínfimo. Leya, 2013.

Cabral, Ivone Evangelista, et al. "Child Health Vulnerabilities during the COVID-19 Pandemic in Brazil and Portugal." *Rev. Latino-Am. Enfermagem*, vol. 29, no.1, 2021, pp. 1-11.

Côrtes, Almir. "Como se toca o oron: combinações de elementos musicais no repertório de Luiz Gonzaga." *Per Musi*, vol. 1, no. 29, 2014, pp. 195-208.

Cluver, Lucie, et al. "Parenting in a Time of COVID-19." *The Lancet*, 2020, www.thelancet.com/action/showPdf?pii=S0140-6736%2820%2930736-4. Accessed 28 Feb. 2023.

Erdtmann, Bernardette Kreutz, and Alacoque Lorenzini Erdmann. "O modelo do sol nascente e razão sensível na enfermagem." *Rev Bras Enferm*, vol. 56, no. 5, 2003, pp. 523-27.

Holliday, Oscar Jara. *Para sistematizar experiências*. MMA, 2006.

Linhares, Maria Beatriz Martins, and Sônia Regina Fiorim Enumo. "Reflexões baseadas na Psicologia sobre efeitos da pandemia COVID-19 no desenvolvimento infantil." *Estudos de Psicologia (Campinas)*, vol. 3, no. 7, 2020, pp. 1-14.

Morin, Edgar. *Introdução ao pensamento complexo*. 3.ed.Porto Alegre: Sulina, 2007.

Morin, Edgar. "Podemos não chegar ao melhor dos mundos, mas a um mundo melhor: entrevista com Edgar Morin." *Instituto Humanitas UNISINOS*, Seção Notícias, 2011, www.ihu.unisinos.br/173-noticias/

noticias-2011/46082-podemos-nao-chegar-ao-melhor-dos-mundos-mas-a-um-mundo-melhor-entrevista-com-edgar-morin. Accessed 28 Feb. 2023.

Morin, Edgar. É hora de *mudarmos de via: Lições do Coronavirus*. Bertrand Brasil, 2021.

Morin, Edgar, and Stephane Hessel. *O caminho da esperança*. Bertrand Brasil, 2012.

Pereira, Alváro, et al. "Retomando as abordagens do cuidado sensível." *Rev. Enfermería Global*, vol. 25, 2012, pp. 356-66.

Santos, I et al. "Caring: Building a New History of Sensibility." *Braz J Nurs.*, vol. 1, no. 3, 2002, pp. 18-26.

Silva Filho, Francisco Bento da, and Symone Fernandes de Melo. "In the Shadow of a Dialogue: Heidegger and the Poetry of Augusto dos Anjos." *Phenomenological Studies – Revista da Abordagem Gestáltica*, vol. 26, no. 1, 2020, pp. 90-97.

Sautchuk, João Miguel Manzolillo. "A poética cantada: investigação das habilidades do repentista nordestino." *Estud. Lit. Bras. Contemp.*, vol. 35, 2010, pp. 167-82.

Teixeira, Enéas Rangel. "O ético e o estético nas relações de cuidado em enfermagem." *Texto Contexto Enferm.*, vol. 14, no. 1, 2005, pp. 89-95.

Appendix 1

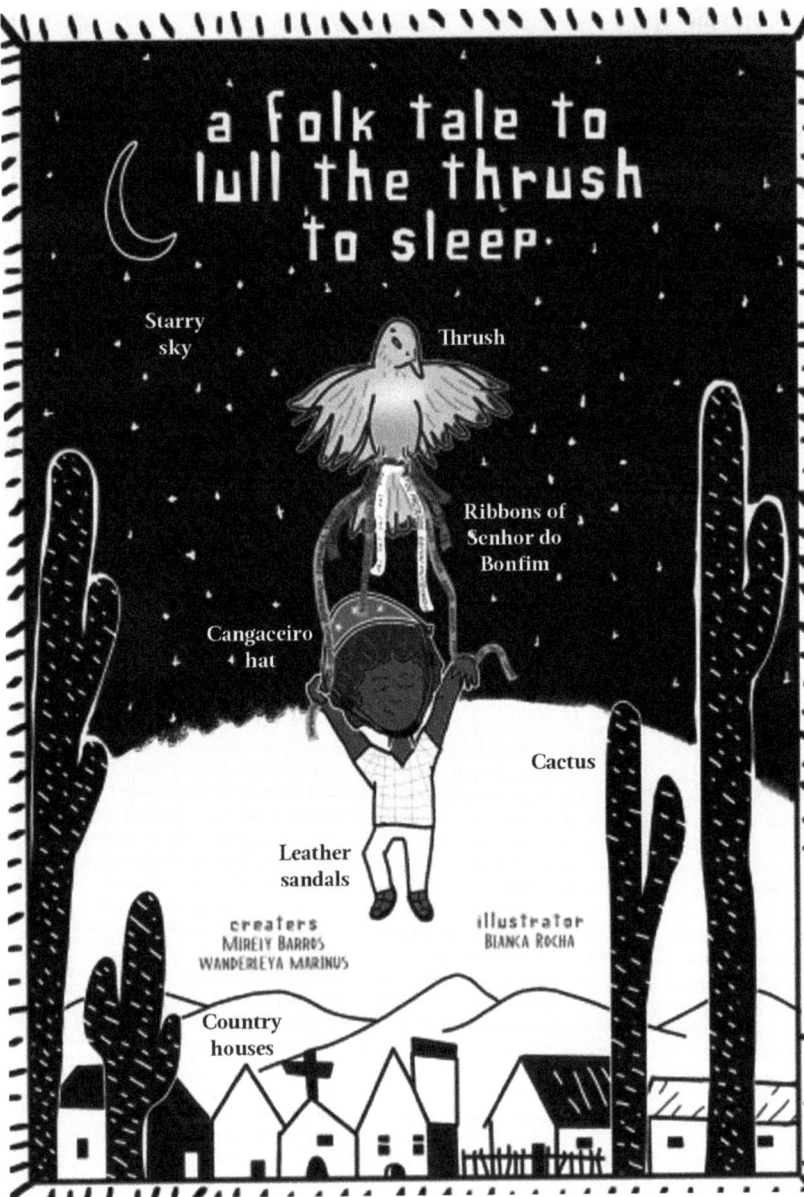

Figure 1.

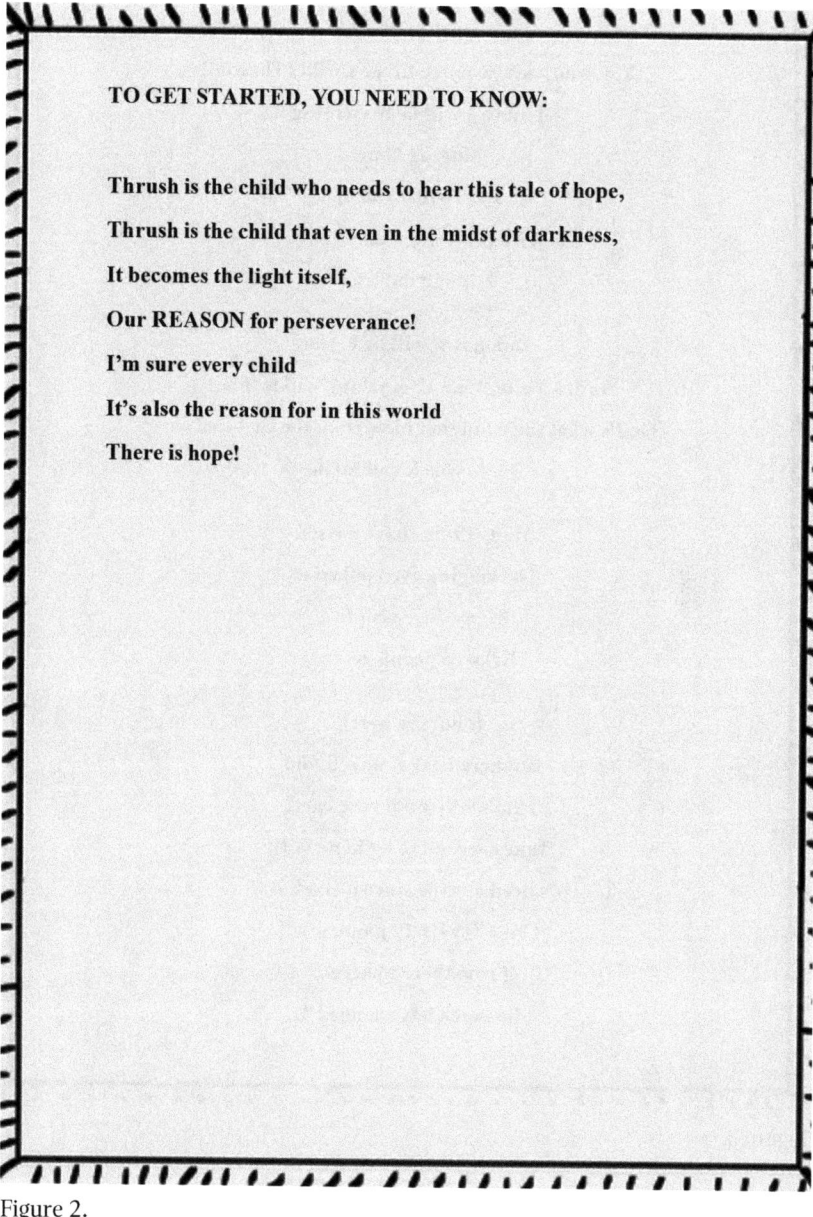

Figure 2.

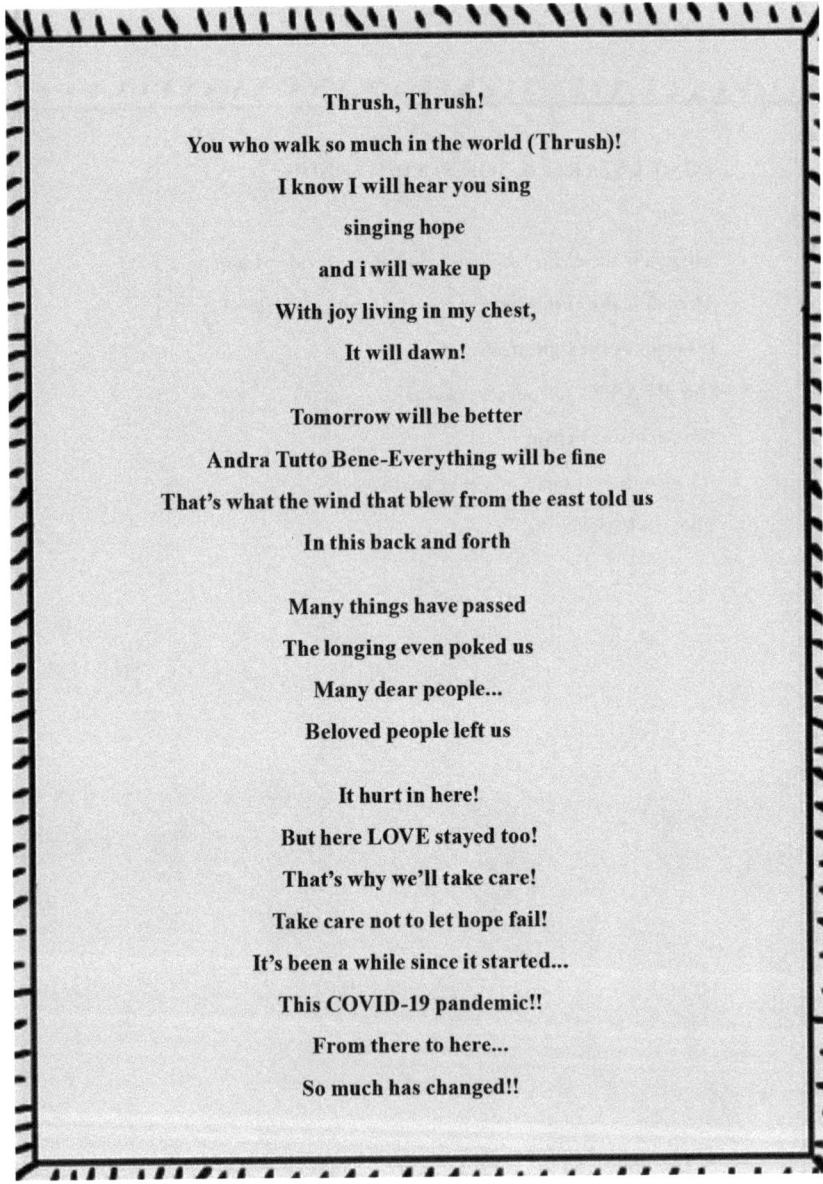

Figure 3.

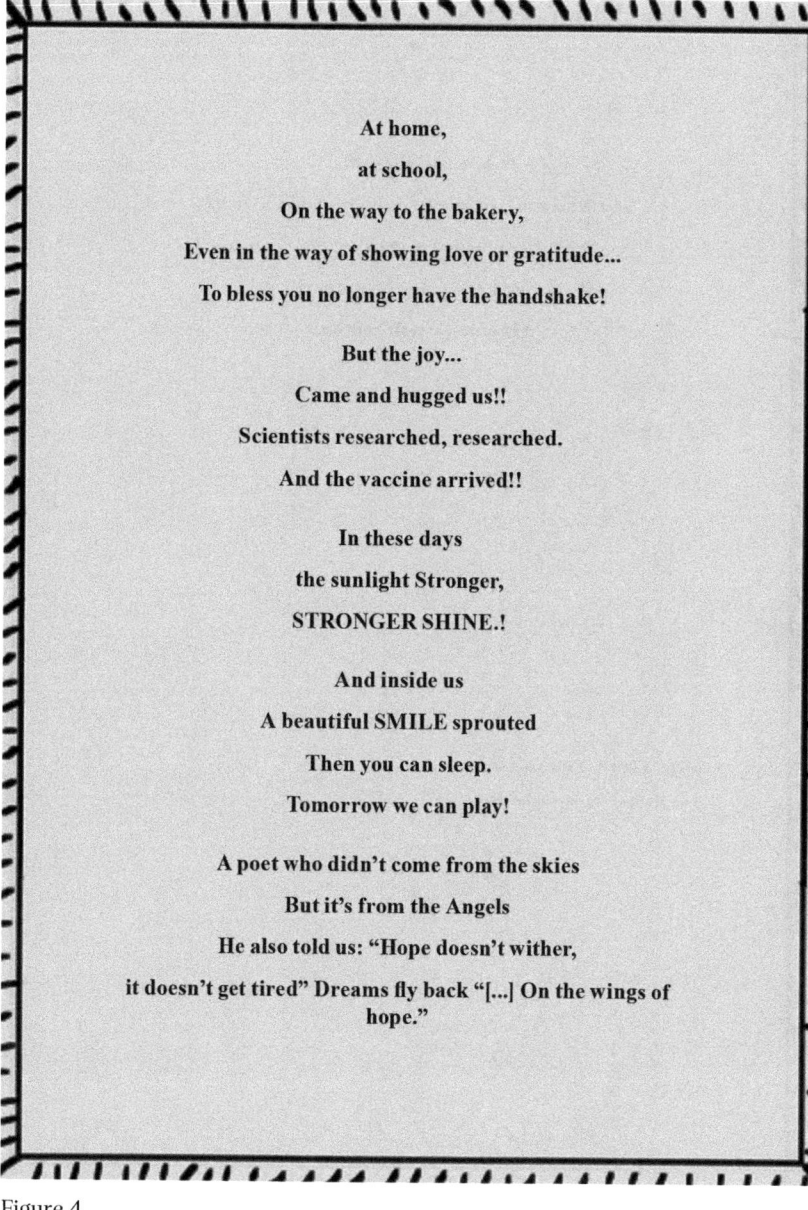

Figure 4.

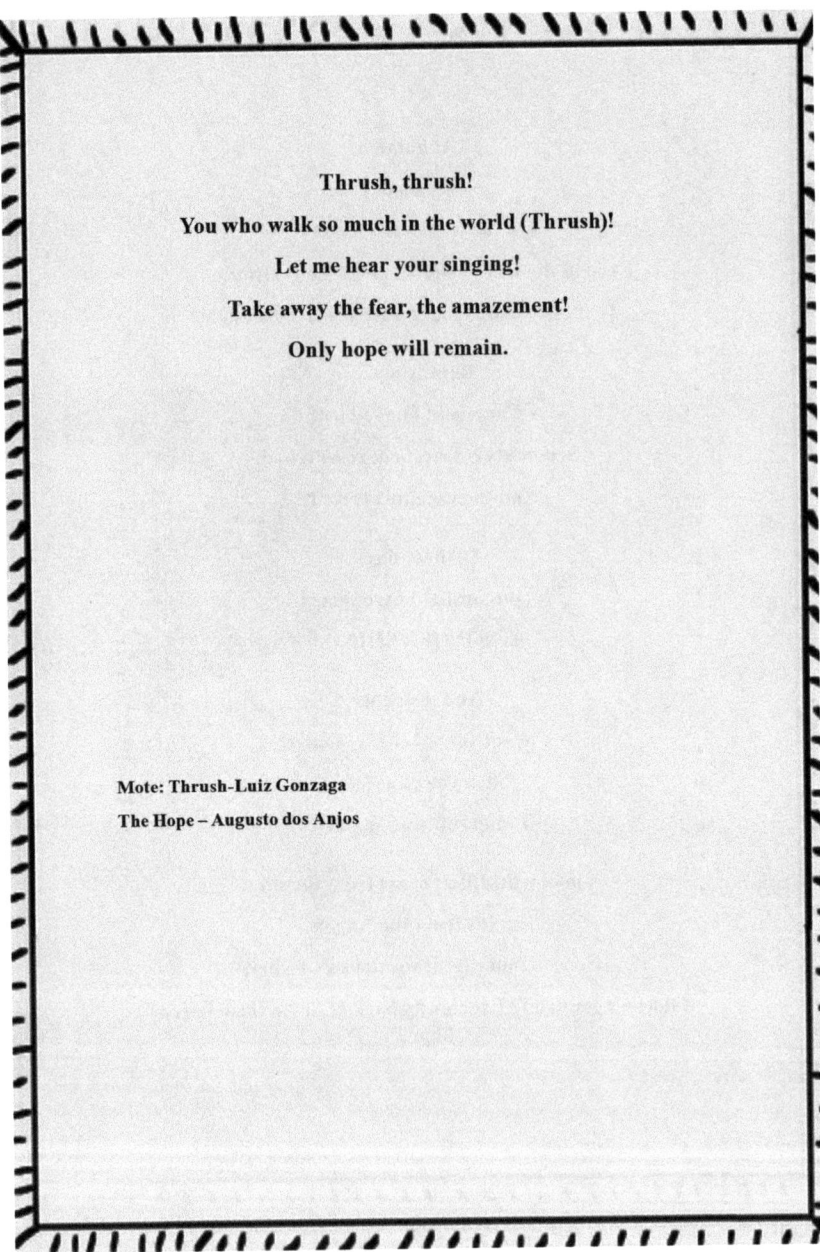

Figure 5.

Chapter 13.

Emotional Support and Academic Expectations: How to Balance It During and After the Pandemic

Ronald Stolberg and Darlene Sweetland

A Recent Case Example from Our Family Therapy Practice

After hearing for the first time how much his son was struggling while in family therapy, a parent said, "I know you say you are depressed." Five minutes later, the parent said, "You are still grounded until you get that math grade up to a B." This was a precalculus class taught online with a technologically anxious instructor.

Parents, teachers, and students have struggled to find the balance between maintaining high academic standards during a time where more children than ever are experiencing mental health struggles. The COVID-19 pandemic has resulted in more academic gaps than at any time we can remember because of the interruption to learning due to various challenges (e.g., distance learning, long-term substitutes, medical issues, financial stress, and personal loss). We hope to help parents and educators explore the important balance between maintaining longstanding traditional academic standards and supporting the mental health struggles of children during this crisis. Specifically, we propose actions that parents, caregivers, and educators can implement to directly improve the mental health of kids in their care. For parents and care-givers, we explore the utility of setting reasonable expectations, rewarding the process rather than the product, and practising self-care behaviour. For educators and school administrators, we offer suggestions for modelling emotion regulation, teaching specific skills in the classroom, and the importance of setting specific goals.

Educators and families are doing their best to make the educational experience a positive one. Yet we hear so much frustration on both sides. Most teachers were never adequately taught how to deliver their curriculum on a digital platform, and few students found it to be an equivalent experience. Remember, none of us were prepared for what our children's education turned into. Some of the more "tech savvy" teachers had an easier time with the transition, but many teachers and school districts never embraced the change. It was the same in family homes. Some had the set up for technology and many rooms to make it work. Yet others struggled with internet connection as well as finding room for everyone to do their work and caregivers available to supervise their children. It was sometimes just a struggle to make sure the children were in front of the screen.

Children missed out on a lot. There is no denying it. First, most of us underestimated the importance of school being the primary source of social interactions for children. For most, their days had been structured and contained. Five days a week in a structured classroom with predictable routines, expectations, and social engagement followed by extracurricular activities were the norm. These are all inherently social activities. School is where their friends are, and it is therefore where they practise making friends, learn cooperative interactions, and figure out conflict resolution. That was essentially impossible to replace during online learning sessions and has been altered for many in the aftermath of the pandemic. Another issue discovered during the pandemic is how difficult it is to support children at home when they are engaged in online learning. We learned how hard it is to be a home teacher, especially if parents and caregivers have multiple children in different grades and schools, or if they have to work. Finally, schools, teachers, and school districts all seem to have taken different approaches resulting in little consistency. Children thrive on consistency, predictability, and the familiar. School no longer provided this anchor.

One middle-school counsellor we spoke with shared that her school has never had the dramatic range in grade-based competencies that they are experiencing in the classroom this year. This results in some of the students being at or above the expected grade level on a particular topic and more students than ever falling drastically below the expectation. She theorized that some parents were fortunate to be able to supplement their child's education during the distance learning periods by utilizing tutors, learning pods, or by simply spending a lot of time becoming their children's home teacher. Other families were stretched thin and did not have the time, financial resources, or family stability to participate in the supplemental support. There was a disparity. The counsellor shared that it was hard to predict ahead of time, but some kids seemed to do well with distance learning, and others really suffered.

A high school English teacher told us that in a typical semester, he has one or two students who fail to engage with the coursework and seem to be too overwhelmed with outside issues to benefit from the course. He shared that since his students returned to in-school learning, it is common to have five to ten students that simply do not do any work. This shows us that there is not only an academic impact of the pandemic but an emotional one as well.

We found the frustration with technology, loss of structure and routine, limits to the benefits of everyday social engagement with peers, and inconsistent academic expectations from the school have had a significant impact on many children's development and mental health.

US Surgeon General Issues Advisory on the Youth Mental Health Crisis

On December 7, 2021, after nearly two years of the pandemic, the US Surgeon General, Dr. Vivek Murthy, issued a new advisory to highlight the urgent need to address the nation's youth mental health crisis. The US Surgeon General's Advisory on Protecting Youth Mental Health outlines the pandemic's unprecedented impact on the mental health of youth and families in the US.

According to the advisory, the pandemic added to the preexisting challenges that these youth faced:

It [the pandemic] disrupted the lives of children and adolescents, such as in-person schooling, in-person social opportunities with peers and mentors, access to health care and social services, food, housing, and the health of their caregivers. The pandemic's negative impacts most heavily affected those who were vulnerable to begin with, such as youth with disabilities, racial and ethnic minorities, LGBTQ+ youth, low-income youth, youth in rural areas, youth in immigrant households, youth involved with the child welfare or juvenile justice systems, and homeless youth. (Surgeon General).

Similarly, in the fall of 2021, a coalition of the nation's leading experts in paediatric health declared a national emergency in child and adolescent mental health:

The pandemic has struck at the safety and stability of families. More than 140,000 children in the United States lost a primary and/or secondary caregiver, with youth of color disproportionately impacted. We are caring for young people with soaring rates of depression, anxiety, trauma, loneliness, and suicidality that will have lasting impacts on them, their families, and their communities. We must identify strategies to meet these challenges through innovation and action, using state, local and national approaches to improve the access to and quality of care across the continuum of mental health promotion, prevention, and treatment (American Academy of Pediatrics).

The Data Support Our Concern

The pandemic has dramatically affected children and teens. According to the Centers for Disease Control (CDC) and the US Surgeon General Youth Mental Health Advisory, symptoms of depression and anxiety have doubled during the pandemic. The data show that 25 per cent of youth have experienced symptoms of depression, and 20 per cent have experienced symptoms of anxiety during the pandemic.

Since the start of the pandemic, hospitals have also seen a noticeable increase in mental health emergencies among children. Between March and October 2020, the percentage of emergency department visits for those with mental health emergencies rose by 24 per cent for children ages five to eleven and 31 per cent for children ages twelve to seventeen. The American Academy of Pediatrics reports that visits to emergency rooms for suspected suicide attempts increased during the pandemic for all youth but with a dramatic 51 per cent increase in suicide attempts for girls.

What Can Parents and Caregivers Do?

Many of us believed that this crisis would pass quickly and that we could weather the storm with just a few temporary sacrifices. The truth, however, is that the longstanding nature of the pandemic has taken its toll. Parents and educators often ask us for suggestions on things they can do to build skills such as academic excellence, resiliency, self-esteem, and confidence. We want this chapter to be solution focussed rather than a retrospective review of the reasons children are struggling. The following pages will provide strategies for parents and educators alike.

An effective and nurturing parent or caregiver has a clear sense of purpose. One goal when raising a student is to encourage academic growth and learning while building self-esteem and confidence. There are a lot of pressures to push students to meet high academic standards. Even during the pandemic, students have been looking forward to and applying for college. That is still on the minds of many high school families. Those pressures have not stopped. The following are strategies that might help parents and their children balance high academic goals while maintaining and strengthening their mental health and resiliency.

Set Reasonable Expectations

Maybe "straight As" was the goal that you hoped for your children. Very few students get a 4.0 GPA every semester. Honestly, most parents we work with say that they just want their child to do their best, but like the example above, they follow it up with "What can you do to get an A?" or "What did you miss?" Students tell us they hear this as "You didn't do good enough." All students have academic strengths and weaknesses that help them in some classes and make others more challenging. When you set reasonable goals with your children, and then they achieve them, you all feel a sense of pride. However, when you set lofty goals, and your child does not meet them, they feel down on themselves—even if they gave a great effort and worked close to their top ability. The objective, especially following a pandemic, is to build self-esteem and confidence by achieving reasonable goals.

Reward the Process Not the Product

We have all heard about rewarding good grades. Maybe it is money for A's or special treats for a great report card. Instead, consider rewarding your child's effort rather than the letter grade. By rewarding how hard they worked, you are reinforcing that work habit. We want to teach that extra time and effort are the goals and that should be celebrated. When the focus is on the grade or outcome, this important message is missed.

Practise Your Own Self-Care

Parenting is a difficult job. It is important to make sure you are caring for yourself. Just like when you fly in an airplane, if anything goes wrong, you need to give yourself oxygen first; otherwise, you cannot care for your children. The following examples of self-care practices are just a few of the many ways to take some steps to care for yourself. With proper self-care, you are more likely to be effectively available to your family and promote mental health for yourself. To start, it is back to the basics.

- **Sleep.** Healthy sleep is vital to your overall health. It rejuvenates you and gives you the ability to focus and concentrate on important tasks. Try to avoid eating and consuming caffeine right before going to bed as that can impact your ability to fall asleep.

- **Nutrition.** Maybe it is too much starch or not enough vegetables. Maybe you just generally do not eat enough. Either way, a healthy diet is associated with lower stress levels and a decreased risk of depressive symptoms. Do not leave out the nutritional foods needed to nourish and balance your body. Eating natural foods, including plants, fruits, vegetables, whole grains, seeds, nuts, and lean proteins can positively impact your mental health.

- **Make Sure to Stay Active.** Setting aside time in your schedule a few times a week for exercise can do wonders to your overall health. Luckily, it does not really matter what kinds of things you do, as any activity and movement are beneficial. Exercise promotes all kinds of changes in the brain, including neural growth, reduced inflammation, and new activity patterns that promote feelings of calm and wellbeing. Before beginning any new rigorous exercise regimens, please consult your physician.

- **Decrease Your Caffeine and Alcohol Consumption.** You may think you need caffeine to keep you focused or to stay awake, but caffeine has been proven to negatively affect anxiety symptoms. A cup of coffee or an energy drink should not be a problem, but when you have too much of anything, it can become harmful.

The statistics shared earlier in this chapter illustrate that children are dealing with more stress and anxiety than ever before. In addition to the pandemic, there are two main reasons for this. First, children are growing up in a fast-paced society with advanced technology that provides instant access to information. Instant gratification has become a way of life. Children of this generation are so accustomed to getting things immediately that they can become easily frustrated, and even anxious, when asked to wait or have something unsettled. A way to increase self-esteem and educational achievements is to reduce anxiety, which is a state of uneasiness and apprehension about future uncertainties. In other words, anxiety often occurs when a person does not know what will happen next. If the pandemic has taught us anything, it is that we have little control over what comes next.

In today's culture of raising children, there is a lot of pressure to provide them with every advantage to get ahead. There is more academic, extracurricular, and social pressure for children now than with past generations. Parents and children hear consistently how hard it is to get into a good college, and the pressure is on them to do more and do it better. This causes tremendous anxiety for children and teens. Here are some ways parents can help their children build the skills to reduce these pressures.

One of the most common mistakes that parents make is failing to recognize the difference between supporting their children and rescuing them. When parents rescue their children from a conflict, they are doing it for them. By contrast, when parents support their children in solving the problem independently, they are encouraging the process of critical thinking and frustration tolerance. When children work to identify solutions on their own, they use problem solving, social skills, and planning while at the same time learning to tolerate the discomfort that comes from not feeling sure about the resolution. This builds resilience and confidence. This process is an essential practise for children and teens, and it is lost when they are rescued.

Children of this generation are so accustomed to getting things immediately that they can become easily frustrated, and even anxious, when asked to wait. Parents can increase confidence in their children by teaching them to tolerate waiting. Parents have the added challenge of raising children in the instant gratification generation. This generation of children and teens has little need to wait for anything, from on-demand movies and television shows to smart phones, texting, and social media. They have instant access to information in almost all aspects of their lives. To compound the issue, parents have also become accustomed to this pace, which often translates into quickly responding to their children's requests and desires, which results in a lot of anxiety when children are required to work out a problem without having a solution right away. The best solution is to build in waiting for things from an early age. Try not to drop everything to respond to the requests or needs of your children immediately You might say, "Give me just a moment, I have to finish this task and then, I would be happy to help you figure out what to have for lunch."

The best way to increase confidence in children is allowing them to develop the skills to have patience and consider resolutions to a problem when it arises. One of the best gifts parents can give their children is to allow them to fix mistakes on their own. Parents will often tell their children: "It is okay to make mistakes. Everyone makes mistakes." However, that message is meaningless unless the children are allowed to fix their mistakes themselves. If a child makes a mistake and a parent jumps in to fix it, it leaves the child feeling upset and possibly shamed. But if the child fixes the mistake themselves, it fosters pride and confidence. It also reduces the fear of making future mistakes, which is inevitable.

It is important for parents to recognize that children of this generation tend to lead scheduled lives, leaving minimal time for the child to independently figure out what to do with unstructured, unplanned time away from the watchful eye of an adult. To help children develop confidence is to allow them the independence to plan, organize, and improvise when they are given unstructured time. Yet that experience is important in developing confidence, particularly as they prepare for their independent life or college. Children and teens need the freedom to make decisions, deal with unexpected outcomes, practise social skills, and make mistakes on their own. Part of the process is making errors of judgment and figuring out what to do about them. This instills knowledge and confidence that children can deal with future unexpected mistakes or outcomes on their own.

For Educators and School Administrators

The pandemic has been difficult for all of us, but educators and school administrators have received an unfair amount of stress and criticism. We usually think of firefighters, police officers or anyone in the medical profession as being frontline critical workers. If parents have learned anything over the past two years, it is that teachers are critical to the wellbeing of our children and that educating children is more difficult than many of us outside the classroom knew. Despite this new awareness, many teachers have been unfairly blamed by parents for many of the problems our children are experiencing today.

Many parents forgot that everyone working at a school was also dealing with their own various problems related to the pandemic. Educators we spoke with have felt overwhelmed, stressed, anxious, and underappreciated. They are expected to be present and resilient, but it is hard to do if you are worn out, underappreciated, and feel unsupported.

The following are a few ideas for improving self-regulation skills in your classroom and school. Self-regulation is the ability to think about your long-term best interests, so you can calm your emotional reaction when you are upset, and allows you to refocus when you are sad. Students often lack the self-regulation skills to always act appropriately, just like us. You may notice that children who fail to self-regulate find it difficult to make and keep friends, interact with others in a positive manner, organize their schoolwork, and appropriately express their emotions. With all the unpredictability during the past couple of years, students have had a lot of strong emotions.

Model Self-Regulation

Share with your students your feelings to make a point. Give them examples about controlling their mood and emotions as well as communicating their own feelings.

- "Everyone, your difficulty in transitioning to reading is frustrating for me because we have worked on it for a long time. Let's refocus and try again."
- "I am not sure how to respond to this, so I am going to take a moment to breathe and think about how to respond. Please give me a moment."

Design Lessons Based on Self-Awareness.

- Teach students how to name their feelings (feeling charts).
- Role play ways to manage and express big feelings during a nonemotional time. It's too late once the emotions take over.
- Help them identify which body parts give them their first warning that they are becoming so angry that they might not be able to control their emotions, such as clenched fists, nervous shaking, sweating, tense shoulders, heart racing. Share your own warning signs.

Teach Specific Skills

- STOP: Stop, think, organize a solution, then proceed.
- Breathing exercises/deep breathing techniques are a great way to relax a classroom and teach self-regulation skills, especially when at the stop step in STOP
- Counting to ten. This is when you count to ten before reacting. The goal is to learn to delay an impulsive reaction. This is great to promote the think.
- Create some space/walk away. This is hard to implement in a classroom but should be rewarded rather than punished. This is needed to organize a solution.

Help Students Recognize When They Do It Right

- Reward positive coping skills and instances of self-regulation. If you see it, point it out, restate what they did correctly, and congratulate/thank/reward them. Remember, they may not know that they utilized a positive skill, but they will like the positive attention.
- Always reward a student for repairing a mistake when they make it.

Personal Timeouts (PTOs)

- If your school or setting supports it, these are a great way to avoid dysregulated mood, classroom disruptions, and bigger problems.
- It rewards self-awareness and reduces big consequences.
- You need to be careful not to let it become manipulative.

Extra Attention

- If there are a few students who need extra practise, try to find time to do small group or individual meetings that feel like special time not punishment.
- Use this time to review strategies and build self-esteem.

Goal Setting Theory

- Teach students how to set goals and help them meet their goals. This builds self-esteem, trust, and a strong trusting relationship between student and teacher.
- Goals should be specific, written down, and be attainable. The smaller and easier steps, the better. "I want to be the best tennis player in the world" turns into manageable steps, such as eating better, practising, watching tennis on YouTube, and getting in better physical shape.

Remind Them of Their New Tool Kit

- Cue them when it is a good time to utilize a new skill.
- Feel free to suggest one of the new skills you know they have learned that might be a good fit for the situation.

- Point out that the skill is in their self-regulation tool kit and how it might help in this situation.

It Never Hurts to Do Mindfulness Exercises

- Teaching them how to calm their brain and body is a great skill to have.
- Mindfulness practise buys you a few minutes of a calm classroom which is always a good idea.
- You don't have to call it mindfulness if that is a trigger word in your school or with certain parents. You can call it "Relaxation Skills".

Summary

School was always difficult for our children, but today, it is even harder. The impact of the pandemic has caused havoc with our educational system and the mental health of some of our children. A parenting and educational approach that balances academic expectations with mental health is so important under the circumstances. Remember to set reasonable goals, reward the effort the children put forth rather than the letter grade they earn, and above all else, practise you own self-care to be the best parent and educator you can be during this incredibly stressful time in our lives. The suggestions, put forth in this chapter, were directed specifically to parents and educators but all the strategies, discussed, can be useful at home or at school. Remember, you are not likely to be able to implement all of the suggestions mentioned above. Start with a few of the ones that resonate with you and know that you have permission to start slowly and build your skills.

Works Cited

American Academy of Pediatrics (2021). A declaration from the American Academy of Pediatrics, American Academy of Child and Adolescent Psychiatry and Children's Hospital Association (2021). Retrieved from: https://www.aap.org/en/advocacy/child-and-adolescent-healthy-mental-development/aap-aacap-cha-declaration-of-a-national-emergency-in-child-and-adolescent-mental-health/

Center for Disease Control and Prevention (2022). COVID-19 Parental Resources Kit – Adolescence: Social, Emotional, and Mental Well-being of Adolescents during COVID-19. Retrieved from: https://www.cdc.gov/mentalhealth/stress-coping/parental-resources/adolescence/index.html

US Surgeon General (2021). Protecting Youth Mental Health: The US Surgeon General's Advisory (2021). Retrieved from: https://www.hhs.gov/sites/default/files/surgeon-general-youth-mental-health-advisory.pdf

Epilogue

Separateness and Connectedness in the Pandemic

Linda Rose Ennis

My final thoughts, in closing this collection, return to the separation-connection model that I introduced and discussed in previous collections. It mostly underscores the pandemic experience, which, as we know, has profoundly affected children and their families, especially adolescents. To reiterate, separateness-connectedness or the "distinction-union" structure is a kind of DNA-RNA of experience, whereby every micro moment or "cell" of experience is made of these moments, although either may be more dominant at any moment (Eigen). There is an intricate interaction between states of independence and dependence, which has clearly played out in the developmental crisis caused by the pandemic, although that balance differs depending on the circumstances and children involved. As Anthony Storr says: "Two opposing drives operate throughout life: the drive for companionship, love and everything else which brings us close to our fellow men and the drive toward being independent, separate and autonomous" (11).

In the precarious balance between isolation and connection that ensued during the pandemic during the early stages, these dynamics were felt most profoundly. Rather than an interplay of separateness and connectedness, the experience was an either-or situation, of being apart or together. This was demonstrated in the approach towards managing the pandemic—whether to focus on academic losses as opposed to children's emotional reactions to the pandemic experience, whether children should have vaccines or not; whether families should or should not visit grandparents, and whether COVID-19-exposed people should self-isolate or not. The focus on either/or thinking resulted in further stress, as the interconnectedness of being apart and together is an integral part of our human makeup.

This volume has addressed the impact of the pandemic on children through three sections: Thinking about Children during the Pandemic; How Children and Their Families Felt; and How We Helped Children Cope. The central issues in the first section included concepts of neoliberalism, individuality, and the lack of publicly funded services for mental health; the influences of technology and narratives of self-expression that lead to self-harm; family participation in the cognitive development of children with learning disabilities in the pandemic period; how attachment informs the COVID-19 pandemic experience; caregivers' actions during the pandemic; and the upside of separation and divorce, as it relates to mothering and co-parenting.

The next section examined how children and their families felt during the pandemic. Topics included the absence of grandparents and its impact on children; a feminist and class analysis of preexisting mental health challenges; mother-child interviews, in which dyads discuss problems specific to COVID-19, such as peer relationships and the perceived effects of social distancing; and how children and adolescents expressed their conflicted experiences in pandemic therapy.

The collection closed with the final chapters, which focused on how children became resilient during the pandemic, and looked forward to a post-pandemic time. The chapters, in this last section, included Anishinaabeg teachings used in one family, incorporating traditional knowledge, to allow culturally centered parenting to create a holistic way of living; a narrative examination of the shared parent-child pandemic experience; another narrative, accompanied by images in an e-book, created to offer children moments of beauty and hope for the current pandemic times in Brazil; and finding a reasonable balance between maintaining learning expectations and supporting children who are suffering from a personal crisis, by offering tips for building resilience at home and in the classroom.

We should examine why children's separation and disconnection from grandparents were so immensely traumatizing for children, grandparents, especially grandmothers, and their families, particularly at a time when we see "intensive grandmothering" in our society, which the pandemic suddenly and totally erased (Ennis). What needs to be additionally explored, related to the absence of grandparents, specifically the impact of absent grandmothers on children and mothers, first introduced in this collection (Kolosov, in volume), is the relationship between "intensive mothering" and "intensive grandmothering." "Intensive grandmothering" is an extension of "intensive mothering." Our society strongly encourages this method of parenting, and it has become accepted and expected, especially for mothers. During the pandemic, intensive mothering had been especially thrust upon mothers to the detriment of their careers. With the grandmothers out of the picture, what became apparent was the important caregiving role that they had often played, which was sorely missed. This absence took its toll on parents, especially mothers, and ultimately on children, who felt their parents' stress, as well as their own upset over the loss of caring grandparents, and missed their caring grandparents, which demonstrates the extent of gender ideology roles that are in place. Intensive mothering is such a heavy load to carry for mothers, that it, often conveniently, spills over to the grandmothers and will likely continue to do so, as anxiety around the pandemic subsides. For children, not seeing their grandparents or worrying that they would transmit the virus to their vulnerable loved ones, was enormously stressful for them.

Additionally, we have not even begun to understand the impact of the pandemic on babies, who were born into it, during it and lived through it, without any connection to other children or with other people outside of their immediate family. These children may experience some anxiety when they are, finally, exposed to others, and they may exhibit heightened separation anxiety when their parents return to work and leave them with a babysitter or in daycare for the first period of time. In addition, it may be difficult for COVID-19 babies to interact with other children if they are an only child and had spent so much time alone at home with their parents for this length of time. Alternatively, COVID-19 babies may fear other adults if they have not come into contact with any adults other than their parents. Having said that, many mothers enrolled their babies in online music and story-time classes and included them in Zoom calls with family and friends, which will help to ease the adjustment from pandemic life to a more normal one.

More work is also needed to explore the theoretical and practical implications of this collection, which will entail addressing the personal needs of parents and children, as well as the responsibility of society to support those needs during normal times and in times of crisis. Those changes will include socialized childcare; an improved and efficient medical system, challenging gender roles, flexible work schedules, and supports for children from low-income families, who may require computers, lunches, and daycare. There needs to be funding in the schools to train teachers to plan and implement online teaching to effectively engage children in situations when in-person learning is not possible. In addition, it is necessary to fund therapy, particularly play therapy, for younger children to communicate their concerns, in such trying times, as noted in this collection (see Gottschalk, Hurd, Jones, and Matlack). We need to hear, through the children's own voices, the extent of their feelings related to the pandemic experience. Perhaps, another volume should be completely devoted to children's feelings about living through such a challenging time and its long-term effects. Further studies should acknowledge that parental stress has greatly affected children, which further impacts children's emotional and intellectual capacities to manage a crisis. The future effects of the pandemic need to be addressed, as they relate to children's socio-emotional development while taking into account their and their parents' social position. As Colleen Russell-Rawlins, concurred recently, related to the impact of the pandemic on children's socio-emotional development:

> Although spending time with family is positive for the vast majority of students because of the social-emotional development, secure attachment, sense of security, love and belonging ... some of the challenges for some students will be the limited social interactions outside their family setting. Without school to attend in-person, or play dates with friends, kids missed out on games and co-operative learning ... some of the health and safety restrictions, which have been necessary—such as physical distancing and masking—have had some unintended consequences because they distort what kids see and hear, impacting oral language development of words and sounds, and could hinder kids' ability to read facial expressions to interpret feelings or meaning. (qtd. in the *Toronto Star*)

Are the kids alright? They were not, but with awareness and support, they, hopefully, will be.

Works Cited

Eigen, Michael. *Contact with the Depths*. Karnac Press, 2011.

Ennis, Linda. *After the Happily Ever After: Empowering Women and Mothers in Relationships*. Demeter Press, 2017.

Ennis, Linda. *Intensive Mothering: The Cultural Contradictions of Modern Motherhood*. Demeter Press, 2014.

Hays, Sharon. *The Cultural Contradictions of Motherhood*. Yale Press, 1996.

Storr. Anthony. *Solitude*. Wm Collins Sons, 1988.

Teotonio, Isabel, and Kristin Rushowy. "C Is for Catch-Up." *Toronto Star*, 21 June 2022, p. A16.

Notes on Contributors

Paloma Gonçalves Martins Acioly, MScN, RN, has eighteen years of experience in nursing. She coordinates an outpatient nursing clinic specializing in surgery, bronchoscopy, digestive endoscopy, and paediatric neurosurgery. She is a member of the Research and Studies Group on Comprehensive Child and Adolescent Health (NUPESICA) and is a senior specialist in neonatal and paediatric nursing, with an emphasis on nursing in child and adolescent surgical health.

Rosane Cordeiro Burla de Aguiar, PhD, MScN, RN, is an associate professor at the Fluminense Federal University (UFF), Aurora de Afonso Costa School of Nursing (EEAAC), Department of Maternal-Child and Psychiatric Nursing in Rio de Janeiro, Brazil. She teaches in undergraduate and graduate programs. She is a member of the Group of Research and Studies in Child and Adolescent Integral Health (NUPESICA). With nineteen years of experience, she is also a senior specialist in the field in paediatric nursing, with an emphasis on child and adolescent health.

Maria Ilk Nunes de Albuquerque is an associate professor, Department of Nursing, Federal University of Pernambuco (UFPE). She graduated in nursing from UFPE and has a master's in public health from the Health Sciences Center/UFPE and a PhD in social work from the Centre for Social and Applied Sciences at the Federal University of Pernambuco (CCSA/UFPE).

Weslla Karla Albuquerque is an adjunct professor in the area of nursing in collective health at the Nursing Department, the Health Sciences Centre (CCS), at the Federal University of Pernambuco (UFPE). Albuquerque has a master's in maternal and child health from IMIP and a doctorate in maternal and child health from IMIP.

Mirelly da Silva Barros is a nurse at the Federal University of Campina Grande (UFCG). She is a specialist in child health at the Institute of Integral Medicine (HDM/IMIP) and a specialist in the neonatal and paediatric intensive care unit at Faculdade Venda Nova do Imigrante (FAVENI). She is currently a master's student in the Postgraduate Program in Child and Adolescent Health (PPGSCA) at the Federal University of Pernambuco.

Renée E. Mazinegiizhigoo-kwe Bédard is of Anishinaabeg, Kanien'kehá:ka, and French Canadian ancestry. She is a member of Okikendawdt (Dokis First Nation). She holds a PhD from Trent University in Indigenous studies. She is currently an assistant professor at Western University in the Faculty of Education. Her areas of publication include practices of Anishinaabeg motherhood, maternal philosophy and spirituality, along with environmental issues, women's rights, Indigenous Elders, Anishin-aabeg artistic expressions, and Indigenous education.

Talita Mendes Bonfim is an undergraduate student in nursing at the Federal University of Pernambuco.

Rebecca Jaremko Bromwich is mom to four teens, a lawyer, a law teacher at Robson Hall Law School, and a law firm manager. She is thriving as a solo parent. She has practised as a member of the Ontario bar for approaching twenty years and has had a simultaneous academic career teaching and researching in legal and sociolegal programs.

Ethan S. Burrow is in the fourth grade, and his favorite colour is blue. His favorite animal has always been a penguin. His favorite season is summer because there is no school. He loves to read books by Jarrett Lerner and the *Dog Man* books written by Dav Pilkey. His favorite holiday is Christmas because of the time with family ... and the gifts! And his favorite thing about himself is his imagination.

Lauren E. Burrow is an associate professor of education studies at Stephen F. Austin State University. She is a MotherScholar of three children with her spouse. With care and intention, she strives for her scholarly, service, and teaching efforts to intersect in projects that encourage community engagement for social injustice changes. The arts, creative writing, and family nature walks are practices that give her spaces to reflect on how to be a better human.

Virna Ribeiro Feitosa Cestari is a nurse and doctoral student in clinical care in nursing and health at UECE and a researcher at GRUPECCE.

Edna Maria Camelo Chaves, PhD, is a nurse in pharmacology and is an associate professor at UECE.

Bridget Cho received her doctorate in clinical child psychology from the University of Kansas and completed an APA accredited internship specializing in child maltreatment at the University of California Davis Children's Hospital. Dr. Cho is an assistant professor of psychology at the University of South Carolina Aiken, where her activities include scholarship, clinical supervision, and teaching. Her research and clinical interests include child psychopathology, parenting and adversity, and culturally responsive interventions for children and families.

Maria Wanderleya de Lavor Coriolano-Marinus is an adjunct professor of the Nursing Department at the Federal University of Pernambuco and a permanent professor of the Graduate Program in Nursing and the Graduate Program in Child and Adolescent Health. She graduated in nursing (bachelor's degree) from the Regional University of Cariri. She has a master's degree and a PhD in child and adolescent health, both from the Federal University of Pernambuco.

Brianne R. Coulombe received her doctorate in developmental psychology from the University of California, Riverside in 2021. Dr. Coulombe is an assistant professor at the University of South Carolina, Aiken, where she teaches graduate and undergraduate courses in research methods, statistics, and developmental psychology. Her research focuses on how important relationships (e.g., parent-child, teacher-child, and peer) support the development of positive social behaviours, especially in children and families facing adversity.

Linda Rose Ennis is a psychoanalytic therapist, a marriage, divorce and parent consultant, a family mediator, an author, and a lecturer. She has contributed chapters such as "Contract-Faculty Mothers: On the Track To Nowhere" (Demeter) as well as "Mothering or Parenting" (Routledge) in addition to many submissions to the *Encyclopedia of Motherhood* (Sage). Dr. Ennis's edited collections include *Intensive Mothering: The Cultural Contradictions of Modern Motherhood* (Demeter 2014) and *After the Happily Ever After: Empowering Women & Mothers in Relationships* (Demeter 2017).

Fernando Figueira has a master's in maternal and child health (CAPES Concept 5) from IMIP (2011) and doctorate in maternal and child health (CAPES Concept 5) from IMIP (2016). She is currently an adjunct professor in the area of nursing in collective health at the Federal University of Pernambuco (UFPE). She has experience in nursing, with an emphasis on maternal and child health, working mainly on the following topics: primary health care, nursing, newborns, family health strategy, and health services evaluation.

Raquel Sampaio Florêncio is a nurse, has a PhD in public health from UECE, and is a researcher at GRUPECCE.

Lêda Maria da Costa Pinheiro Frota is a physical therapist, has a PhD in rehabilitation sciences from the Federal University of Minas Gerais (UFMG), and is a board member for the Centre for Early Treatment and Stimulation (NUTEP).

Karina Rangel da Silva Garcia, MScN, RN, is a quality manager in a tertiary hospital and a registered nurse at the maternity unit. She is a member of the Group of Research and Studies in Child and Adolescent Integral Health (NUPESICA) and is a senior specialist nurse with eight years of experience in neonatal intensive care.

Kiley Gottschalk is a white, cisgender female as well as a licensed clinical psychologist in Newton, Massachusetts. She works in a community mental health centre and is in private practice, where she sees children and adults. She is also a candidate in training at the Massachusetts Institute for Psychoanalysis.

Bianca Rocha Gouveia graduated in art and media from the Federal University of Campina Grande (UFCG) in 2019. Currently, Bianca has an ongoing specialization in the cinema and audiovisual production course at the Corporate University (UNICORP) and conducts research in the areas of cinema and photography. She also participates in festivals and exhibitions on national audiovisual circuits with independent productions, such as the short film *Rock*.

Meredith G. Higgins, M.A., is a graduate student in the counselling doctoral program at Texas Woman's University. She engages in research related to child-parent relationships, peer victimization, and the role of bystanders in situations of relational aggression.

NOTES ON CONTRIBUTORS

Brenda Elize Nunes da Hora is an undergraduate student in nursing at the Federal University of Pernambuco.

Rebecca Hughes's current research is grounded in inclusive education in the areas of gender, equity, and media literacy. In her present work teaching both technology and literacy at OISE, University of Toronto, Dr. Hughes leads students in a critical examination of issues associated with the use of media and technology, with an emphasis on promoting inclusion, equity, and diversity.

Tracey Hurd is a white, cisgender, and female mother as well as a licensed clinical psychologist who sees children, adolescents, and adults in a private practice in Wellesley and Concord, Massachusetts. She is a candidate in psychoanalytic training at the Massachusetts Institute for Psychoanalysis, where she is concentrating on relational and intersubjective self-psychological theories and practice.

Angela Jones is a white, cisgender, female licensed clinical psychologist in private practice. Her interest in children began in childhood with her younger sisters. This inspired work in summer camps in both English and French, in a residential therapeutic program, and currently in clinical practice where she sees children and their families, adolescents, and adults. She is a candidate in psychoanalytic training at the Massachusetts Institute for Psychoanalysis with a focus on intersubjective self-psychology.

Jacqueline Kolosov's creative as well as scholarly writing appear in a wide range of venues, including *The Sewanee Review, The Southern Review, The Writer's Chronicle,* and *Studies in American Indian Literature.* She has published several YA novels, and her fourth collection of poems, *Talons, Wings,* and a story collection, *Exit, Pursued by a Bear,* are forthcoming in the autumn of 2023. Originally from Chicago, she now lives in Lubbock, where she is Professor of English at Texas Tech University.

Maria Estela Diniz Machado, PhD, MScN, RN, is an associate professor at the Fluminense Federal University (UFF), Aurora de Afonso Costa School of Nursing (EEAAC) (Rio de Janeiro, Brazil) and is associate director of the Department of Maternal-Child and Psychiatric Nursing. She teaches in undergraduate and graduate programs. She is a member of the Group of Research and Studies in Child and Adolescent

Integral Health (NUPESICA) and is a senior specialist with 30 years of experience in neonatal and paediatric nursing.

Laura Matlack is a white, cisgender female as well as a licensed clinical psychologist and parent in Cambridge, Massachusetts. She came to clinical work through a first career working with adolescents in classrooms, playing fields, dining halls, and dormitories. Currently, she works at a community mental health centre and is in private practice, where she sees adolescents and adults.

Hillary Di Menna is the mother of a roller-skating teen. The two wild haired whirlwinds share a noisy apartment in Toronto, with three black cats, a little black dog, and a drummer, where they write love letters to the moon. Hillary has an MA in Gender Studies and has been published in over forty publications, including the Demeter Press collection *Mothers, Mothering, and COVID-19*.

Thereza Maria Magalhães Moreira is a nurse, lawyer, as well as a postdoctorate in public health from the University of São Paulo (USP). She is an associate professor at the UECE.

Francisca Charlenny Freitas de Oliveira is a specialist in special education and distance education and has a master's in child and adolescent health from the State University of Ceará (UECE).

Vitória Andrade Farias de Oliveira is an undergraduate student in nursing at the Federal University of Pernambuco.

Eny Dórea Paiva, PhD, MScN, is an associate professor at the Fluminense Federal University (UFF), Aurora de Afonso Costa School of Nursing (EEAAC), Department of Maternal-Child and Psychiatric Nursing in Rio de Janeiro, Brazil. She teaches in undergraduate and graduate programs. She is an editor for the *OnlineBrazilian Journal of Nursing*. She is a member of the Group of Research and Studies in Child and Adolescent Integral Health (NUPESICA) and is a senior specialist nurse with twenty years of experience in neonatal and paediatric nursing.

Vera Lúcia Mendes de Paula Pessoa is a nurse and a postdoctorate in public health from the Federal University of Ceará (UFC). She is an associate professor at the State University of Ceará (UECE), is coordinator of the postgraduate program in clinical care, and a researcher at the

Epidemiology, Chronic Care and Nursing Research Group (GRUPECCE).

Luciana Rodrigues da Silva, PhD, MScN, RN, is an associate professor at the Fluminense Federal University (UFF), Aurora de Afonso Costa School of Nursing (EEAAC), Department of Maternal-Child and Psychiatric Nursing in Rio de Janeiro, Brazil. She teaches in undergraduate programs and residency nursing programs. She is a member of the Research and Studies in Child and Adolescent Integral Health Research Group (NUPESICA) and is a specialist in neonatology with twenty-two years of experience.

Lisa H. Rosen is an associate professor and director of the undergraduate psychology program at Texas Woman's University. Her research focuses on parent-child communication and exploring ways that parents can best support victimized youth.

Linda Rubin is a professor of psychology and licensed psychologist at Texas Woman's University. Her research, clinical, and teaching interests target traumatic stress and violence against women. She has offered empirically based intervention to college students who experience domestic/dating violence, sexual assault/rape, and stalking.

Adélia Karla Falcão Soares is a nurse at the Federal University of Pernambuco (UFPE) and a specialist in child health at the Hospital das Clínicas of the Federal University of Pernambuco (HC/UFPE). She has a master's degree in the postgraduate program in nursing (PPGENF) at the Federal University of Pernambuco.

Ronald Stolberg, PhD, is a licensed clinical psychologist and a professor at Alliant International University in San Diego, California. As a family therapist for twenty years, he specializes in working with children and their families. He is the coauthor, with his wife, of the award-winning book *Teaching Kids to Think: Raising Confident, Independent, and Thoughtful Children in an Age of Instant Gratification*. Dr. Stolberg is married and has two college-aged children. In his spare time, you will find him reading a good book or at the beach.

Darlene Sweetland, PhD, is a licensed clinical psychologist with a private practice. Her specialty is assessment and treatment for children and teens who are challenged with such things as emotional, learning, attentional, and behavioral disorders. She is the author of *Teaching Kids to Think: Raising Confident, Independent, and Thoughtful Children in an Age* *of Instant Gratification*, which is a Nonfiction Book Association award winner and a Publisher's Weekly Select 2015 Parenting Title. It has been translated into nine languages.

Melinda Vandenbeld Giles is a feminist author and anthropology/English lecturer at the University of Toronto and Lakehead University. Melinda's publications include her Demeter Press-edited volume, *Mothering in the Age of Neoliberalism;* her coedited volume, *The Routledge Companion to Motherhood,* and her Inanna feminist novel, *Clara Awake.* Melinda's work also appears in many Demeter Press-edited collections, *Current Sociology, JMI (Journal of the Motherhood Initiative for Research and Community Involvement), Development (Journal of the Society for International Development),* and *Canadian Woman Studies.*

Tuppett M. Yates, PhD, is a professor of psychology at the University of California, Riverside. Dr. Yates draws on her integrative training in clinical and developmental psychology to investigate relational and regulatory mechanisms undergirding risk and resilience in adversity-exposed paediatric populations.